OFF GUARD

The story of the earliest drug scandal in

professional football… as told by one of

the best linemen to ever play in the NFL.

D1617541

Walt Sweeney

with

Bill Swank

Off Guard: The Story of the Earliest Drug Scandal in Professional Football . . . As Told by One of the Best Linemen to Ever Play in the NFL.

"Awarded With a Future; Ruling for Sweeney Puts Blame on NFL" by Luke Cyphers, copyright *Daily News*, L.P. (New York). Used with permission.

ISBN 978-1-893067-12-7

printed in the United States of America

Foreword

Off Guard is the story of one of the most gifted athletes ever to play professional football, Walt Sweeney. He played thirteen years without missing a game and played in nine Pro Bowls.

Merlin Olsen, one of the greatest defensive tackles ever to play had this to day about Sweeney. "If I had to play against Sweeney every week, I'd rather sell used cars."

Follow his battles on the field, in the courts against the NFL and with his own personal demons. It covers an era in football before drug testing.

"Drugs were tested on us. We were told that steroids were vitamins that would make us bigger and stronger and that we would be fined if we didn't take them. Amphetamines and pain killers were passed out like candy," Sweeney says.

Sweeney, a first round draft choice, second player drafted in the league, signed his first professional contract on national television. Thirteen years later he had to use a revolver to collect his final contract. What happened to this small town New England kid to turn him into a lunatic?

The story goes beyond his football days and follows him through a variety of jobs, rehabs and into his lawsuit with the NFL. Sweeney puts a humorous spin on what many consider a tragedy.

Will McDonough, Sportswriter
Boston Globe

The NFL's
Persona Non Grata

I love the game of football. I am grateful for the opportunity to have played professionally. My playing days were, thanks to the NFL, high times indeed.

I loved playing in the League. It wasn't until later that I paid the price for taking the drugs my team provided. It was with a sense of irony and even sadness that I had no choice but to sue the league that gave me the opportunity to play for a living. The NFL helped turn me into an addict and addiction left me unable to earn a living after football. This wasn't exactly a fitting end to my glory days on the field. As Chad and Jeremy crooned back in the 1960s, "They say that all good things must end someday."

In 1995, I won the first round in my legal battle with the National Football League Players Association. The NFL was ordered to pay me $1.8 million in disability payments after a federal court ruled the League had pushed drugs on me. The NFL threw a challenge flag and, in 1997, the appellate court overturned the ruling of the lower court.

Fifteen years have passed. More broken bodies are piled like cordwood, but the National Football League remains apathetic.

My drug addiction is directly related to the game. It was the San Diego Chargers trainers and doctors who gave pre-game amphetamines to rev me up, post-game sedatives to bring me down, pain killers as "needed" and steroids, said to be vitamins, for better health.

I considered taking drugs as normal for game day preparation as putting on my game face. Better living through chemistry.

It took a long time for me to realize that medication was exploitation especially since drug use was rampant within the Chargers organization. I have accepted my responsibility in this matter. Nobody held me and forced a fistful of pills down my throat, but I ask the NFL to own up to their responsibility for providing the drugs.

The NFL's complicity in dealing with rampant drug usage in the 1970s involved a cover-up that included trading several members of the San Diego Chargers, including me, to other teams. When I was with the Washington Redskins, after eleven years with the Chargers, head coach George Allen said he'd buy a truckload of pills if it would make us win.

Well, the Chargers brought in truckloads for a long time and encouraged their players to take plenty of drugs. Did it help us win? That's debatable, but drugs certainly made me feel bulletproof. It was after football that my bulletproof shield got lost at the cleaners.

Steroids have permanently stained Major League Baseball's record book. Drugs, including steroids, never caused the same public outrage in football as they did in baseball. The fans want bigger, stronger, faster football players. Football is a violent game. The NFL has instituted several rule changes to protect the players. A cynic might say rather than being concerned about safety, the NFL wants to protect its investment in the players. When they are used up, the League has to buy some more.

I never missed a regular season game during my career. I played in 181 straight games. Nine Pro Bowls were my reward for the job I did on the field. I earned respect from other players, coaches, sportswriters and the fans by playing like a savage turned loose on his prey. I had job security; I was untouchable. I never worried about being replaced. Football legends Sid Gillman and Al Davis told me that I belong in the Football Hall of Fame, but it's tough to get invited to the party when you've piss in the host's punch bowl.

Perhaps my success on the gridiron can be traced to my early dysfunctional family life. It wasn't exactly *Leave It to Beaver*. It was more like *Destruction Derby*. What would you expect from a working class Irish home with six boys? My story is about a long struggle. I'm just glad to still be here to tell it.

This book is dedicated to my wife, Nanci
You said I'd miss you ... and I do.

Growing Up Sweeney

"Stop running around with all those whores." My mother's voice shrieked across the marsh like the constant cry of the seagulls battling over fish. I was probably around five or six years old when I first remember hearing Mary Ann McCormick Sweeney's dating advice to my older brothers. I knew she was talking about women and I was pretty sure it wasn't in a good way. My own relationships with the opposite sex were probably affected by her ranting.

In the early 1920s, my mother moved to Boston from Nova Scotia in search of employment. She left her brothers, hers, her parents and her past in Canada. I know nothing about them. Mary Ann McCormick met and fell in love with Jack Sweeney, the son of Irish immigrants. Together, they had seven children. I have one older sister and five older brothers. I am the youngest, five years younger than my closest brother. The rest of the gang were born about a year apart. I'm sure my birth had nothing to do with Planned Parenthood.

I know a little bit more about my father's family, because I grew up close to my Grandfather Jim, my (great) Uncle Henry, and their sister, my (great) Aunt Mary "Bones" Sweeney.

Once there had been three brothers in County Kerry, Ireland: James, Henry and my namesake, the Reverend Walter Francis Sweeney. The poverty that swept the Emerald Isle made it an easy decision for Jim and Henry to take that gigantic step halfway across the world to America. Their sister, Bones, would join them later. Brother Walter had job security with the Catholic Church and chose to stay in the green hills of his homeland.

Jim and Henry worked long and hard to take advantage of the new opportunities that came their way. They settled in the small town of Cohasset, about twenty miles south of Boston. The Boston area was comfortable for them as there were more Irish in Beantown than in Ireland.

Henry, who had a way with numbers, took a job with an accounting firm and quickly advanced within the company. Jim went to work for a dairy farmer and, although he didn't make as much money as his brother, he made enough to buy a small house near Henry's much larger home. He courted and married Rose Sullivan, the daughter of a local shopkeeper, and produced two sons, Jack and Edward.

Uncle Ed joined the Navy as soon as he was old enough. He became a career man and rose to the rank of Captain. My father, Jack, did what most men in the community did. He went to work at the Fore River Shipyard as a ship fitter. Fore River was the largest employer in the area. Jack was more interested in working and hanging out with his friends in the local taverns than settling down. He was thirty years old when he married my mother. Mary was twenty-five and worked as a domestic for one of the wealthy families near my grandfather's house.

After they were married, Jack and Mary rented an old ramshackle dwelling on Jerusalem Road, across the marsh from my grandfather's house. Jerusalem Road is one of the wealthiest streets in all of New England. Jack and Mary lived at the wrong end of Jerusalem. On the east end of the four-mile road were huge mansions overlooking the Atlantic Ocean. Reportedly during Prohibition, Joe Kennedy smuggled booze ashore through the many tunnels in the cliffs that surrounded the village of Cohasset.

The house where Jack and Mary settled was on the edge of Little Harbor. It is one of the most beautiful locations in the country. Several motion pictures have been filmed there including *Witches of Eastwick* and *House Sitter.* The home where I grew up was a real blot on the landscape. Rough-hewn logs held up the second-story porch. I can remember being told to stay off one end of the porch for fear it would collapse. The tide would come in and surround three sides of our house leaving only the front entrance dry. Growing up, my home was a constant source of embarrassment, especially when the elementary school bus would stop to pick me up.

My father was killed when I was two years old. Today, his death would be ruled a homicide, but back in 1943, it was considered an unfortunate incident. On a cold December night, Jack Sweeney wondered what happened to his bus. It was midnight and he had just finished his shift at the shipyard. The South Shore bus was always prompt, but that fateful night it was fifteen minutes late. When I was born, my father switched to the second shift. The money was better, but he didn't get to see much of his kids. He was on his way to work when they were getting out of school.

When he finally boarded the bus, there were fewer passengers than usual. Jack had taken this thirty-minute ride hundreds of times. It crossed the Fore River Bridge, traveled through the working class town of Weymouth, past beautiful Hingham Harbor, and finally down Route 3A into downtown Cohasset.

It started to rain as the bus stopped in front of Colonial Pharmacy. Jack stepped off and waited for the bus to pull away before crossing South Main Street. Halfway across the thoroughfare, a 1941 Ford slammed into him. He was dragged a mile or so before he was finally freed from the rear axle. My father was discovered later that night, barely clinging to life. He was taken to the hospital where he died in the early morning hours.

Thanks to a witness, the police were able to locate the killer's vehicle. A piece of Jack's sweater hung from the axel. Unfortunately, in those days, felony hit and run drunk drivers didn't face the penalties they do today. I was told the drunk only did six months in

jail and received no fine. My mother's task of raising seven children alone was daunting. She had very little money and she was
dealing with a rather unruly bunch. Donald was the oldest. He
was followed by James, Louise, John, Robert, Bernie and last, but
not least, me.

With the exception of my sister and my brother John, they
were all hard drinkers and brawlers. My family was known as the
drunken, brawling Sweeneys. The quality of their lives and the lives
of those around them were made significantly worse by alcohol.

When my brothers couldn't find someone to fight, they fought
with each other. Some of my earliest childhood recollections are
drunken brawls in my own house. Sometimes, these conflicts were
life threatening. There were incidents when guns were pulled, when
brothers threw each other from the second story porch, when the
cops had to come to restore order. It became a constant cause of
terror and humiliation for me. I can remember hiding under the
bed for hours at a time until the brawls simmered down. The fights
usually ended when one of them needed medical attention or the
police finally arrived.

The reputation of the Sweeney boys was well known in Cohasset
and throughout the small neighboring towns. It was a source of
embarrassment, but not enough to prevent me from following in
their footsteps, at least the drinking part.

I was also ashamed that my mother was a maid. She could neither read nor write. At the time, I was unable to appreciate her
many other virtues. She was a loving and caring mother. She was
extremely honest and hard working. What Mary lacked with her
ABC's, she made up for with common sense. Despite being known
for having the rowdiest kids in town—she was fighting a losing battle trying to get the Sweeney brood to behave—we were also known
as the cleanest family around. Although our house was a run-down,
three-bedroom dump that we rented for twenty dollars a month, it

was immaculate. My mother would work eight to ten hours a day cooking and cleaning for others. Then she came home and to take care of us. She was weary, but worked till the early morning doing our wash, mending our clothes and cleaning the house.

Suppertime at the old homestead was a joke. I imagined that other families sat down and ate together. My brothers straggled in at various times. Without hesitation, my poor mother would wait on each and every one of them as if she were working in a restaurant.

She was our sole support although my eldest brother, Donald, contributed a few dollars a week. One of the biggest regrets in my life was not helping my mother learn to read and write. Realistically, there wasn't time. She was too busy working as a maid and caring for us.

Since my mother worked during the day, my sister Louise assumed much of the responsibility for my upbringing. Eleven years my senior, she took me everywhere. I remember riding in her bicycle basket. She always made sure I had gifts for Christmas and my birthday. Like our mother, Louise had a strong sense of responsibility to the family. She went to work for the telephone company right out of high school and didn't marry until she was forty years old.

My mother and sister bore the brunt of my brothers' drunken fights and antics. They were embarrassed and psychologically battered. This sad pattern of my mother and sister trying to hold things together continued throughout my childhood. Alcohol fueled the chaos. Each time my mother would get a little ahead, one of them would get into trouble.

Bernie embezzled a few thousand dollars from the department store where he worked and took off for Florida with the wife of a mid-level Mafia boss. Fortunately the police caught him before the mob did. He spent two years on a Florida chain gang. My mother had to borrow money for his attorney fees, but the heartache she suffered took a much greater toll.

We were all good athletes, excelling in football, track, baseball, and basketball. Bobby was an excellent southpaw pitcher and led Cohasset High to a state championship in the early fifties. I was told that both the Baltimore Orioles and the U.S. Army drafted him. Unfortunately for Bobby, the army's claim took priority. He spent two years in Korea. Apparently he had a tryout with the Orioles after his discharge from the service, but either he didn't make it or never had it. I don't think he was ever quite the same after Korea.

Rumor has it that Bernie was offered a football scholarship. He was a pretty good fullback and the only bright spot on a Cohasset High team that had gone five years without winning a game.

After watching them play sports in school, I wanted to follow in their footsteps. In junior high, I was just an average size kid. Once I got into high school, I grew a couple of inches and gained twenty pounds every year. With only forty-eight kids in my class, all the same guys played all of the sports. I was the center on the basketball team, ran the 100 and 220 in track, but my true love was football.

When I was ten years old, I told the milkman I wanted to play professional football when I grew up. He laughed and said I wouldn't be big enough. My senior year at Cohasset High I was 6'3" and weighed 220 pounds. Since our school was so small, we played class "C" ball. I was the biggest and fastest guy in the league and finished fourth in the state in scoring with 120 points. My average touchdown run was thirty-five yards. My high school years were probably the most fun I have ever had playing football.

Even though our school competed in the tiny Mayshore League, I had about twenty-five scholarship offers from schools around the country. If you have talent, college scouts will find you.

After weighing the plusses and minuses of each, I picked Syracuse University because the drinking age in New York was eighteen. I've told that story many times over the years. Apparently my humor pissed off the university administration. I learned from a friend who's the sports editor of the *Syracuse Herald* that I was named to the All-Century Team at Syracuse. The other guys who made the team were flown in for the weekend festivities (banquet, football game, etc.) The school didn't even give me a phone call. I can't really blame them, though I think that I should have been included because of my football ability and not my inability to kiss ass.

In high school, I could drink twice as much as my friends. I would drive them home. I thought it was a gift from God. At the time, I didn't realize it was a curse from Hell.

SU

Football fans know Syracuse University as Syracuse, but all the students and alumni call it SU. Head SU football coach Ben Schwartzwalder talked me into reporting for practice with the varsity a week before the rest of the freshman recruits in 1959. I was going to be a tight end and defensive end instead of a running back and defensive back. This was when I realized that the transition from high school to college football wasn't going to be that difficult for me.

When I started working out with the varsity, many of the players razzed me for being stupid enough to report early. Ben also brought a couple of other freshmen in early. After practice, I gravitated toward the varsity players and hung out with them in the bars. After all, school wasn't going to open for another two weeks and I badly wanted to fit in. Once I figured out the guys who could drink like me, I hung with them. Senior Roger Davis, winner of the Outland Trophy for best college lineman, and junior end Dave Baker were two of the upper classmen I was drawn to.

Back in those days, SU gave out about thirty football scholarships a year. My freshman year, they brought in about twenty-five fullbacks and ten quarterbacks. Ben's reasoning was that fullbacks were big and fast enough to play just about any position and the quarterbacks could become defensive backs. My switch to tight end was a relatively easy adjustment. I had been catching passes from my brothers since I could walk, but learning how to block was the toughest thing I had to do. Playing defensive end came natural to me.

Freshmen couldn't play on the varsity back in those years. We had our own team and schedule. It was a very exciting time for me. We had some pretty good talent including John Mackey, who went on to become a Hall of Fame tight end for the Baltimore Colts, and Dave Meggessey, who played seven years for the St. Louis Cardinals. Our freshmen team went undefeated, emulating the varsity. In our final game against Army, I caught eleven passes. The coaches loved me. Later *Sports Illustrated* touted me as the greatest tight end to ever play at Syracuse. That was some heady billing, because Fred Mautino, first team All-American, was currently playing on the varsity.

The varsity became National Champions in 1959 rolling over everyone they faced. They were loaded with talent. Players like the late Ernie Davis (1962 Heisman Trophy winner), Roger Davis, Art Baker, Bruce Tarbox, Dick Easterly and Dave Sarette to name a few. SU went on to beat the University of Texas in the Cotton Bowl and became the number one team in the country. It was also acclaimed to be the best college team of the decade.

The first half of my freshman year was a success. I made the jump from high school to college football and became one of the most highly touted players in the best college football program in the country. Everybody treated me like I was special, but I didn't feel so special. I had confidence on the football field. Off the field, I was full of self-doubt, shy and just didn't feel good about myself. It was only when I drank that I felt as good as everyone thought I was. The only difference in my drinking pattern between high school and college was now I imbibed after every practice instead of after every game.

The Clover Club is where I did most of my drinking. It was located in one of the worst slums in Syracuse in a derelict building about a mile down the hill from campus. For reasons unbeknown to me, the football team had taken over the bar years earlier. Prior to that, it was known for brawls, stabbings and on-going ethnic wars between blacks, poor whites and Native Americans. These three groups seemed to delight in combining forces against SU football players. You could buy a Carlings Black Label beer for two bits and a T-bone steak for a $1.25. If you didn't feel like drinking alone, the bartenders Irv or Phooey would always be happy to join you.

Another of my watering holes was the Open Door, a blue-collar bar located downtown where you could get a shot and a beer for forty-five cents. Economic reasons drew me to these to joints because money—the lack of it—was always a problem. A lot of guys on the team had "sugar daddies", rich alumni that would give them money. I wasn't one of them. My roommate, John Charette, a 240-lb. fullback from New Hampshire, and former Golden Gloves champ, used to sell his blood and weekly meal ticket for money. Because of my fear of needles, I just sold my meal ticket. My mother and brothers sent me what little money they could and Tom Welsh, the scout who recommended me to Syracuse, would give me a few dollars when he was in town.

When I had a couple of extra bucks, I went to the Tecumseh Club. It overlooked a beautiful golf course and was the local haunt for the sorority and fraternity crowd. I would ogle the coeds until I drank enough to actually work up the courage to talk to one of them. A gang-bang in high school was the extent of my sexual experience, and, as I recall, it wasn't that much fun. Five guys and a big, farm girl being a sperm receptacle.

I really didn't give much thought to dating my first year at Syracuse. When I did get in the mood, which was usually after drinking, I'd occasionally pick up a hooker outside of the Clover Club. Having sex with these hookers was sort of like masturbating as far as not having to look your best. You didn't have to take a shower, brush your teeth or, for that matter, comb your hair. I'll never forget the first one. She placed her mouth to my ear so I could hear some kind of electronic medical device she used. It might have been an early pacemaker.

From my freshman year until I left Syracuse four years later, alcohol would cause me a lot of problems. When I was in school, alcohol was not allowed in the dormitories. After the first semester, every one had a week off until the second semester began. Most of the student body left the campus to go home and visit their families. Since I couldn't afford that luxury, I remained at SU with three of my teammates. We bought some beer and had a party in my room. Needless to say we were caught and had to appear before student court. I was called to appear as a hostile witness:

"Since the school was closed during semester break, I didn't think the rules applied!" I argued.

The Dean of Men spoke. "That's right, Mr. Sweeney, you didn't think."

I guess they didn't buy our defense strategy, because we were all put on probation. The coaches loved me during my freshman season, but I quickly fell out of favor after that episode. My roommate, Charette, and I began to cut classes for days at a time. We were either downtown drinking or sleeping it off in our room. Fortunately for me, with Syracuse winning the national championship and me being a freshman "hero in waiting," football fever was rampant among the faculty. They looked away which enabled me to remain eligible to play despite grades.

Joe Szombathy, my tight end coach and liaison between the faculty and the football department, summoned me to his office.

"Walt, we're getting a number of phone calls from members of the community about your drinking and carousing."

"Joe, I admit to the drinking, but I have not caroused." I wasn't quite sure what carousing meant, but if I was being accused of it, it couldn't be good. "Coach Schwartzwalder has never, and he isn't going to start now, put up with this type of behavior from one of his players," Joe plowed on, ignoring my smart-ass remark.

I believed what Joe was saying about Ben. He had been a highly decorated paratrooper in the elite Army Rangers during World War II.

At one of our earlier meetings, he told the team, "Some guys liked to stab the Germans, but I liked to stab them and twist the blade." His nickname was Bantam Ben, because of his short stature and 150-lb. weight.

I shrugged off Szombathy's lecture. He was a square who didn't know how to have a good time. But I did tell him that I would take it easy.

When spring practice rolled around in April, I realized that being a football player set me apart from the rest of the student body. While I was busting my ass on the practice field every afternoon, most of the other kids were heading out to the lakes in their convertibles to party.

The coaches disregarded the rave notices they had given me the past autumn and put me on the third team. SU had six full teams that comprised the varsity unit. The second team was almost as good as the first and probably played just as much. For the most part, the third team was made up of sophomores that could play at a varsity level. The fourth team consisted of "red shirt" players. These guys were sophomores who would practice everyday, but didn't suit up for games. By not playing in any games, they would still have three years of eligibility left. It was a good deal if you needed extra time to graduate.

I saw fifth- and sixth-teamers who should have been starting, but because they were on the coach's shit list for one reason or another, they were relegated to being blocking dummies for the guys that played. I had made a mental note to stay off Schwartzwalder's shit list.

I remained in Syracuse that first summer and took on a job working construction. I felt it would be good for my physical conditioning plus it paid more than the job I had had the previous summer as a lifeguard. The construction job was interrupted in July when I had to fulfill a 28-day commitment to the U.S. Naval Reserve. For some unknown reason, I joined the U.S.N.R. when I was a junior in high school. I spent two weeks training at the Great Lakes Naval Training Center during summer vacation before my senior year in high school. About thirty seamen recruits from the South Shore area flew to Chicago. We were met by a Navy bus at O'Hare and driven to the training center. "What must I have been thinking?" kept crossing though my mind during this entire journey.

"Sweeney, pick up those butts by the garbage cans!" Squad leader Travis was shouting out orders.

"Fuck you! You pick 'em up." I was sick of this prick giving me orders. After all, he was the same rank as me, a lowly seaman recruit. As a result of this little outburst, I had to appear before the base commander.

"Sweeney, you have absolutely no military bearing about you and if you don't start towing the line, we're going to send you home." I should have thanked him and let them send me back home.

The only other thing I remember about my fortnight with the Navy, besides the career advice from the commander, was going to Milwaukee with David Patterson.

David was a childhood pal and we had joined the reserves together. After being at Great Lakes for a week, we were given Sunday off. We decided to go to Milwaukee and drink the beer that made the city famous. During the hour-long train ride, we anticipated those ice cold Schlitz long necks. In Milwaukee, we confirmed the drinking age was eighteen. We were seventeen and they checked IDs very closely. Since we couldn't drink, we decided on tattoos. Made sense to me. We couldn't alter our minds, so why not permanently change the surface of our epidermis?

We ended up at Dietzel's Tattoo Parlor. After perusing Dietzel's artwork, I opted for the cheapest one available, a dagger through a heart next to a rose, for three bucks. David chose some similar dramatic designs. Thirty minutes later, two young seaman recruits walked out the door marked for life.

I was the center on our basketball team during my senior year in high school. I thought I was hot stuff because of the tattoo. I was the only kid in the league dumb enough to get one, an athlete way ahead of his time. Five years later, following my rookie season with the Chargers, I realized society frowned on such body artwork. I decided to have it removed. In the off-season, the plan was for a doctor to incrementally excise a portion of the tattoo from my forearm and stitch the incision. The procedure would be repeated three times and I would only be left with a hairline scar. After two doctor visits, the stitches broke open while playing basketball. I abandoned the project and now have half a tattoo with a three-inch scar beside it.

In August, I reported to the Brooklyn Navy Yard for what I thought would be a 28–day cruise. I was assigned a destroyer escort that never left port. My job was to paint the identification numbers on the bow. Halfway through my tour of duty, my lower right leg became infected from a jackhammer cut incurred during my construction job. The remainder of my cruise was spent at the Long Island Naval Hospital. A heating unit with four bulbs was placed over my swollen leg. At night, a sheet was placed over the unit and two of the bulbs were turned off. My first night in the hospital, someone forgot to turn off the bulbs. My leg was badly burned. To this day, I still have the scars.

When I was finally discharged from the hospital, it was time for me to report to fall football practice. After two weeks on my back, I was in terrible shape. By the third game of the season, I was promoted to first team. We were the defending National Champions with a seventeen-game winning streak on the line when we faced the University of Pittsburgh Panthers.

My first start and assignment was to block and defend against their senior, All-American end, Mike Ditka. This guy was a big, strong, mean coalminer's son from Western Pennsylvania. Ditka gave me a run for my money and we lost the game.

Syracuse University did not have a shortage of good-looking girls. Unfortunately, these girls from New York City, Long Island and New Jersey did not frequent the same recreational establishments that I did (the Open Door and the Clover Club.) Usually when I was in these places, I was well lubricated. I could shoot the shit with the best of them, but my clever conversation fell on the ears of derelicts and hookers.

A friend of mine from the dorm, George Thomas, had been nagging me to meet this girl that sat next to him in one of his classes. I wasn't one for blind dates or any dates for that matter. George persisted and I finally agreed to meet her.

I was pleasantly surprised to say the least. Her name was Jean Wagner. She was a sophomore from New Jersey. She had gorgeous auburn hair and I thought she was beautiful. She had a personality to match her looks. I found her easy to talk with, which was something new for me. We started dating and for the first time in my life, I had a girlfriend. Jean was a moderate drinker and I didn't drink nearly as much when we were together. When we weren't together, I made up for it.

The summer between my sophomore and junior year, I decided to stay in Syracuse with the same construction company I had worked for the previous year. The plan was for Jean to go home for a month and return for summer school. While she was in New Jersey, I took a room in a run down building within walking distance of the Clover Club. I felt right at home in the neighborhood.

I did all my drinking and took most of my meals at the Club. My cholesterol must have been sky high with all those buck-and-a-quarter steak and French-fries dinners, but this was before we worried about such things.

After stumbling home from my favorite bar one night, I went to bed and fell asleep with a lighted cigarette. Smoking was a nasty habit I picked up as a fifteen-year-old soda jerk at Delory's Drugstore in Cohasset. Everyone in my family smoked. There I was, after a hard day of making frappes and scooping ice cream, surrounded with all these bright colored packs of cigarettes. What could I do?

Getting back to my story. An hour after going to bed, I woke up gasping for air in a room engulfed in smoke. I managed to find the window and jumped out forgetting I was on the second floor. Luckily I managed to escape the building unscathed and never went back. The only thing I left behind were some old work clothes. The incident didn't temper my drinking, but it was the last time I ever smoked in bed.

Jean arrived for summer school and the rest of the summer went smoothly. She was a bright girl, but wasn't really interested in going to school. Jean decided not to return for her junior year, but came up for an occasional weekend in the fall. Once football season was over, I went down to her home for several visits. As much as I missed Jean, I enjoyed the freedom I had when she wasn't around. It allowed me to drink the way I wanted, when I wanted, and with whom I wanted.

Joe Szombathy called me into his office before the fall semester started.

"Walt, unless you get your grade point average up, you're not going to be able to matriculate next semester."

I had no idea what he was talking about. It sounded like some sort of disease with a drip. "Uh huh," I muttered.

He gave me a list of gut courses. Classes that even football players could pass. Two days later, I registered for some history classes (my major), Rhythm and Dance, and Marching. We had twenty-five football players and two girls in Rhythm and Dance. We learned how to ballroom dance and how to do the Irish Jig. I learned to dance well with guys, but to this day, I can barely dance with a woman. We had a lot of laughs and received A's in both dance courses, which helped our eligibility.

Jean would call me at 10:00 p.m. every night. Sometimes (most times) I would be half in the bag, but I tried my best to come across sober. I wasn't always successful and when she did bust me, it always led to an argument. After one such phone call, I was so pissed, I went back to the bars.

I was drinking at a bar on the north side of town and the booze wasn't making me feel any better. It was putting me in a darker mood. This happened so many times before when I drank while something was bothering me. The booze always made me feel good for a short time, but the results were always the same. A dark cloud would seem to engulf me. A couple of stools to the left, some biker types were looking for trouble. I was wearing my varsity letter jacket. They said SU football players were pussies. Sober, I probably would have ignored them. They didn't look particularly tough or big. If I hadn't been drinking, I would have gone out of my way to avoid a fight.

I said, "My grandfather once told me that no matter how hard you rub, you can't put a polish on a turd." (I still don't know where that came from or why I said it.) It must have really disturbed them, because the one closest to me charged like a wild bull. I caught him with a forearm shiver that stopped him in his tracks. Banging blocking sleds with my arms for years had finally paid off. Before he had a chance to recover, I grabbed him and heaved him over the bar causing extensive damage to some glassware, not to mention some probable bumps and bruises on him. My adrenaline was pumping now. The booze was giving me an invincible attitude. His compadre was running out the door. "Go Orange, you asshole!" I shouted.

The University heard about the incident and I lost my scholarship for my senior year. I tried to explain that I was defending the honor of the school, but they didn't seem to give a shit.

Schwartzwalder called me into his office and read me the riot act. After five minutes of chastisement, he told me that a wealthy alum would pick up the tab for my tuition so I could continue to play ball for SU. I guess Ben was expecting me to be grateful and repentant, but I wasn't. I felt no obligation to the University, because I had come to realize that the football program was making big bucks for the school. I was one of their main hired guns.

The idea of school spirit and "win one for the Gipper" and all that bullshit had worn off a long time ago. We all knew I was there to play football. The Athletic Department and the coaching staff could figure out the details to assure their investment would keep paying off. I couldn't blame them for not being particularly fond of my piss poor attitude, but they knew I always gave 100% on the field.

Jean and I decided to get married during the summer of 1962. I had one more year to go at Syracuse, but we knew we loved each other. Our only real difficulties had to do with her concerns about my drinking. I thought marriage would settle me down and that I would be able to control it. I didn't realize it then, but anytime you have to control something, it's already out of control.

We were married in my hometown of Cohasset and spent our honeymoon on Cape Cod. We got an apartment just off campus in Syracuse. I worked construction for the remainder of the summer and prepared for my last year of college football. I had been getting letters and feelers from all the pro teams since my sophomore year. I was sure I had a future in professional football.

My drinking slowed down considerably. The coaches were elated that I was now married and settled down. They were expecting a big year from me. I withdrew from all extracurricular activities that involved the team (banquets, parties, etc.). Ben frowned on this, but I really didn't care. At this point, I just wanted to have a good season and be selected by the pros in the draft.

We had a strong team in 1962. If we won our last game of the season against Notre Dame at South Bend, we were assured an invitation to the Orange Bowl.

We were ahead by two points with three seconds left on the clock. Notre Dame was attempting a 55-yard field goal which was nearly impossible for a college kid back in those days. With no time left on the clock, the ball was snapped. I charged in from my right end position and ran over the holder. I was called for roughing the holder and we were penalized 15-yards. With no time left on the clock, they kicked a forty-yard field goal and won the game.

After the game, I couldn't hold back the tears in the locker room. I felt even worse because Schwartzwalder give the game ball to me. My penalty cost us the Orange Bowl and hundreds of thousands of dollars in gate receipts and television revenue. The NCAA (National Collegiate Athletic Association) announced a week after the game that there was no such penalty as roughing the holder. Notre Dame should not have been given an extra down. They also said Syracuse actually won the game, but Notre Dame would have to concede. They never did. I'm still remembered at Syracuse as "the guy that lost the Notre Dame game." *Sport's Illustrated* called me the only "fighting Irishman" on the field. There used to be a bar in South Bend that won't allow anyone in unless they know who Walt Sweeney was.

Sittin' in High Cotton

In early December 1962, I was thrilled beyond belief when the San Diego Chargers made me their number one draft choice. I was the second player chosen by the eight teams in the American Football League.

The Kansas City Chiefs selected Buck Buchanon, the 6'8", 280-pound defensive tackle from Grambling, as the first player in the draft. Al Davis, an assistant coach under Sid Gillman, had attended several of the SU practices. On the days that I knew pro scouts were in attendance, I would run a little faster and hit a little harder. Al spoke with me after one of his visits and told me he was impressed with my speed, athletic ability and temperament.

The National Football League held its draft a few days later. The Green Bay Packers told me in mid-November that I'd be their number one pick. When that didn't happen, I was disappointed. From what I understand, they didn't select me because I went high in the AFL draft. They thought I had a prearranged deal with San Diego. The Cleveland Browns later selected me in the sixth round.

I was feeling terrific as we prepared for the final game of the season in Los Angeles against UCLA. My life-long ambition of playing professional football was about to be realized. Not only that, I had been a number one pick as one of the top prospects in the country. I thought I had the world by the tail as the SU team headed west.

As we landed in Los Angeles, the balmy breezes blew in my face. The palm trees swayed. California seemed like heaven after leaving Syracuse where the snow was already up to my ass. After a short practice at the Coliseum, we bussed to Santa Monica and the Ambassador Hotel. We checked into our rooms and I was ready for a few pops. Why not? It was my first time in California and it was my last game as an amateur. With these rationalizations in tow, I hooked up with a couple of fellow thirsty Orangemen— Hank Hutner and Len Slaby—and we headed for the bars on Santa Monica Boulevard. After playing "I Left My Heart in San Francisco" a dozen times and downing eight or nine beers, we decided to head back to the hotel. After all, we did have a game the next day.

I had two messages at the front desk. One was to call Jean and the other was that Sid Gillman and Al Davis were waiting for me at the Coconut Grove, the famous hotel restaurant. Jean would have to wait. I was in a state of panic and paranoia was running deep. Here I was, their number one draft choice, half in the bag the night before a game. I raced up to my room and proceeded to eat a whole package of breath mints and splashed a generous portion of Old Spice aftershave on my face.

As I rode down in the elevator, I thought I was going to blow my life's dream. Jean was pregnant and we needed the money that pro-football would provide. I had never thought about doing anything else. It never occurred at the time that meeting these two gentlemen the night before my last college game was highly unethical. The Browns had told me they couldn't talk to me until after the UCLA game. The competition to sign players between the NFL and the two-year old AFL was fierce. It was a time when some teams would literally hide their high draft choices until they were under contract.

By the time I reached their table, I was sweating bullets and could hardly talk. Between the mints and aftershave, I must have smelled like a French hooker. We shook hands and Sid asked me if

I wanted a drink. I wondered what he meant by that. Could he tell that I had been drinking? Get a grip on yourself, I thought.

"I'll have a coke," I blurted out. I gradually settled down as they talked about their plans for me in San Diego.

"Walt, I think you would make a great middle linebacker. You have the quickness and the speed and the size," Sid explained. All this sounded fine to me. Had they asked me to jump off the roof of the hotel that would have been fine, too.

I said, "The Browns want me to play defensive end."

"I think the Browns are wrong. I think with your talent, you could cause a lot more damage at middle linebacker." With the niceties and chitchat over, with Sid got down to business.

"We are prepared to offer you a two year, no cut, no trade, contract for $15,000.00 a year and a $5,000.00 signing bonus," he said.

Al Davis looked at me like he couldn't believe how lucky I was that Sid was making me this fantastic offer. I was so elated that no one said anything about my drinking that I probably would have signed anything. Al pulled a standard contract out of his jacket pocket, filled in the figures, and I like the moron that I was, I signed it.

Signing me before my collegiate football career was over was illegal and highly unethical as far as the NCAA was concerned. Of course, this is only true if you get caught. There wasn't any reason for anyone to get caught, because I honored the contract. Some rearranging would have to be done. The game was to be nationally televised and they (Gillman and Davis) would hold a press conference after the game when I would sign another contract. I readily agreed. Hell, I thought I was shitting in high cotton. If any one asked about my weight, I was to tell them I weighed 245, ten pounds more than my actual weight. Sid said it sounded better.

We beat the Bruins the next day. I had a great game, sacked the quarterback several times. That was to be expected. After all, I was a pro playing with amateurs. John Mackey had a great game, too. We were interviewed on TV after the game. As I walked away from the interview, a representative from the Browns was tugging on my arm.

"Walt, the Browns will give you anything you want."

"I've already signed with San Diego." Remorse swept over me like a dark cloud.

I told myself that it's too late now and try not to think about the thousands of dollars I lost because of signing so quickly with the Chargers. As I had done with unpleasant thoughts so often in the past, I blanked them out of my mind.

Gillman, Davis, reporters, and TV cameras were in the end zone waiting for me to appear. With cameras on me, I signed my second contract in as many days, and officially became a San Diego Charger. The next day, as I sat on the plane heading back to Syracuse, I couldn't help think about how alcohol had cost me a lot of money.

I was sitting next to Mackey, who had been the second round draft choice of the Baltimore Colts. John and I had been teammates for four years. Although we didn't run in the same social circles, I considered him a friend. He was a fraternity type guy and I liked the saloons. John and Ernie Davis, our Heisman Trophy winner the previous year, had roomed together. John was well versed in the going rates for high draft choices. Every team in the NFL and AFL wanted Ernie Davis, but the Cleveland Browns got him. At the College All-Star Game, It was discovered Ernie had leukemia. That didn't stop Art Modell, the owner of the Browns. He tried to get Ernie to suit up to be in the same backfield with another legendary Syracuse back, Jim Brown. It would have been a big-ticket seller for the Browns, but Ernie's failing health didn't allow this to happen. Ernie died about a year later. We lost a great athlete and a great guy.

I soon realized why John wasn't too excited about my signing with San Diego. "Number one draft choices are getting between ten and twenty-five thousand just for signing. For salaries they are getting between fifteen and thirty thousand," John explained.

"What did you get for signing?" he asked.

Since I was such a high selection, I should have been on the high end of the money. As I listened to John, I was getting hot under the collar. To make matters worse, I was embarrassed. Thanks to my stupidity and a few beers, I had made a huge blunder. I found out later that Baron Hilton, owner of the Chargers at the time, was trying to spend as little money as possible. In my case, the Chargers got much more than they paid for. They weren't so lucky in other instances. A few years later, in a cost cutting measure, they passed on drafting Alan Paige and took Ron Billingsley instead. Paige went to the Hall of Fame; Ron didn't. Moves such as these weakened the very strong team we had my rookie year in 1963.

After my signing, I began a period of ego-building activity. As a number one pick, I was invited to all the major post-season all-star games. The North South Game, the Senior Bowl, the Coaches All-America Game and the centerpiece of the summer, the College All-Star Game, held in Chicago on August 3, 1963. The game pitted the nation's top seniors against the defending National Football League champions, the Green Bay Packers. The *Chicago Tribune* sponsored the game and all proceeds went to charity. Since its inception in 1934, the All-Stars had only beaten the pros eight times. It was generally understood that the "champs" had all the guns and weren't about to be beaten by a bunch of college "punks." Practice for the game started in mid-July, about the same time the pros opened training camps. The owners and coaches hated this game, because it took their top draft choices out of training camps and put them three weeks behind their counterparts. Then, of course, there was always the injury factor. On more than one occasion, an All-Star incurred a career ending injury.

Before I left for Chicago, Jean and I rented an apartment near San Diego State College. Jean was eight months pregnant. At the time, it never occurred to me that I should forego the game and stay home to help out. After all, I could have lots of kids, but there was only one All-Star Game. Besides, her parents were in town to help and that eased my mind. Her father, Bob, was a vice-president in charge of the elevator division for Westinghouse. He had done well over the years and had made several good real estate investments. He was thinking about early retirement. Jean and I were hoping they would retire in the San Diego area. Jean's mother, Constance, was a very sweet woman. We hit it off right away. Jean had great parents. I liked them a lot.

The All-Star team was quartered at Northwestern University at Evanston, Illinois, about a thirty-minute drive from downtown Chicago. My roommate was Tony Liscio, an offensive tackle from Tulsa drafted by the Dallas Cowboys. Otto Graham, the great Hall of Fame quarterback of the Cleveland Browns and one of my childhood heroes, was our head coach. I was pleased to learn I would play defensive end. This would be another opportunity to show the Chargers that defensive end was where I belonged. They would forget the notion that I could play middle linebacker. The two-a-day practices in ninety-degree muggy heat were brutal.

I made friends with another defensive end, Don Brumm from Purdue, who the St. Louis Cardinals had drafted. Brumm had his car, so everyday after our second workout, we headed for the bars on Rush Street to replenish the fluids we left on the practice field. We would drink in these joints up until the last minute and then rush back to Evanston for our eleven o'clock curfew. Most evenings we made it back in time, but there were a few times when we didn't. Graham, the head coach of the Coast Guard Academy and a strict disciplinarian, was furious when we were late. After practice, when the rest of the team headed for the locker room, we ran extra sprints and laps for punishment. They were torturous with a bad hangover, but our vows of "never again," were soon forgotten once we hit the showers. It's amazing how much abuse the human body can take when it's young. After our next curfew violation, Otto was so pissed that he threatened to send us home! Imagine being kicked off the team by one of my childhood heroes. That would be quite traumatic. We promised to cool it and were allowed to stay on the team.

News of my drinking reached San Diego. Jack Murphy, sports editor of the *San Diego Union*, was in town covering the game and tagged me with the nickname "Suds." I could see that explaining this to Jean would not be an easy task, especially when she was about to give birth.

Game day finally rolled around. The team had nothing scheduled. No pre-game meal or meetings, just show up at the stadium to get taped and dressed for the game. Six of us piled into Brumm's car and headed downtown. One of our teammates had a friend with a suite in one of the better hotels just ten minutes from the stadium. The plan was to hang out for a couple of hours before we went to Soldier Field.

Our pre-game meal consisted of about six beers apiece. It was the only time in my life that I had drank before a game. It seemed strange to me that we had half a dozen of the best pro prospects in the country and yet none of us hesitated in throwing down the beers. In the car on our way to Soldier Field, we ate mints, chewed gum, gargled mouthwash and shot the shit about everything except the game.

As I slowly worked my way into my uniform, it started to dawn on me that in a couple of hours I would be on the field playing against the NFL champs. On one hand, I was anticipating bringing my game to the next level. On the other hand, I was full of fear. I didn't know what to expect. I didn't want to be embarrassed. I wanted to look good against the Packers and show the people in San Diego, who had been reading Murphy's accounts of my off-field behavior, that I was worthy of being the Chargers' top draft pick.

As I was sitting in my locker trying to get my head together, I was wishing I hadn't consumed all those beers. I was feeling sluggish and disconnected from my body. Absent was the hyperactive urge to hit something, which I usually had in the locker room before a game. Worried about the beers, I went into my "overcompensation" mode and had a great game. I was flying by Forest Gregg, the Packer's All-Pro offensive tackle, sacking Bart Starr and nailing Jim Taylor in the backfield several times. The College All-Stars played superbly that night. We beat the Packers 24–21. It was the last time the All-Stars would beat the world champions. The game was discontinued in 1977. Vince Lombardi, the legendary Packers coach, was embarrassed and beside himself with anger. His nearly invincible team had been beaten by a bunch of college boys. I wonder what he would have thought if he had known that six of the All-Star starters had a pretty good buzz on.

Suds Sweeney

The flight from Chicago was on time and Jean was there to meet me. I could tell by her demeanor that she was upset. We had been separated a lot that summer. I had been in Buffalo for a week in June during the Coaches All-America Game and now I was returning from three weeks in Chicago.

"Hi," I said bending down to embrace her.

"Hello," she replied casually. I was expecting a warmer welcome. Didn't she love me as much as I loved me?

"How's the baby? I can't wait to see her!"

"She's fine. My parents are watching her until we get back to the apartment." By the tone of her voice, I felt more like an intruder than the father of her child. Our daughter Kristin had been born a week earlier.

As I got my luggage, Jean brought the car around. I had to remove the local sports page from the passenger seat before I got in. I started reading and discovered why Jean was so cool. Jack Murphy's column jumped out at me.

"Walter Francis Sweeney, the brawling Irishman from Cohasset, Mass, is coming to town." From then on, Murphy referred to me as "Suds." He praised my play against the Packers. I would be a tremendous asset to the Charger defense. He also made some offhand and not very subtle remarks about how my residency in San Diego wouldn't hurt the local bar business.

"I thought that was all behind us, Walt."

"C'mon Jean. You know how these sportswriters are. They like to stretch the truth to sell newspapers." If anything, in this case, they were giving me a break.

"Are you saying that you weren't out drinking every night?

"For Christ sakes, I had a few beers after busting my ass for five hours on the practice field in ninety-degree heat! What's wrong with that?"

"You know how I feel about you hanging around bars and getting drunk!"

I was trying to stay calm, but underneath I was seething. Thanks to Jack Murphy, my homecoming was a disaster. I had to blame Jack. I couldn't take responsibility. Sometimes I wonder if growing up without a positive male role model was the reason I was such a lousy husband. My brothers were my only examples. They had their own problems with the sauce and with women when they had them.

I kept my mouth shut for the remainder of the ride home. I hoped we could get along until I left for training camp the next day. Gillman was anxious for me to get with the program because I was already three weeks behind my fellow rookies. Early the next morning, Jean drove me the sixty-miles to Boulevard where the Charger training camp was located. I'm not the type of guy who looked forward to training camps of any kind, but because of the tension on the home front, it didn't seem like a bad place to escape the situation.

Sid had sent me some brochures about a million-dollar dude ranch (this is back in the days when a million-dollars was a million-dollars) where the team would be housed for summer camp. The ranch was called Rough Acres. The brochures made the place look like a first class operation. We drove through downtown Boulevard in about five seconds. I did notice two bars, the Oak Knoll Tavern and the Gopher Hole. I was sure I'd become quite familiar with both of these fine establishments.

We spotted the sign for Rough Acres and took a long, sandy road. A run-down motel office was at the end of the road. I kissed Jean goodbye, grabbed my bags and headed up the stairs to the entrance. I introduced myself to Frances Beede, one of the Charger secretaries. She gave me a room key and directions. As I headed to the room, I couldn't help but notice how run-down this place was. Those photographs in the brochure Sid sent me must have been taken several decades earlier. I got to my room and my roommate, Pat Shea, was sprawled out on the bed. After playing second team guard at the University of Southern California, Shea had been a walk-on the year before. Because of his work ethic, strength, and combative nature, he became a starting guard with the Chargers in 1962. We shot the breeze as I put my gear away. My first impression was that he was as big a fuck-up as me. I liked him right away.

"The team had a pretty good laugh when they read in the paper that you're a big drinker. Some of the guys were heckling management for drafting a lounge lizard."

That was just what I needed to hear on my first day in camp. Shea filled me in on the schedule:

7:00 a.m.	breakfast
7:30 a.m.	taping
8:00–9:00 a.m.	team meeting
9:30–11:30 a.m.	practice
12:00–3:00 p.m.	lunch break
3:00–5:00 p.m.	practice
6:00–7:00 p.m.	dinner
7:00–9:00 p.m.	team meeting
9:00–11:00 p.m.	Gopher Hole/Oak Knoll Tavern
11:00 p.m.	curfew

My first night in training camp, prior to curfew I'm sure, Shea took me to a nearby motel to meet some of the players who were having a private party. There were five guys sitting around the room drinking beer watching a teammate perform cunnilingus on a woman on a bed in the corner. After shaking hands all around with the beer drinkers, the guy with the girl lifted his head out of her crotch and introduced himself. Without blinking an eye, he returned to his activity.

Whenever the team rode on a bus, which was quite often, the muncher insisted on the last seat next to the window. He was always looking into cars hoping to catch somebody getting a blowjob. He said that if he were ever fortunate enough to discover a couple in the act, he would give up his seat. As far as I know, he occupied the same seat until he left the game in the late 1960s.

The backs would lift weights after the morning practice and the linemen would lift in the afternoon. Sid Gillman was the first coach to hire a full time strength coach, Alvin Roy of Baton Rouge, Louisiana. I didn't even know where the weight room was at Syracuse. They had a volunteer program, but I didn't participate. Since the Chargers were paying me, I figured I had better do what they told me to do.

A ball boy came by the room and told me that Sid wanted to see me before practice. As I waited in his outer office, I wondered what he wanted. Was it to welcome me to camp? Was it to ask me about Jack Murphy's column? What was it? He appeared in the doorway and I followed him into his office.

"Walt, I know you have been playing defense in these All-Star games and we talked about you playing middle linebacker for us, but we have a problem. We've had a rash of injuries in the offensive line, especially at guard. The coaching staff and I think that you would make a dream guard."

My ears couldn't believe what they were hearing. While Sid was talking about a "dream guard," I thought I was having a horrible nightmare.

"Okay," I replied, but I didn't feel okay. A guard, shit. What next? Where was Al Davis? Al had said I'd be a perfect middle linebacker.

Between the time I signed with San Diego and the time I reported to training camp, Al had been hired as the head coach of the Oakland Raiders. After he took the job, he phoned and said that he hoped that I didn't think he was running out on me. I thought that was pretty cool. I don't think too many coaches would have taken the time to do it. Al Davis was, and is, a class act.

"Playing guard will be totally foreign to me, but I'll give it my best shot."

As a tight end at Syracuse, most of my blocking consisted of double-teaming with the offensive tackle or throwing body blocks downfield. I did very well in that phase of the game, but I had no pass protection experience. I was usually in the pass pattern.

"I know you will, Walt. That's why we made you our top pick. After lunch, I want you to see Alvin Roy and he'll set you up with a weight program."

All of a sudden I was on shaky ground. I cruised through high school and college ball wasn't that tough. I figured coming in here as a defensive player would have been hard enough, but I'd probably be able to hold my own because of my quickness and speed. Besides, defense is more natural. An offensive lineman has to be disciplined, and discipline wasn't my long suit. They have to learn different blocking techniques for various situations. It wasn't going to be easy.

Ever since I was in Little League, I always looked up to coaches as father figures. I strove to be the best because I wanted them to like me. I offered no opposition to Sid when he told me that I would be a guard. I wanted him to like me.

Alvin Roy, a former USA Olympic strength coach, was a likeable guy from the Deep South. He noticed the Russians were getting amazing results from an anabolic steroid called Dianabol. He thought the San Diego Chargers should take it, too. We didn't know a steroid from a vitamin and, as a matter of fact, Alvin told us they were vitamins. They would make us bigger and stronger.

Everyday at training camp, Alvin would come around at lunchtime and watch each of us take these two little pink pills. If we didn't take them, we were fined fifty dollars. Now fifty bucks doesn't seem like much these days when players make millions, but back then that's what we were given for an exhibition game. That's what I was feeding my family with until the season began.

I remember the Chargers All-Pro offensive tackle, Ron Mix, gave Sid a medical book that described the harmful affects of anabolic steroids. It was during a team meeting. We all watched as Sid thumbed through it. A few minutes later, he threw it on the floor.

"This was written by a bunch of doctors. What do they know about football?" And that was that.

I only took Dianabol for three weeks during that first training camp. Years later, Mix told me that it was always available for the decade we played together. There were guys who took it for years. I saw one of our guards put on fifteen pounds of muscle in three weeks.

I hated training camp. I hated the weights. I hated the sweltering heat. I hated the sandy practice field, but the thing I hated the most was becoming an offensive lineman. I had been a high scoring running back in high school. At Syracuse, I had dependable hands on offense as a tight end, but defensive end was my forte. Now, in my opinion at that time, I had sunk to the lowest position on a football team—an offensive lineman. I knew these guys were necessary, but whenever I watched game films, I usually just watched myself. When I did look at the linemen, they reminded of a bunch of big guys leaning on each other.

To make matters worse, I was in lousy shape when I showed up. As Jerry Magee, the beat writer for the *San Diego Union*, so aptly put in it his column: "Sweeney looks like a mouse that crawled out of a beer barrel."

One day, I overheard Alvin Roy talking to Sid. "I think you made a mistake drafting Sweeney."

I remembered those words when I was assigned to play on all of the special teams in my Charger debut.

We drove into downtown San Diego and Balboa Stadium for the second exhibition game of the season against the Raiders. I was in Chicago when the Chargers beat the Oilers in the opener. Sam Gruniesen, a big redheaded center/guard, rode with Shea and me. Sam was a solid citizen, a good family man and a real student of the game. After Shea and I roomed together for a week, Sid split us up. Sam became my roommate. I guess Sid figured that mischievous boys like Shea and me shouldn't be living together.

We pulled into the parking lot about 4:00 p.m. Game time was at 6:00 p.m. and the temperature was in the high eighties. It seemed much hotter in that old locker room. Our head trainer, Kerney Roebe, and two assistant trainers were busy taping ankles. As I waited in line for my turn, I noticed that some of the players were reaching into Kerney's pocket and pulling out a small brown jar. They opened the jar and helped themselves to these orange triangular pills. Shea told me that the pills were Dexedrine or speed. He suggested that I ought to try them. Speed was new to me. The only drug I had taken up until this point was alcohol and that was just fine with me. I thought speed, as the name implies, made you run faster. If one could make you faster than two would work even better. Four would make you as fast as "Bullet Bob"

Hayes. I didn't realize that it made your heart race at what seemed, a thousand-beats-per-minute.

As Kerney was taping, I reached into his pocket, extracted the bottle ever so carefully, and helped myself to half a dozen pills. I've always been a pig: food, booze and now these magic little triangles. Kerney turned to see who was in his pockets this time.

"You too?" he asked and I slid back to my locker like a thief in the night.

I took all the pills and proceeded to dress for the game. I didn't expect to see any action in the offensive line, but I was ready to start on all the special teams. A sense of well-being started to spread through me. The usual pre-game jitters seemed to be absent. I felt unusually sharp during pre-game warm ups.

Feeling sharp though, doesn't necessarily mean you are sharp. As I was giving Lance Alworth some helmet slaps, a pre-game ritual we shared the many years that we played together for the Chargers, my body was buzzing with nervous energy. I thought to myself that this was too good to be true. A job that lets you get high and, in some cases, encourages it. Perfect for someone like me who was already altering his mind with alcohol.

Oakland won the toss and, eagerly waiting for the opening whistle, I took my position next to the kicker. I was the first player in Oakland territory and made the tackle on the 12-yard line. I was beating wide receivers downfield and made four out of five tackles on punt and kickoff coverage. In ensuing years, the team press guide said that I became a favorite of the San Diego fans during my rookie year due to my "Herculean" efforts on special teams.

After the game, I thought my heart was going to explode.

"Shea, I took six of those pills and I feel like I'm jumping out of my skin." I muttered this in the general direction of Pat.

"I'll go get Kerney." Kerney was there in a flash.

"Why did you take so many?"

"I don't know! There weren't any instructions on that bottle in your pocket!"

"Alright, alright. Take it easy. The good news is you're not going to die and the bad news is that Sid will hear about it."

"Fuck it!"

"I assume you're going home after you shower."

"Yeah."

"I'm giving you two Seconals. It's a strong barbiturate. After you've been home for a couple of hours, take them and go to bed."

That was the last time that happened. I cut the dosage in half and everything was hunky-dory. Speed didn't enhance my performance, but it sure made me feel good on game day. It did allow me to play hurt—probably when I shouldn't have.

My rookie year was a real eye opener. They say an army moves on its stomach, but I concluded that a football team moves on its drugs. I discovered that drugs were an integral part of the San Diego Chargers. As I got to know guys from other teams, I realized it was just a part of football that I never knew existed. Some guys told me that they had been playing on speed since high school.

One year we were playing the Raiders in an exhibition game in Oakland and our trainer forgot to pack the speed. He ran over to the Raider locker room before the game and borrowed some of theirs. They probably wouldn't have been so generous if it was a regular season game. They had "black beauties," probably to match their uniforms, but they worked the same as ours and the game went on.

Speed for football spawned a whole other industry. Every team stocked cases of saliva stimulant. You would squirt this lime-flavored liquid on a little wad of cotton and place it in your mouth. It kept you from getting "dry mouth," a common symptom of amphetamine use. Before I knew about saliva stimulant, I would chew gum during a game and inevitably it would end up all over my face and facemask.

In the autumn of 1963, Jean, Kristin and I moved to the beautiful seaside community of Del Mar. I was driving to San Diego when I heard on the radio that President Kennedy had been assassinated. I went numb after the news bulletin. It was earlier that summer that we watched President Kennedy's motorcade going down El Cajon Boulevard in San Diego. I was from "Kennedy Country." We all loved the Kennedys no matter if they were good, bad, or ugly. The NFL played their regularly scheduled games that Sunday after the assassination. Out of respect for the President, the AFL postponed their games for a week. I thought the NFL should have also cancelled their games.

We had an 11–3 record my first year and all my playing time was on special teams. We beat the Boston Patriots, 51–10, in San Diego for the American Football League Championship. The game was played before of a whopping crowd of 30,127 laid-back fans. Our quarterback, Tobin Rote, picked the Patriot defense apart with pinpoint passes to Lance Alworth and Keith Lincoln. Lincoln rushed for 206 yards and Paul Lowe added 94 more on the ground. Our defense shut down Babe Parelli and the rest of the Patriot offense. The winner's share was about $1,700. The Patriots came to San Diego about a week before the game to escape the terrible East Coast weather. Rumor had it that several Patriot players went to Black's Beach—San Diego's nude beach—and got such bad sunburns on their genitalia that they were unable to play in the game.

I thought that would be the first of many championships, but we never won another in my eleven years with San Diego. Perhaps the Chargers should have continued to make steroid use mandatory. My good friend, Ben Davidson, former great defensive end for the Oakland Raiders, says the Chargers will never win because there are too many sailboats, beaches, and good-looking women to name a few of the many distractions in San Diego.

In my day, most of the players worked during the off-season with the hope of developing another career after football. My first couple of years in San Diego, I sold pickups and campers. I also did their TV commercials. Our sales lot was located in downtown San Diego and I spent more time in the bars than I did at work. This was back when the military was the number one industry in San Diego. Broadway was lined with go-go bars, tattoo parlors, billiard halls and locker clubs where the sailors stored their "civvies" while in port. Naturally, there were plenty of bars. I tried to share the wealth and hit them all.

My relationship with alcohol started at a fairly young age. I was always a shy kid with little confidence and a lot of fears. My Uncle Henry had an old cow in a pasture with a huge fence around it. Even though it was fenced, someone had to walk with me until we'd pass that "evil" old cow. During the Korean War, my brother Bobby kept telling me that the Chinese were going to bomb us any day. That, coupled with the fact that everyone was building bomb shelters, kept me terrified for months.

When I was about ten years old, I started watching the *Gillette Friday Night Fights* at my Grandfather Jim's house. I loved Jim and looked forward to those times together. I always had cookies and cocoa while Jim nursed his Ballantine Ale. One night, he gave me a glass of his ale. It was like a magic elixir. I don't think I was a very happy child growing up. I remember being very moody and most of my moods were on the down side. By the time I was in high school, I drank every weekend. When I drank I was no longer shy or afraid. I had that "Dutch courage" going for or against me depending on how you looked at it. I would do things drunk that would make me shudder when I was sober. I had a reputation for being a fighter. I'm not sure how that came about, because I can only remember being in a couple of fights. My philosophy was look crazy and no one will fuck with you. Of course it helps if you're bigger than most people. I had seen this work for my brothers. The only difference was that my brothers really were crazy!

Sometimes, just to drink the way I wanted, I'd tell Jean that I had to go to Los Angeles on business. She thought she was married to a normal person and had no reason to think otherwise. I would make the two-hour drive to LA and start looking for a hotel with a good bar. If it passed the test, I would check in. To pass the test, it had to have booze, a bartender, and be within stumbling distance to my hotel room.

On one such memorable trip, I checked into a hotel about 10:00 a.m. and immediately went to the bar to pound down the scotch and waters. At 260 pounds, I could consume a lot of booze and look reasonably sober right up to the very end. Then I would completely fall apart.

One of the cocktail waitresses had taken a shine to me and we made plans to meet in my room when she got off work at midnight. It was about 10:00 p.m. and I had already been drinking for twelve hours. I wouldn't think about cheating on Jean if I was sober, well...maybe I'd think about it, but I wouldn't act on it. One of the problems with booze is that it causes you to make bad decisions. I was sitting at the bar in a light gray suit and was having trouble controlling my bowels. As a matter of fact, I shit my pants. Mortified, I scooted out of the lounge as quickly as possible and hoped that nobody noticed the stains on my pants. Once in my room, I worked at getting the stains out of my trousers before jumping in the shower. Out of the shower and into some clean underwear. I wore the same suit, because it was all I had and back to the bar to claim my date. Apparently the "gild had gone off the lily" because she was long gone.

My first arrest for drunk driving was during the off-season. Several of the Chargers—Paul Maguire, Bob Zeman and Dave Koucerok—owned the Surfer Lounge in Pacific Beach. The bar was right on the beach. Many an afternoon, I just sat there to watch the waves pound the sand and the sun sink into the ocean. Our punter, Paul Maguire, worked the day shift and had a good following. This guy should have been a stand up comic instead of a bartender or a punter. It was probably a good training ground for his ESPN broadcasting job.

One afternoon after listening to Maguire's jokes, watching the surf and drinking, I headed for my car. Two blocks later, the police stopped me for an equipment violation. Unbeknownst to me, I had a taillight out. I reeked of alcohol. I was taken downtown to police headquarters and booked. I had to call Jean to come down and bail me out. Naturally, she was pissed off and disappointed!

The one thing I did do right in the off-season was to join a gym and follow the program Alvin Roy had set up for me. I was going to be in top shape for 1964. I wanted to be a starter.

Time for Serious Business

In mid-July, I reported to training camp in Escondido, about thirty miles north and inland of San Diego. We weren't welcomed back at Rough Acres because of a questionable scene in the rookie show the previous summer. One of our players simulated jacking off a donkey. There was a pending law suit against the Chargers and the owners of Rough Acres filed by the Society for the Prevention of Cruelty to Animals.

I was glad to be in Escondido. Although it was hotter than hell in the summer, it had a lot more watering holes than Boulevard and it was only thirty minutes from San Diego. Sam Gruniesen and I were rooming together again. We were housed at the TraveLodge and took our meals at Palomar Lanes, a bowling alley Sid owned adjacent to the motel. Sid had a beer and pizza party our first night in camp. All the guys who were on the team the year before were given AFL Championship rings. The rings were nice looking and, thinking this would be the first of many rings, I had the brilliant idea of having mine made into a charm for Jean's birthday. That was my first and last ring.

I was promoted to starting left guard because of the great job I had done on special teams the year before. Usually starters didn't play special teams, but I was an exception to the rule.

Some of the guys who didn't hit the bars stayed behind at the TraveLodge and had some serious card games. Thousand of dollars were at stake and finally Sid put a stop to it. Gambling was too much of a distraction. Losing money to a teammate was not good for team moral.

The two hours that I had to drink—9:00 p.m. to 11:00 p.m.—weren't long enough for me. Several times a week, I would sneak out after bed check. Besides taking the chance of being fined, I risked the wrath of Sid Gillman which would have been worse. I liked Sid and he liked me. I didn't want to ruin our relationship, but once "demon rum" kicked in, the little common sense I might have had went right out the window.

Practicing football with little sleep and a hangover was brutal in the Southern California summer heat. There were many times I promised myself that if I could just get through practice, I'd straighten up and fly right. But it was the same old story, out of the shower and off to the races again.

On August 7, 1964, while I was in training camp, Jean gave birth to our son, Patrick McCormick Sweeney. This was an era when having babies was considered "women's work." After conception occurred, my part was done. However, I did manage to get to the hospital about twenty minutes after Patrick was born.

Our head trainer, Kerney Roebe, retired and was replaced by Jimmy Van Duesen. We had new pockets to pick and Desbutol replaced Dexadrine. Desbutol was speed with a little bit of downer so you wouldn't get too far out there. This was before drug testing. As a matter of fact, drugs were tested on us. Desbutol was so good that they took it off the market a few years later.

I did all right the first two games of the season, especially for a guy who never played guard before. What I lacked in technique, I made up for in quickness and aggressiveness. When I was leading sweeps, my cross body blocks always brought the defenders down. Our star halfback, Paul Lowe, had this to say: "Following Sweeney is like following a flashlight in the dark."

I was by no means an accomplished guard. I had a long way to go, but I realized it might not be as tough as I first thought.

"A day at the beach," was a phrase used when your opponent wasn't that good. My first two games were "days at the beach." I wondered how many times my opponents would say that about me?

Our next three games were on the road. We were headed east for Buffalo, Boston, and New York. After the Bill's game, we would stay in Niagara Falls for a week to prepare for the Boston Patriots. When the Boston game was over, we would fly to New York and stay at Bear Mountain, a resort about fifty miles north of the city. We would be there for a week as we prepared for the New York Jets. It was our only long trip of the season—seventeen days—and everybody looked forward to it. It got us away from the wife and kids for a couple of weeks and there was always that great Canadian beer. It was also a chance for me to see my mother and the rest of the family.

Playing against the Bills, I would face my first real challenge. Tom Sestak was Buffalo's All-Pro defensive tackle and the premiere defensive lineman in the league. I failed my first true test and was completely embarrassed. According to the local sports page the next day, "he handled me like I was on "roller skates." Sestak was all over John Hadl who had taken control at quarterback. It's hard to throw the ball when you're flat on your back. Hadl took out his frustrations by screaming, "Can't you block that son of a bitch, Sweeney?"

I had never been so humiliated in a football game before. I decided that was never going to happen to me again. If I couldn't block someone legally, I would do anything to keep him off my quarterback. I became quite adept at various holding techniques and knowing where the referees were. I would say that I was a desperate player who played with a lot of fear rather than a dirty player. Dirty players don't care if they hurt people. I didn't want to hurt anybody. I just wanted to do my job. I became a master at cut blocking, leg whipping, and as a last resort, the facemask pull-down.

We played the Patriots the following weekend at Fenway Park, home of the Boston Red Sox. I was fortunate enough to see my childhood hero, Ted Williams, play here in the 1950s. I loved it when he flipped off the fans after they heckled him.

It seemed like we played in a different place every time we came to Boston. One year it would be Fenway, the next it would be Harvard Stadium or Boston College Field.

We won a close game. It was hardly a repeat of the championship game earlier that year. I had a chance to spend Saturday afternoon with my family and also have a short visit with them after the game before we caught a plane to New York.

About twenty minutes into the flight, Sid's voice came over the loud speaker:

"It wasn't pretty today, but we got it done. Everyone is to be at Bear Mountain for dinner at 6:00 p.m. tomorrow night. Busses will be at the airport for those who want to go there tonight. Those who are not on the busses are on their own as far as transportation is concerned. Congratulations on the game and if you stay in the city, take it easy."

Everybody started clapping and cheering after Sid's announcement. A night off in the "Big Apple." We couldn't believe it! The speed I took at half-time was kicking in along with the in-flight beers. I was ready for a night off.

The plane landed in Newark about 7:00 p.m.. Pat Shea, Bob Zeman, and I took a cab into New York. Zeman was a hard-hitting safety who had been with the Chargers two years earlier, but was traded to Denver. Now he was back. From what I gathered, the team was flying home after a victory and Zeman had gotten very drunk. He vomited on Mrs. Baron Hilton, the owner's wife, and passed out. Some of his fun-loving teammates proceeded to stuff celery and carrot sticks into all the orifices in his head. The next day, Bob was a Bronco.

With twenty-four hours off and a pocket full of speed in the city that never sleeps, Shea and I managed to slide a few extra Desbutols out of Van Dusen's side pocket pharmacy. After hitting a few bars, we found ourselves at Sullivan's on East 71st Street.

"Who do you guys play ball for?"

"Who wants to know?" asked half-in-the-bag Zeman.

"Timothy O'Hara and this is my friend, Michael Regan."

"We're with the Chargers," piped in Shea.

"We were at the game," O'Hara said.

It turns out that O'Hara and Regan were off-duty civil servants, a cop and a fireman respectively. We shot the shit with these guys for a while and then decided to move on. O'Hara and Regan, who were becoming bigger assholes by the minute, wanted to go along with us.

Zeman, who was about sixty pounds lighter than Shea and me, was feeling his booze and growing hostile. I could see trouble coming and we hustled Bob outside. New York's finest trailed behind. We made it apparent that we didn't want them with us, but they still followed. If these guys had a death wish, Shea and Zeman would have been happy to oblige.

"Get away from us you faggots!" Bob yelled.

That's all it took. A brief scuffle ensued. O'Hara and Regan ended up stretched out on the sidewalk. No one was hurt and I thought it was over. We got about a block away and here come these two crazy drunks after us. After a few minutes of cursing and shoving with me being the referee, the cops showed up. Shea was smart and took off. I should have followed, but up until this point, we had done nothing wrong. The cops had Zeman and me with our backs up against the side of a brownstone. All of a sudden, the fireman, all 5'6" and 160 pounds of him, lunged out at us. Bob and I, standing side by side, reacted by putting our arms up and shoving him backward onto the sidewalk. He hit his head on the concrete and was knocked out cold. When the ambulance arrives to take him to the hospital, he's still unconscious. Oh how I should have taken off with Shea, because Zeman and I were arrested.

We were sitting in a police station while the authorities in the next room were deciding what to do with us. We popped the remaining Desbutols and thought the whole thing was a joke until they booked us for felonious assault. In the span of thirteen hours, we toured eleven different New York jails. At one of these police stations, we were sitting behind a table when they brought in a couple of hookers to be booked. We were wearing suits and ties and the ladies began flirting with us. They thought we were detectives. They went slack-jawed when we were cuffed and led out of the building.

Every hour or so, we were moved to a different precinct until they finally dumped in The Tombs where we were released to the custody of the Chargers. Bobby Hood, the assistant equipment manager, drove down from Bear Mountain to retrieve us. We arrived in time to join the team for dinner. As Zeman and I entered the dining room, we were greeted by the very loud voice of our 6'9", 320 pound defensive tackle, Ernie Ladd: "What kind of birds don't fly? Jailbirds!"

Our teammates found a lot of humor in our plight, but I didn't think it was so funny. It had been a rough week for me and I was full of silent rage. My only mistake was being in the wrong place at the wrong time. Jean wasn't speaking to me. I had embarrassed her again. The East Coast newspapers had the story on the front pages.

Two San Diego Chargers Arrested for Felonious Assault

The San Diego papers had similar headlines. I called my mother in Boston and Jean's parents in New Jersey and told them it was all a big mistake.

We appeared in court the day before our game with the Jets. I tried to slouch my 6'4" frame down as low as I could. Zeman and

I stood next to the squat fireman in front of the judge. All charges were dismissed.

We were lucky because after the fireman hit his head, he went into a twenty-four hour coma. It cost Zeman and me $750.00 each for a lawyer. We had to give a guy that used to be in the District Attorney's office $500.00 and the arresting officers $100.00 each just so they would tell the truth. I was still pissed at game time and took out my frustrations on my opponent. We won the game and I had my best day as a pro.

We won our division, but lost, 20–7, to Buffalo in the championship game. I fared much better in my rematch with Tom Sestak. I was chosen to go to the AFL All-Star Game. I felt especially honored to have made the team since the players, not the sportswriters, chose those who went. The game was to be held in New Orleans. I was looking forward to a week in Dixie. Making the team was a reward for the players that excelled during the season, but the game itself didn't mean much.

On my first day in the Big Easy, I was hanging out with Keith Lincoln, the Chargers leading rusher, and Johnny Robinson, Kansas City's All-Pro safety. Robinson had played college ball up the road at LSU and was well connected in New Orleans. We were set up with everything from massages at the exclusive New Orleans Men's Club to high price hookers from the Absinthe House on Bourbon Street.

On a rainy Tuesday night, I was out bar hopping with fellow Chargers, Ernie Ladd and Earl Faison. It was slow around town and we decided to go back to the hotel. We hailed a cab. The driver stopped and told me that Ladd and Faison couldn't ride in his cab, because they were black. I had heard about discrimination all my life, but to my knowledge, I don't think I had ever seen it before. It was the first time that I felt guilty about being white. The next day, the game was pulled out of New Orleans and moved to Houston.

Back in those days, the AFL had their All-Star Game in different cities to test the market for future franchises. They (the AFL) backed off New Orleans, but the NFL, recognizing a lucrative market, did not.

Disappointed about leaving New Orleans, we checked into the Shamrock Hilton. Houston wasn't one of my favorite cities. I had been there several times to play the Oilers and that's where the fun ended. Maybe it was the liquor laws that didn't agree with me. You had to bring your own jug into a private club and buy setups. A player from the Oiler organization arranged a temporary membership at a private club called the Dome Shadows. As the name implies, it was very close to the Astrodome. I spent the rest of the week sucking up the sauce at the Shadows. I don't remember who won the game, but I do remember throwing up on the defensive tackle I played against.

Clever Maneuvers That Should Have Worked

Two years had passed since I signed with the Chargers and now it was time to negotiate a new contract. This was prior to player agents and I hated this aspect of pro football. My line coach, Joe Madro, once told me I had an exalted opinion of myself. This is the same guy that said: "For ratio of size and speed, Sweeney is best lineman in the game."

When it came to talking contract and asking for money, I had a very difficult time. On the one hand, I thought I was a real hot commodity and on the other, I didn't feel like I was worth what they were paying me. I guess it had a lot to do with my alcoholism and low self-esteem. In the time before free agency, you either played for what a team offered you or you didn't play at all.

As I drove to the Chargers office at the Lafayette Hotel, I was dreading my meeting with Sid. I knew if I hit the Red Fox Room downstairs and had five or six cocktails to bolster my courage, I would probably do better. On second thought, it was 10:00 a.m. in the morning and it might be a bad idea to show up smelling like a distillery. Besides, the bar wasn't opened yet. I was drunk when I signed my first contract and that certainly didn't help.

My meeting with Sid took about five minutes and it went something like this.

"Sid, I went to the All-Star Game last year and I think I should be paid accordingly."

His responds was automatic, "I've seen more bums come through those All-Star games than you can shake a stick at,".

My big bargaining ploy had been shot down within thirty seconds of my arrival and I didn't have a back-up plan. If you didn't make the All-Star team, he would be quick to point that out. There was no way I could win dealing with him. I signed a progressive three-year, no-cut, no-trade contract for $20,000, $22,500 and $25,000. I didn't have enough confidence in my own ability to go after more money, so I went for security. To tell the truth, I was happy to get that contract and felt very fortunate to be playing pro football. The average guy on the street was probably making about five-six grand and busting his ass for the whole year. I was getting paid relatively well for something I loved and only worked for five months out of the year.

I had a BA degree in history and there wasn't any way that I could make that kind of money anywhere else. I know the best place to live is where you make your money and after living on the East Coast most of my life, I didn't want to leave San Diego. Neither did Jean.

Paul Maguire, San Diego restaurateur and punter, went to Sid and told him he wanted to buy a house. Sid assured him he would be on the team for the upcoming season. He recommended that Paul should buy it. Two weeks after escrow closed, Sid traded him to Buffalo.

With a new three-year contract under my belt, I hit the gym in the off-season with renewed enthusiasm. I was in excellent shape when I reported to camp in Escondido. I was switched from left to right guard. We ran a lot of sweeps. Sid wanted his fastest linemen, Ron Mix and me, on the right side. That was fine with me, because I felt more comfortable on that side.

It was a cloudy Friday afternoon when we checked into the Kansas City Hilton for our Sunday opener with the Chiefs. Maybe it's because I'm an alcoholic, but I used to pay particular attention to the bars we passed en route from the airport to the hotel. Muncher looked for blowjobs while I looked for an interesting lounge to slide into when we had some spare time. On this ride, nothing struck my fancy.

We had a couple of hours to kill before dinner, so Sam and I caught a cab for the End Zone which owned by the Chiefs defensive tackle, Big Ed Lothamer. Ed was a nice guy that I met the year before at the All-Star Game. We had a standing invitation to his place anytime we were in town. We hooked up with Bill Lenkaitis, our second year center behind Sam, and we were off to the End Zone.

As we walked in, I heard Lothamer yell, "Hey, Sweeney, over here!"

After introducing Sam and Bill, we started bullshitting each other about how much respect we had for one another's team. With that out of the way, we got down to the business at hand of catching a buzz.

The place was full of Chiefs fans who had been drinking since they got off work. When word got out that we were with the Chargers, the drinks started flying our way. Why not get the opponents drunk? Maybc it would make the Chiefs job easier on Sunday.

Within half an hour, half a dozen more Chargers piled into the already over-crowded saloon. Lothamer introduced Bill and me to a couple of his waitresses who were dressed in sexy little referee outfits. As the warmth of the booze spread through my body, I could feel any good judgment I might have had start to slip away. The girls were very suggestive and it appeared we wouldn't be disappointed if we came back after curfew.

Sam and I were lying on our beds watching the eleven o'clock news when trainer Jimmy Van Duesen knocked on the door.

"Sweeney. Are you there?"

"It ain't Richard Nixon." (Alcohol makes me clever.)

"How about you, Gruneisen?"

"Yeah."

We listened as he made his way down the hallway, knocking on doors and checking to make sure the rest of the players were in their rooms.

"Shit! I forgot to get my Seconals from him."

The year before, I had started taking Seconals the night before a game to get a good night's rest. They knocked me out for about seven hours and, before you drift off, the high is very mellow.

Sam laughed. "I thought you and Lenkaitis were sneaking out. You won't need them."

"We are, and I won't, but you know how suspicious he is. He thinks he's Dick Tracy. He knows I always take the Seconal on the road."

"There are forty other ball players on this team and I don't think you are foremost on his mind. Stop being so paranoid."

"Yeah, maybe."

He was right about that. I did worry too much. It was usually about me trying to cover my ass for being in the wrong place at the wrong time or for some similar lack of judgment.

I mulled over my options. If I got caught breaking curfew, I would be fined a thousand dollars. Even worse, I would be exhibiting a piss poor attitude and incur the wrath of the coaches. On the other hand, there was the good probability of getting laid. After giving this about thirty seconds of careful consideration, I made my decision. "See ya later, Sam."

Whenever the team stayed at a hotel, I always made it a habit to check the premises for exits. At midnight, I went by Bill's room and we walked down five flights to the basement before making our unseen departure from the hotel. I felt like I was in a spy movie. All I needed was a trench coat.

We caught a cab and returned to the End Zone. Bill was a bit on edge. If we got caught, it would be a lot harder on him than it would be on me. He was a backup center and I was entrenched in the starting line with a bright future. We were still in the cab and I was paying the driver when I spotted Jackie Simpson, our linebacker coach, and Bum Philips, our defensive line coach, coming out of the End Zone.

"Take it around the block!" I shrieked at the cab driver. Bill gave me a puzzled look. He hadn't seen the coaches. Nothing is ever easy I thought. I was always swimming up stream.

The bar was even more crowded than it had been earlier. Lothamer was still there. No curfew for the home team. Ed bought the first round and I noticed Bill getting friendly with Ellie, his now off-duty waitress friend. When my eyes finally adjusted to the dim lighting, I scanned the bar looking for my referee, Jenny. She was involved in deep conversation with a man at the end of the bar. She had a worried look on her face. Being the sensitive man that I am, I felt something was awry. When her friend left for the men's room, I walked over to her.

"Are we still on?" I asked.

"I have to work until two." She replied. She seemed to have lost some of the eagerness to spend time with me. I was getting a little hot under the collar.

"Are we still on?" I repeated the question.

"I think so."

"What's that mean? You told me that you wanted to see me and I risked getting fined by sneaking out and now you say you only think so. What the hell does that mean?"

"My boyfriend unexpectedly dropped in. That was him I was talking to. He went to call his wife and he wants to come over to my place when I get off work."

Usually I would back off if there was a husband or boyfriend involved, but this guy had a wife, so as far as I was concerned, fuck him.

"So, we won't go to your place. We'll get a motel room." I reached for her hand and gave her my most endearing smile and a look I hoped would make her think that I would take care of her. I slipped my arm around her waist. "So let him get angry. He'll appreciate you more." The relationship expert had spoken.

"He's taken his anger out on me before. He hits me and he carries a gun" she said!

Even with my brain clouded with scotch, this was beginning to sound like a bad situation. I found myself I wishing I were back at the Hilton in a deep Seconal slumber.

My endearing smile must have switched off when she mentioned the gun. She must have noticed my hesitation and her interest seemed to have rekindled. (Women, go I figure.)

"I'll have Joe come over with Bill and Ellie for a little while. Then I'll get rid of Joe and then you come up." Jenny's stupid idea seemed to make sense to my muddled mind.

As I've said before, common sense isn't one of my strong suits and this wasn't my kind of scene. But the more I drank, the less I became concerned about consequences. I informed Bill and Ellie of the plan. Ellie got Jenny's key and since she was already off, she left with Bill. I stayed at the bar and drank.

Jenny lived two blocks from the bar. Joe's yellow Cadillac was parked in front of her apartment building. When the bar closed, I went across the street and had some greasy eggs at an all-night diner. When the Caddy was gone, I would make my appearance. At quarter to three, I was leaning against an old oak tree across the street from her place smoking a cigarette. Was this guy was ever going to leave? My patience was wearing thin. I gave it fifteen more minutes before entering the building. I lumbered up the dark narrow stairway to the second floor and knocked on Jenny's door. Joe answered. I was relieved to find out he was much smaller than he appeared in the bar. "Yeah." He growled.

"I'm here to see Jenny," I said as I pushed passed him on into the living room where Lenkaitis was sitting on the couch with Ellie. Jenny, who had come into the room from the kitchen, was now standing facing me.

"Who's this guy?" Joe said in kind of growling whine.

"He's a Charger, too. This is Walt," Jenny told him.

Joe's eyes narrowed as he gave me the once over. I tried to return his scowl, but for all I know, I probably gave him one of my endearing smiles. I had way too much to drink.

"Come on in the kitchen, Joe. I want to talk to you," Jenny said.

Joe knew instinctively things didn't look good for him and he was getting pissed. They left the room and I sat down.

"Good timing," Bill said with a chuckle.

"Hey! Fuck you! I should have left your ass and gone back to the hotel. This is right up there on my most-stupid-fuckin' ideas list! Who needs this shit?"

I reached for the jug of whiskey on the coffee table and took a good-sized pull. The voices from the kitchen came through the wall as muted snarls and pleadings. They grew louder and sharper.

"Fuck you then, you dirt bag whore!" were Joe's parting words as he slammed the door.

Jenny appeared from the kitchen, a bit shaken, but with a coy look on her face.

"Alright, Babee!" I yelled as I pushed myself from the chair with as much dexterity as six hours of drinking would allow. We shared two or three more drinks with Bill and his waitress and retired to our respective bedrooms. Jenny and I slipped out of our clothes and into bed. I was about to perform a highly erotic act when I went out like a light. After all the bullshit I went through to be with this girl, any girl, I pulled a typical Sweeney stunt.

An hour and a half later I was wide-awake. I tried to arouse Jenny, but she wasn't going for it. She rolled over and went back to sleep. I made my way in the dark to the other bedroom to see if Ellie might still be awake. Bill and Ellie were both sound asleep. I was trying to reach her over Bill's big body when a shot rang out. Bill sat straight up, knocking my ass on the floor.

"What? What the hell was that?"

Two more shots and the sound of breaking glass.

"It's that nut case, Joe. I came in here to warn you," I said, hoping that he didn't notice me trying to grope his girlfriend.

"Let's get the hell out of here!" Bill rolled on the floor and grabbed his clothes. Ellie ran into the closet and closed the door behind her. I crawled toward the other bedroom. Jenny had the lights on and looked terrified. I hit the off button and pushed into my clothes.

"It's your fuckin' boyfriend!" I crawled into the living room with her close behind…more shots, more broken glass.

"That crazy son of a bitch is downstairs shooting the windows out!" Bill yelled.

"There's got to be a back way out of here," I said.

We found a set of stairs right off the kitchen. We were in the backyard when a police van containing the SWAT team came flying down the street screeching to a halt in front of Jenny's building.

"Jesus Christ," I whispered as we watched these guys in black vests and rifles fanning out over the street.

"This looks like a TV cop show."

"I'm not hanging around to see the ending," said Bill. He took the back wall like an Olympic hurdler and was in the next street by the time I was over the wall.

That Sunday at the stadium, while taking our warm-ups before the game, I kept checking the stands. I was more nervous than usual, because I couldn't help but wonder if #78 was in the cross hairs of Joe's gun.

Mean Joe Who?

Others have always said that I was a better football player than I thought I was. Even with Joe Madro saying I had an "exalted opinion" of myself, it had more to do with ego than with confidence in my ability as a professional offensive lineman. In high school and college, I thought I was as good as anyone else and better than most. But when they put me at guard, my confidence level went in the shitter. I became desperate and played with a lot of fear. I dreaded the thought of being embarrassed in front of thousands of fans more than the fact that the quarterback might get dumped on his ass.

From 1964 to 1969 I was voted to go to all six American Football League All-Star Games. After the merger between the NFL and AFL in 1970, the AFL All-Star Game was history. The NFL All-Star Game is called the Pro Bowl and I played in 1970, 1971 and 1972. As mentioned before, the All-Star team was chosen by opposing players. It was more gratifying to make this than some of the other All-Pro teams. I made my share of those teams, also. Over the years, I was selected to AP, DPI, and *The Sporting News* first and only combined AFL/NFL All-Pro team in 1968. The Thousand-Yard Club of Green Bay chose me "Lineman of the Year". I felt honored to make these various teams, but the thing I got the biggest charge out of was an article that didn't appear in *Sports Illustrated* in the early seventies.

We were playing the Pittsburgh Steelers at San Diego Stadium in San Diego. The Steelers had some great teams back in those years. Terry Bradshaw was at the helm and they had the notorious "Steel Curtain Defense" led by that great defensive tackle, "Mean"

Joe Green. We had our typical mediocre San Diego Charger team. The offense wasn't that bad, but our defense was Swiss cheese.

Tex Maule, legendary *SI* sportswriter, was in town to cover the game. The Steelers used a 4–3 defense, which meant Mean Joe would be right in front of me all day. Maule's feature was to be titled, The Demise of an All-Pro Guard. Joe Madro filled me in on the details of the proposed article before the game. If I was going down, I'd be going down swinging.

Mean Joe didn't touch our QB, John Hadl, all afternoon. I used every trick in the book against Green and even blocked him legitimately a couple of times. He couldn't believe the shit I was doing. At one point, he switched sides with their other defensive tackle, Ernie Holmes. I guess he wanted to show Ernie what he was up against.

Now Holmes was a guy who while stuck in traffic one afternoon on the Ohio Turnpike, took out his hunting rifle and started shooting at the traffic copter. He was not somebody you'd want to piss off. I showed Ernie a few tricks too. The Steelers beat us that day, but I did my job against Joe. The whole composition of Maule's article had to be changed. Joe was a great football player, but he really wasn't that mean. Mean rhymes with Green. I should have dubbed myself Sweeney the Meanie. Naw, that sounds like a sissy.

Raquel Welch dated Joe Namath in 1972 and said, "He speaks a language all women understand. He's actually very sweet and intellectual. You have to be brainy to play quarterback."

To prove you have to be brainy to play a sex goddess, she added, "I would never go out with a guard." Raquel didn't know that *Cosmopolitan* magazine asked me to pose for their centerfold.

That same year, the National 1,000 Yard Club Foundation presented me with the NFL's 1971 Outstanding Blocker award in Menasha, Wisconsin. After the ceremony, we went to Fuzzy

Thurston's bar in Green Bay. He called me over and said I was "too pretty" to be a guard. Fuzzy is very sweet and intellectual.

The secret to playing professional football for a long time is to miss as many training camps as possible. They are designed to get a player in competitive condition and to teach new players a team's system. For the veteran who stays in condition, training camp does little more than extend the season. The grueling two-a-day sessions put unnecessary mileage on a player's odometer since barring serious injury, a player lasts only a certain number of years before wear and tear break his body down. Linemen usually take more punishment because they hit, or get hit, on almost every play.

Training camp is where players earn their money. The fun starts once the real games begin. I had only missed two training camps in my eleven years with the Chargers. I missed my rookie camp because of the All-Star Game, but we had our own murderous schedule preparing for the Packers in Evanston, Illinois. I missed two weeks in the mid-sixties because I smashed my car up on the way to camp. Jean was back east with the kids visiting her parents and I was out drinking the night I was to report to camp. On my way to Escondido, I misjudged a curve and wrapped my car around a tree. I wasn't cited for the accident, but the car was a total wreck. I had a gash across my forehead that required eight stitches. The only good thing about it was that I couldn't wear a helmet for two weeks.

In 1972, I didn't report to camp, because I was holding out for more money. I felt I was not paid as well as the other teams paid their perennial All-Pro linemen. I retained an agent, Dick Mangiarelli, to negotiate my contract for the 1972 season. He informed the team that I was not reporting to camp until it was completed. Dick had a company called PAMCO (Professional Athletes Management Corporation) and some of my teammates had signed with him. I figured the Chargers had been screwing me since I had first signed with them, but I also realized that it was no one's fault but my own. It's hard to ask for a raise when you're always questioning your own self-worth.

The entire thing proved to be a disaster. In my opinion, Mangiarelli was a good guy, but I wasn't too sure about his negotiating abilities. The Chargers fined me $500.00 for every day I wasn't in camp and as my agent, he missed scheduled meetings with team management. Most of the time, I thought he was working more for the Chargers than for me. He was like most of the people I hired during that period of time. I hired them based on their personality rather than their qualifications. The lawyer I hired to represent me in my divorce with Jean was a drinking buddy who specialized in real estate law. Jean did very well in the final settlement.

In an effort to create leverage so my agent could negotiate a better deal, I told the team that I was thinking about retiring. I worked full-time for Hunt/Wesson Foods for two off-seasons and told the press I was taking some time off to think about my future. In reality, I was sitting around my South Mission Beach apartment with my teammate and friend, Pete Barnes, who was also holding out for a better deal with the team. Barnes was an excellent linebacker and a dope-smoking buddy. During this stressful period, we went through a lot of Zig-Zag rolling papers.

One day, Pete and I had an appointment with Harland Svare who had replaced Sid as head coach and general manager. We were to meet with him at the University of California at Irvine where we now had training camp. We smoked a couple of joints during the ninety-mile drive to Irvine and became so paranoid that the team would give us a blood test, we turned around and returned to San Diego. The whole thing was a fantasy, because they didn't even have drug testing at the time. How could they? They were passing out the drugs. Pete thought everyone got high. He thought President Nixon was smoking the real good stuff. I signed about a week later for what they offered me in the first place and Pete was traded to the Patriots. The only good thing about it was that I missed most of training camp.

When I finally reported, I learned that the complexion of the team had changed considerably with Svare's new talent. He brought in a whole bunch of guys to join me in my favorite pastime of altering my state of mind. Deacon Jones, Dave Costa, Tim Rossovich, Lionel Aldridge and Jerry Levias to name a few of the new faces. Dope smoking, rather than drinking, had become the predominant extracurricular activity. It became so flagrant in our dormitory that the assistant coaches refused to come in for bed check. They were afraid to tell Svare what was going on. The Chargers also obtained Johnny Unitas and my old college teammate, John Mackey, from the Baltimore Colts.

"Those boys are in there burning that rope again." Johnny U. said as we walked down the hallway of our dorm.

Most of the players Harland acquired were past their prime, but he was hoping to pull off a "George Allen." George had been very successful with the "Over the Hill Gang." His Redskins got extra mileage out of experienced vets, but there was only one George Allen.

Marijuana created a serious rift among the players. Some of the straight guys—beer guzzling good old boys and religious zealots alike—began resenting those of us who sat around our rooms catching a buzz with pot. John Hadl got angry with me, because I no longer would hit the bars in neighboring Newport Beach with him. After a hard day on the practice field, it was easier to smoke a joint and drift off in front of the TV. John always knew when I was out of weed, because I'd be back in the bars with him.

Harland ran a different kind of camp than most NFL head coaches. He was laid back. He was a good guy, but coaching just wasn't his racket. Harland had been a great linebacker with the New York Giants in the 1950s, but great football players do not

necessarily make good coaches. At one point, he was the youngest coach in the NFL when he headed up the Los Angeles Rams in
the early 1960s. He hadn't been very successful in that endeavor
and the only reason he was hired in San Diego was because he
was a kiss-ass buddy of current Chargers owner Gene Klein. Baron
Hilton had sold the team to Klein in 1969.

In most training camps, once two-a-day practice sessions are
over, the mornings are used for skull drills and the afternoons for
practice. In Harland's scheme of things, we had our meeting and
practice in the morning. We had the afternoon off. After lunch
each day, Rossovich, Costa, and I would toke up and head to the
Pacific for some bodysurfing. Half the team hit the beach and the
other half hit the links. Unitas was amazed. In his sixteen years
with the Colts, even though there was a course beside their training camp, not once did he get a chance to play golf.

Early in the 1972 season, I tore some rib cartilage and was getting shots of painkillers before each game. When the season began,
I was tipping the scales at 260 pounds. As we approached the half
way mark, I was down to 240. I had developed walking pneumonia
and had a hell of a time keeping weight. I still played in every game
despite constant pain. I was severely weakened, but proud that I
hadn't missed a game in my ten years with the Chargers. When I
was living with Jean and the kids, I was much healthier. During the
season, I only drank after a game. I didn't smoke marijuana until
Jean and I divorced. If I had been single from the beginning of my
career, I never would have played as long as I did. Self-discipline
has never been my long suit.

I'm sure the marijuana and cigarettes didn't help my pneumonia, but I didn't want to stop either vice. I got through practice
each day by constant self-medication with generous portions of
codeine cough syrup kept in my locker. After practice, I would use
a machine that medicated my lungs with Microefferin. My health

continued to deteriorate. By the end of the season, I was extremely run down and weighed only 228 pounds.

Our last game was against the Chiefs in Kansas City. I was having a tough time trying to block Curly Culp. Curly weighed 280 and was a former NCAA heavyweight-wrestling champion. He was as quick as he was strong. I was leg-whipping, cut-blocking, holding and using every trick a desperate man could come up with. My offensive line coach, Forest Gregg, pulled me out of the game just before halftime. There really was a God after all. Ralph Wenzel, my backup, took over and did a good job for the remainder of the first half.

I nearly collapsed in the locker room at half time. I chewed up 30 milligrams of speed and washed it down with some cough syrup. This was a precautionary measure just in case, for some unknown reason, I might have to go back into the game. I got on the lung machine and sucked down as much Microeffrin as I could hold. While the coaches were discussing second half strategy with the team in the next room, I was stretched out on a table in the training room. I didn't give a fuck about the first half or the second half or anything else at this point. I was perspiring profusely. My eyes were burning, but I felt so weak I couldn't lift my arm to wipe the sweat away. I could hear Forest Gregg calling my name. He found me laying on the training table.

"Oh, there you are. You're starting the second half."

I couldn't believe my ears! I felt like I was half dead. I barely had enough strength to get off the table. My ribs felt like Rocky Marciano had been pounding on them. We were in last place in our division and this was the last game of the year. I guess Gregg's dislike for me outweighed any compassion he might have mustered for my situation. It was the only time in my life I didn't want to go into a football game.

"Let Ralph take it. He's doing a good job." Gregg gave me a cold and taunting look.

"No way, Sweeney. You're not getting out of it that easy."

The redneck was going to show the dope-smoking hippie who was boss.

"Hey, Walter, you can handle it. You don't think I'd send you out there if there was a chance of you getting hurt?"

I should have told him to get fucked, but figured I'd better save my strength. I was going to need it. I don't remember much about the remainder of the game. I know we lost, but that was nothing new.

I worked hard in the off-season to build myself up. I didn't get rid of any of my bad habits, but did hit the weights more than I'd ever done before. Food became a major priority. In the past, if I were on a two-day bender, I wouldn't eat because that meant the drinking was over.

I got my weight back up to a solid 255 pounds. By the time 1973 training camp opened, I could bench press 435 pounds, a personal best for me. I wasn't the strongest guy in the league by any means. I wasn't the strongest guy on our own team. Our left guard, Doug Wilkerson, could bench 550. I didn't make it in football because of my muscles. I made it on desire, heart, or attitude, whatever you want to call it. I'm a natural 200-pounder. For years, I had to pump iron and force-feed myself at times to keep my weight up.

That summer, I picked up a roommate. For a short time in the 1960s, I owned a beer joint called The Huddle. I sold the bar after a couple of months, because Jean didn't think the bar business was my cup of tea. One of the barmaids gave me a black lab puppy. The kids named the dog, Magee. Jean scoffed that I wasn't responsible enough to be a pet owner, but I showed her.

Magee and I became inseparable. He was brought up in The Pennant and The Beachcomber, two of the most popular bars in South Mission Beach. Magee would lie under my barstool while I drank. Everybody loved him, well almost everybody. He was the

only dog allowed in these bars and a few of the other dog own-
ing customers resented it. Hey, I didn't make the rules. When my
faithful companion wasn't in the bars with me, he was out running
around on the beach. He cost me a small fortune in tickets from
the "dog narcs."

Thanks to Magee, I once had to spend the night in jail. Actually,
I managed to get thrown in the slammer all by myself. After being
booked for drunk driving, the cops ran a warrant check on me.
Sure enough, I had failed to pay Magee's latest ticket. Instead of
being released right after I was booked, I had to stay in jail for eight
hours. Magee and I had a serious discussion about his carousing
when I got home.

Despite making $65,000 a year, I was nearly broke at the start
of training camp. Two households and my bad habits were expensive to maintain. There were other drains on my finances. Two
years in a row, I invested in Imperial Valley lettuce. The Imperial
Valley is about a hundred miles east of San Diego. Lettuce was
usually a good investment, but torrential rainstorms wiped out the
crops and my money. I also invested $20,000 in a limited partner-
ship that purchased commercial property in Sacramento. Six of
my teammates also took a chance on this venture. We all lost our
money. The whole thing turned out to be a scam.

There were other bad investments like the time Magee and I
were sitting in The Beachcomber. I overheard a woman trying to
sell the owner a life insurance policy. Considering it was only ten
o'clock in the morning, I had a pretty good buzz going. I told her
I might be interested in some insurance. We agreed to meet at my
apartment which was only a block away.

She wasn't particularly attractive, but I had been drinking for a
while and that was enough to arouse some sexual interest. I left the
bar and she showed up twenty minutes later.

"I really need some life insurance. I've got two kids and an ex-wife and I need some coverage. I'm a busy guy and I don't feel like listening to a sales pitch."

I was busy all right. Busy getting fucked up!

Before she had a chance to reply, I hit her with this charmer:

"If you go to bed with me right now, I'll sign up."

"Okay," she said as she began to slip out of her clothes.

She caught me a little off guard. I bought a hundred thousand dollars worth of term life insurance. The policy cost me a hundred a month for the next three years before I finally dropped it. One of my teammates thought four grand was a little steep for a piece of ass. I might have done better to patronize whorehouses than to buy a piece of the "Rock."

The Chargers 1973 training camp opened under the same conditions as the previous year. Dope smoking was rampant. We enjoyed the same body surfing and golfing schedule. We had lost players to other teams via trades or guys being picked up on waivers. Departed players talked about the blatant drug use among the Chargers. Rumors spread throughout the league and into the Commissioner's office. Jack Murphy kept writing articles that referred to so-called drug problems on the team.

In one article, he quoted unidentified sources. I guessed they were the guys who were traded or cut. The sources talked about how the team had two busses that transported the players from training camp to exhibition games. One bus was called the "Benny" bus. The "Benny" bus was reserved for the guys that took amphetamines for the games and the other bus, which was almost empty, was for the guys that didn't. Svare's attitude, and the attitude of other coaches and team management ranged from ignorance to "don't rock the boat."

Svare attempted to face the drug issue by bringing in psychiatrist named Arnold Mandell. The good doctor was head of

Psychiatry at the University of California in San Diego. He was also a friend of Harland's. He had been with the team since Harland had become head coach the previous year. His main role, as far as I could see, was kibitzing with the players and writing prescriptions of Desoxyn. Desoxyn was pure speed and we told the good doctor how many milligrams and the quantity we wanted. He was happy to oblige. No more fishing in trainer's pockets. We took the prescriptions to a pharmacy in Irvine and they were entered on the Charger's account. The only reason I took speed was to play football and Mandell had given me enough to play for two more years. This was the third type of amphetamine I had been given since joining the Charger team. It was, by far, the most potent.

I remember going to Mandell early in the 1972 season.

"Doc, when these Desoxyns wear off after a game, I get so depressed I'm almost suicidal."

"After you get home and you feel the speed start to wear off, smoke a joint."

He was absolutely right. I found myself smoking it in case I "might" get depressed. It was sort of like preventive medication. Marijuana joined booze as my favorite mind-altering drug. Mandell told me that when he was on the golf team at San Diego State, he used marijuana to slow down his back swing.

In 1976, he published *The Nightmare Season*. In his book, he tried to justify his rational for all the speed prescriptions. He claimed players were using street drugs for football games. He wanted to know what might be in player's system in case surgery was required after a game. In all my years of pro football, I never knew anyone that took street drugs to play. They may have used street drugs in high school, but in the pros, it was all pharmaceutical.

Farewell SD, Hello DC

South Mission Beach is a mile long strip of land, wide as two football fields, bisected by Mission Boulevard that runs from the Big Dipper Roller Coaster in Belmont Park to the Mission Bay jetty. Laidback Mission Bay is on the east side of the boulevard and the mighty Pacific on the west. It has beautiful white sandy beaches, palm trees and bikinis. At one time, it was my favorite haunt in San Diego. Wikipedia lists me as a "notable resident," but I haven't been a resident since the 1980s. South Mission has a liquor store, a small market and two signature bars, The Pennant and The Beachcomber. I lived there for about ten years and have a lot of fond memories about the place.

I first moved there in 1971 when Jean asked me to move out. I rented an apartment on the ocean side of the boardwalk. It was the perfect place for me to ease my pain and guilt from the breakup. When I looked out my front window, it was like opening a *Playboy*. The girls might not have been as glamorous, but they were in my front yard. More importantly, they were (at least in my mind) available.

I smoked my first joint, snorted my first line of coke and dropped my first hit of acid in South Mission. I got along with just about everyone. Most of the locals were sports nuts and I certainly was a big sport. I would get falling down drunk with them during the week and on Sunday afternoon, I'd be at San Diego Stadium battling for glory on the hometown team. They loved this. I was their hero. Of course, there are exceptions to every rule and I did step on a few toes.

Jack Elliot is someone that comes to mind. Jack owned The Pennant back in the 1970s. It was a real blot on the landscape. It had the dirtiest men's room this side of the Tijuana. One night, after my tenth International Stinger—an ass kicker of a drink—I decided to help remodel the men's head by flushing a "seal bomb" down the toilet. It blew the porcelain throne to smithereens and the walls looked like they were shot with a shit gun. Jack wasn't 100% sure that I did it, but he was sure enough. I was on his shit list for a while. I paid for that toilet many times over with all the money I spent, so I wasn't terribly concerned with how he felt about me. Other than that incident, I usually didn't bother anyone or cause any trouble. I generally try to get along with everybody. I was a friend of the two guys who owned The Beachcomber and the guy that owned the liquor store. The local dope dealers also loved to see me coming.

I remember one Saturday afternoon at the Beachcomber. The place was packed. People were standing three deep at the bar waiting to get their drinks. I was with Jack O'Hallaran, the boxer who became an actor. Jack was about six-foot-six. He was a scary looking guy and most of the roles he played in the movies were tough guys.

Apparently Jack really had to go, so he took a leak in a guy's pocket as we stood packed around the bar. The guy was wearing bib overalls and Jack was a foot taller than him. The poor guy looked up and said, "Do you want me to shake it for you?" We left right after that and went across the street to my apartment.

During the off-season, I would pick up my kids from school on Friday afternoon and take them down to my place at the beach. We always had a good time together. The rules were a little less stringent at my place than they were at Mom's. If the beach wasn't enough for them, Sea World was a five-minute drive. Belmont Park, the local amusement center, was a two-minute stroll down the boardwalk. The kids and I enjoyed these visits together. I didn't need any alcohol or drugs to make me feel good when they were with me. Occasionally, after they went to sleep, I'd step outside and smoke a joint. That was the exception rather than the rule. On Sunday evening, I would take them home to El Cajon, about fifteen miles east of San Diego. From Sunday to Thursday, I would party. Maybe party isn't the right word for it. It was more like self-destruct. There were many 'round the clock bouts with booze and drugs.

Harland Svare might not have been the greatest coach in the world, but he had a big heart. During the season, it was standard practice for the team to stay at a hotel the night before the game. He allowed me to bring the kids to the hotel and let them spend the night with me. A lot of coaches wouldn't have allowed this. Every team in the National Football League starts each year with a clean slate and hopes of making the playoffs or, better yet, the Super Bowl. Although we were terrible in 1972, I was optimistic and eagerly looked forward to playing against the Redskins as I drove to the stadium for our home opener.

We fumbled the ball three times in the first eleven minutes and the Skins turned every one into a touchdown. We got our asses kicked, because of stupid mistakes. It was to be a preview of a long, miserable season. The speed they were giving certainly wasn't helping us play any better. Maybe we should have talked to the Redskin's pharmacist and found out what they were using.

After the first five games, we had one victory under our belt. The more we lost, the more the rumors flew. They ranged from marijuana and speed usage by certain players to the one about players being tailed by narcs from the Commissioner's office. My personal favorite was that indictments against certain players for possession with intent to sell were coming from the District Attorney's office. I knew I was innocent on that. I liked the stuff too much to ever sell it.

Paranoia was rampant on the team. Owner Gene Klein was rumored to be sticking a coke spoon up his nose. In addition to the players, the trainers were allegedly doing speed for the games. I know at least one was using speed, because I was giving it to him. Mandell responded by writing more scripts for speed. He told us not to smoke grass for a few days before game day, so we would be more aggressive. Lack of aggressiveness was never a problem for me.

Harland formed a grievance committee to discuss the players' use of drugs and any other problems that might come up. A representative was chosen from each segment of the team. I represented the offensive line, Deacon Jones the defensive line and so forth. There were six reps. Half of us took speed and smoked marijuana. I would say that fifty percent of the team was doing drugs, so the straight players and the druggies were being equally represented.

The Charger fans were tired of spending good money on an inferior product and were becoming increasingly hostile. Most of their rage was directed at Svare. On several occasions, the police had to escort him out of the stadium. Gene Klein put up with about as much as he could and finally replaced him as head coach. Svare maintained his position as General Manager.

With four games to go and the Chargers solidly entrenched in last place, Harlan choose our backfield coach, Ron Waller, as the interim head coach on the basis of handwriting analysis. Unbeknownst to me, Harland had everyone's handwriting analyzed at the beginning of the season. I wish I had known about it. I would have added a few extra loops to my signature. No telling how far I could have gone in the Charger organization.

Waller's first game as head coach was in Denver against the Broncos. We didn't know what to expect as he gathered the team in the crowded locker room. "All right you guys, let's go out there today and show the Broncos and the people back in San Diego that we are not a bunch of drug addicts and bums."

I couldn't believe my ears. I was as fired up for the Broncos as I had been for every game I ever played. There was never a game I thought we couldn't win, no matter what the odds. I never thought of myself as a drug addict or a bum. I certainly wasn't thinking of the people in San Diego. I was pissed all right...pissed at Waller. I felt like grabbing the skinny little prick and slapping him.

Waller continued, "Go out there and knock the dog shit out of these mother fuckers. Kick 'em in the nuts. Make them wish they were never born. And now," he continued as he turned to the man beside him, "Father Mulcahey would like to lead us in prayer."

My anger shifted to silent laughter. As I looked around the room, I saw some of the guys out-right laughing. By some quirk of fate, we won the game. I don't think it had anything to do with Waller's pep talk or the good Father's prayer. Even a blind pig finds an acorn once in a while. We lost the next three games. Waller and the rest of the coaching staff were fired.

A week after the season ended, Tommy Prothro was hired as the new head coach of the Chargers. It wasn't too long until I received a call from him.

"Hello, Walt, this is Tommy Prothro," he drawled.

"I just traded you to the Washington Redskins. I wish I had had you when you were hot."

"I'm still hot. Thanks for the information."

As I hung up the phone, I found myself wishing that I had given him some shit. Something intelligent with a little bit of class like: "Stick it in your ass, you fat fuck."

As an offensive lineman, I had been taught to be aggressive. In the past when faced with adversity, I usually shot first and asked questions afterwards. More often than not, I usually lived to regret those outbursts.

I was stunned. I had given the Chargers my best for eleven years. I played hurt and never missed a game. I had distinguished myself

as one of the top linemen in the game and now I was being dis-
carded like an old shoe. The initial shock didn't last long. Those of
us who played the game knew how it was. Football is a business just
like any other business. The next call was from Jerry Magee with
the San Diego Union. "Walt, You've been traded to the Washington
Redskins for three draft choices. What's your reaction?"

"It's about time I got out of the minor leagues."

As I hung up the phone, I couldn't help chuckling to myself. I
couldn't go gracefully. I had to take the last shot. The once mighty
Chargers had fallen on hard times.

After a few days of thinking about the trade, I realized it was
the best thing for me. The Redskins had a great coach in George
Allen. He had gotten them to the Super Bowl in 1972. They lost to
the Dolphins, but at least they got to the big game. I would be finishing my career on a winning team.

The downside of the trade would be separation from my kids
for six months. Having them with me every weekend, except when
the team was on the road, probably afforded me more time with
them than the average guy that worked from eight to five and lived
at home. Kristin was now eleven and Rick was ten. They were old
enough to fly. Maybe they could visit me during the season.

Later in the month, I would learn my reputation around the
league. I was chosen to participate in the All-Pro Olympics in
Miami Beach. This was a gathering of top players from around the
league competing in various events for cash prizes. The forty-yard
dash, tug o'war, blocking sled races and other contrived contests
of that nature. In one event, I was teamed with "Mean" Joe Green
in the two-man sled race. We won our first heat and took second
place in the finals.

The night before the competition, I attended a cocktail party at
the hotel where we were staying. A nationally prominent network

sportscaster approached me and asked, "Walt, do you have any rolling papers?"

I had never met this man before and was somewhat taken aback. He was carrying a brief case under his arm and continued, "I've got some real ass kicker pot here."

He insinuated it was inside the case he was carrying.

"I'm afraid to leave it in the room. Security or the maids might find it."

Talk about paranoia. I shook my head and walked away. I was pissed that somebody who didn't know me would ask such a personal question.

Later that evening, Bob Hayes of the Dallas Cowboys, asked if I had any speed for the next day's competition. As in the case of the sportscaster, I had never met Hayes before. Being obviously known around the league as a doper made me feel very uneasy.

The day after the event in Miami, I was due to fly to Washington to meet with George Allen. I got drunk with big John Matusak after the competition and missed my plane to DC. I didn't call Allen to let him know that I wouldn't make it for our meeting, but choose instead to show up a day late. As his secretary escorted me into his office, George was pacing back and forth behind his huge desk. "Walt, if we ever have a scheduled meeting again and for some reason you can't make it, LET ME KNOW!" '

"George, I assure you this will never happen again."

"Walt, do you want to play for me?" '

"Absolutely, I have a lot to prove and I can't think of anyone else I'd rather play for."

"Get back to San Diego and get ready for the season."

I couldn't wait to get out of his office, out of D.C. and back to California to the beach and my pals. Getting off to such an inauspicious start with my new coach made me very uncomfortable. I hated pissing him off before I even put on a Redskin uniform. So much for first impressions.

About a week later, on a Sunday morning, I was sitting in the living room of my apartment with Tim Rossovich and Dave Costa. We were passing a joint and sipping beers when a knock on the door interrupted us. I was surprised to see Jerry Gross standing in my doorway with a copy of the *San Diego Union* in his hand. Jerry was a local TV sports reporter and a guy that I liked. We had tipped a few together over the years. He unfolded the newspaper and the front-page headlines sprang out.

Charger Players and Management Fined for Violating NFL Drug Policy

"What's your reaction to this?" He asked as he pointed to the paper.

My first reaction was to faint. I pulled myself together and offered Jerry a toke of the joint I was holding. As I've said before, nobody ever accused me of being too smart. The weed wasn't helping matters. Now I just wouldn't offer a toke to just anybody. I wasn't that stupid, because Jerry was a friend of mine. I was sure he wouldn't broadcast it. Maybe I should have fainted.

The article stated that the Charger organization was guilty of giving amphetamines, a drug on the NFL taboo list, to its players. The team was fined $25,000 and eight players were nailed with fines ranging from $1,000 to $3,000. I felt relieved to be a $1,000 man. The team owner, Gene Klein, former head coach Harland Svare, and the real head coach, Dr. Arnold Mandell, were also fined. It had listed the names of the San Diego Eight: " Deacon" Jones, Tim Rossovich, Coy Bacon, Dave Costa, Rick Redmond, Jerry Levias, Bob Thomas and Walt Sweeney. With the exception of Redmond and me, Harland brought the rest of the players to the Chargers the year before. It also made vague references to our involvement with the use of marijuana.

Harland had been fined $5,000 for "failure to exercise supervisory control over the players." He was placed on probation along with the eight players. I wondered what they meant by "probation." I thought a person had to be convicted to be put on probation.

Rozelle also fined Klein $20,000 for "supervisory omissions" by his staff. As Jerry spoke, he gave me a pained look as he glanced at the now extinguished joint still in my hand.

"I have a camera crew with me. Will you come out on the patio and do an interview?"

"Why the fuck didn't you call first?" I could feel the anger starting to rise—not at Jerry—but at the whole ugly scene.

"I've been calling you all morning, ever since the story broke. There was no answer."

I had a bad habit of unplugging the phone and forgetting about it. Then I'd wonder why nobody ever called. My mind was racing a hundred miles an hour. I had known something was up, because Rozelle's investigators had been snooping around and talking to various Charger players. I had no idea I would be involved like this. I was with the Redskins.

"Give me a minute." I said as I closed the door and walked inside.

"Did you hear that bullshit?" I asked the boys.

"Yeah, we heard. What are you going to say?" Rossovich asked.

"Don't say we're here," Costa added.

"What do you take me for, a fool?" I could hear them chuckling as I headed for the bedroom to throw on a shirt.

Before Gross showed up, I had knocked back about six beers with a little cannabis. I had a pretty good buzz going. I looked in the mirror to comb my hair and saw Robert Redford looking back. I knew if I had shoes, they would be shining too. I went back outside where Jerry and his cameraman were waiting. We set up in a corner of the patio with my back to the Pacific.

"I know you have been traded to the Redskins, Walt, but it has been reported that when you were on the Chargers last year, that you were one of eight ballplayers who have been fined and put on probation by Commissioner Rozelle for violating NFL Drug Policy."

Jerry stuck the mike in my face and waited for my reaction. I looked into the camera with all the sincerity I could muster and said, "I'm appalled. I don't know where they get their information, but I assure you my attorney will get to the bottom of this."

The only attorneys I knew handled drunk driving cases and I knew plenty of them. Gross gave me a funny look. I don't know what he expected, but I certainly wasn't going to admit to anything. We were both hoping that the smell of marijuana wafting through the screens in my apartment wouldn't reach the small gathering of onlookers who had gathered to see what was going on. Most were my neighbors and they had already seen the morning papers.

Someone yelled, "Atta boy, Walt. You tell him!"

"The hell with Rozelle!" Shouted another observer.

Then a voice from inside the apartment. "Yeah, fuck 'em. Ain't no dope being smoked around here."

I recognized Costa's deep voice.

"That it, Jerry?"

"Yeah, Walt. Good luck with the Redskins." He looked at me like I'd need a lot more than luck.

"Like I said before, it's good to be out of the minors. I'm really glad to be out of this mess, believe me."

Gross laughed. As he turned to leave, I headed for my front door and received a small round of applause from the bystanders. The story made headlines in all the newspapers across the country. *Time, Newsweek, Sports Illustrated* all reported on the disgrace that had befallen the Chargers. If I hadn't been involved, I would have had a good laugh, because the whole situation was a joke. Basically, we were fined for taking drugs that the team was giving us. The whole league was doing it, but the Chargers took the fall. Most of the articles called the situation the worst drug scandal in sport's history. The San Diego Eight had their faces splashed all over the network as well as local news shows. I again found myself trying to convince loved ones that the news reports were wrong and not to believe them.

I took my kids out to dinner the day after the story broke. I tried to explain it was all a mistake. They said they understood, but I could tell by their eyes that they were hurt and upset. I knew that they had been proud of me for my fame as a football player. Now that image had been tarnished. I felt that I had let them down. I had let them down. My relationship with Kris and Rick was the only thing that kept me going at times. Despite my drinking, drugging, and self-obsession, I tried to be a good father. It would be tough to make this year up to them, because I'd be in Washington for six months.

To help ease the pain, I bought a new Mercedes. I cut back on the sauce, but smoked a lot of weed. Marijuana was my medicine. I was the doctor and the patient. I never got violent on weed. I never was arrested for driving under the influence of marijuana. And, last, but not least, it always put me in a better mood.

I was supposed to report to Redskin training camp in Carlisle, Pennsylvania in mid-July. I got in excellent shape during off-season, but labor negotiations between NFL management and the Players Association broke down. The possibility of a walk out loomed on the horizon.

Sure enough, we went on strike. We had been playing without a contract and wanted one badly before training camp. After working out in the morning, I would go to the Chargers training camp at the University of San Diego and walk the picket line with the other veteran players.

George Allen was pressuring me to report to camp. All the camps were open and stocked with rookie draft choices, free agents, and journeymen trying to extend their careers with one last shot. George wanted me there to learn new system. Being a strong union man, I refused to relent to this pressure. Besides, this was the first time since college that I was on the beach in August. Eventually the two sides agreed to a new contract. The strike ended by the third week of August and I went off to Pennsylvania.

The Mind May Have Punted, But the Right Moves Were There

I had to fly to Los Angeles to catch a connecting flight to Pennsylvania. As I was boarding the plane, I saw my old pal and teammate, Deacon Jones. Deacon had been dealt to the Redskins, too. The Chargers shed the San Diego Eight. The plague of the league had either been traded, cut, or signed with the newly formed World Football League. Retirement wasn't an option for me. As far as I was concerned, I was at the top of my game.

"Hey Deac," I said as I moved towards him in the half empty plane.

He grinned as he reached for my hand. "You look like you're in shape for a change, Sweeney."

"Fuck you, Deac."

I couldn't help laughing. It was truly good to see him. He is one of the funniest men I know and shooting the breeze with him would make the five-hour flight seem a lot shorter. I hadn't seen or talked to him since our names and faces were plastered all over the news.

I ordered a double scotch, Deacon a double gin and we told the stewardess to keep them coming. She seemed more than willing to oblige. Four drinks down the hatch and we both became more sociable.

"You know, Sweeney, the eight of us took the rap for the whole team. You know as well as I do that three-quarters of those guys were doing the same thing that we did."

"Absolutely. How about three-quarters of the whole league."

"That's right!" Deacon agreed.

"What's George Allen like? I only met him briefly when I showed up late."

Deacon was a member of Allen's Fearsome Foursome defense with the Rams before they traded him to the Chargers.

"You fucked up there, Sweeney."

"Really?" I didn't like the sound of that.

"Don't worry about it. He eats and sleeps defense. You're an offensive lineman. He probably won't even know you're there."

I liked the sound of that better. He now turned to a more serious subject.

"Hey, Walt, did you bring any weed?" All of a sudden I was Walt.

"No, I didn't. I didn't want to take any chances being on probation and all."

"Now why do you want to lie to me like that?" He whined.

Well, he was right about that. I had an ounce stashed in my luggage.

"Listen, Sweeney, I know you too well. I know you don't go anywhere without it."

"I do have a little, but you can't have any." I lied again.

"After all we've been through, why do you want to do me like that?"

"I don't want to be a detrimental influence on you."

"Well ain't this a bitch!" Deacon muttered as he put his head in his hands.

The next thing I remembered, I was riding down the Pennsylvania Turnpike with Deacon. Bubba Tyrer, a trainer with the Redskins, was behind the wheel. From what I was told later, Deacon and I were so soused that we became the fodder of amusing stories Bubba would tell for years.

Because of the strike, we had less than a week to prepare for the Hall of Fame game in Canton, Ohio. The game signified the kick-off of the exhibition season. It was the wrap-up of the weeklong prelude celebration and festivities Canton bestows upon the current class of Hall of Fame inductees. George Allen always had great defensive teams. He was a genius in that department. I was brought in to bolster a weak running game that featured star running back Larry Brown. They wanted someone with enough speed to get in front of him on sweeps. At thirty-four, I had retained my speed. My mind might have been gone, but I still could move out.

Sonny Jurgenson and Billy Kilmer or as they were known to their teammates—Roach and Whiskey—were the quarterbacks. Joe Theisman, fresh out of the Canadian League, backed them up. Allen had brought a number of former Rams including Maxie Baughan and Diron Talbert along with him to Washington. For the most part, the "Over-the-Hill Gang" was a bunch of guys in their thirties who had played all over the league. George was a great motivator. He had a way of getting extra mileage out of older players.

It was extremely hot and humid the night we played the St. Louis Cardinals in Canton. We were stuffed into a small high school locker room, a lot of griping and bitching. We beat the Cardinals in a sloppy game. No one expected a thing of beauty. After all, we had less than a week of preparation.

As it was with the Chargers, so shall it be with the Redskins. I noticed my teammates around the water cooler popping pills. They weren't salt pills. The only difference was the team wasn't dispensing the speed. The players were going to private physicians and getting what they needed or what they thought they needed. Professional football is a violent game. It's unrealistic to expect a lineman over thirty, who is smashing into someone on every play, to go without stimulants. There are exceptions to every rule, but not many. Drugs have been around football long before I began playing and they are still prevalent today. The football establishment tries to promote a squeaky clean image, but it's just so much bullshit. People that have been around the sport such as players, coaches, trainers, and doctors know the real low down.

I had a pretty good game. I came to camp in good shape and the terminology was basically the same as it had been in San Diego. Charlie Waller, the Redskin's offensive coordinator, held the same job in San Diego. He was instrumental in the Redskins trading for me.

After the game we flew back to Pennsylvania. We arrived in Carlisle around 10:00 p.m.. We had to practice the next day, so everyone stayed in camp. Diron Talbert, a good old boy from Texas and a pretty good defensive tackle, invited Deacon and me to his Winnebago for drinks. They had been teammates in Los Angeles.

When I stepped into the RV, I was impressed. It was over thirty feet long and it looked quite comfortable, at least comfortable for drinks. Deacon had arrived before I did. He was seated at a table with Kilmer, Talbot, and Len Haus, the old All-Pro center for the Redskins. They were drinking beer and Jack Daniels bourbon. I took a beer and grabbed a seat. Deacon and Talbot were reminiscing about their days with the Rams. I chatted with Kilmer and Haus. I was coming down from the speed I had taken for the game.

"Does anyone want to smoke any of this?" I asked as I pulled a big fat joint from my pocket. As soon as the words came out, I regretted opening my mouth. They looked at me like I was some kind of child molester. I never could understand how some people could get falling down drunk on booze, but look down their noses at marijuana. I like to cover all the bases and use both. Even that prick Jones acted like he didn't know me.

I put the joint back in my pocket. I really didn't give a shit what these rednecks thought. As far as Deacon was concerned, I'd make him pay later. After that, I gravitated toward the younger players on the team. Most of them got high and I joined them.

My roommate was a ten-year vet, Ray Schoenke. I think Ray had played every position in the offensive line at one time or another. What he lacked in natural ability, he made up with hard work. He was half-German, half-Hawaiian and very much a political animal. He had been a big McGovern supporter in his bid for the presidency in 1972.

Unlike previous camps with the Chargers, I didn't spend much time in the local bars. At thirty-four, I couldn't drink for half the night and practice the next day. Because of the strike, we had some marathon practices and meetings. By the end of the day, I barely had enough strength to sneak off by myself, smoke a joint and crawl back to my room.

Schoenke had trouble sleeping one night and was looking through my shaving kit for some sleeping aids. He fumbled through my assortment of pharmaceuticals: Disoxyn for the games and an occasional practice, Seconal to get some sleep the night before a game. After the game, I usually had difficulty with sleep. The speed would keep me up all night no matter how much I drank which was usually a lot. I would take six Seconals before I went to bed. They would knock me out, but only for a couple of hours. I would wake up and replay the game in my head, always fearful that I hadn't played well. More often than not, I got the job done. But I couldn't help worrying about it until I saw the game films the next day.

The shaving kit also had Dalmane, a non-narcotic sleeping pill and a bottle of Percodan, a strong pain reliever. There were also about a half a dozen joints. The Chargers had provided everything except the weed to me. Schoenke joked the next morning about how nervous he became just looking through my shaving kit.

The next weekend, we beat the Eagles in Philadelphia. We arrived back in Carlisle around 8:00 p.m. and George gave us our first night off since we had been there. Deacon and I decided to go into D.C. for a little relaxation and amusement.

We drove into town in a new Oldsmobile that a car dealer let me to use for the season. In return, I gave him the two season tickets the Redskins allotted me. You had to bump a twenty-year waiting list to get Redskin tickets. When I left the Chargers, you couldn't give the tickets away.

Franny O'Brien's was one of several restaurants that former Pittsburgh Steeler Franny owned. It was one of the favorite haunts of the Redskins in downtown D.C. O'Brien's had great steaks, a warm and friendly atmosphere and, usually, some good-looking, available women at the bar. If you played for the Redskins, women were never a problem.

After a couple of hours of my scotch and Deacon's gin, mixed with shots of Irish whiskey the patrons bought for us, we were feeling no pain. We decided to head for the bars in Georgetown. They were only a few miles away. Two blocks from O'Brien's, we had a head-on collision at an intersection.

I must have blacked out, because the only thing I could recall was sitting on a park bench while a hobo was trying to sell me his shoes. There was no car, no Deacon, and I was bewildered to say the very least. I pulled myself together as best I could and stumbled across the park to the nearest police station. It was about four blocks away. I walked in and there was Deacon trying to explain to these cops what had happened. As I made my entrance, he looked up and pointed at me:

"There he is. That's who I was talking about! Tell them what happened, Sweeney! You know, you pulled me from the passenger side and put me behind the steering wheel!"

"Are you off your fuckin' rocker?" I replied, wishing I was that smart.

I couldn't believe what my good pal and teammate was saying. The cops weren't buying it either. The cops thought he was nuts until I showed up. Obviously I bolted the scene, but I couldn't remember. The scariest thing about the whole accident—it turned out to be a fender bender—was that neither one of us could remember who was driving. The damage was minimal to both cars and no one was injured. Deacon got a ticket for running a red light. What could have been a serious situation turned out to be a routine traffic ticket. Hail to the Redskins. The police loved their team as much as everyone else in the area. They cut us some slack. Perhaps if I had been held accountable for my actions, I wouldn't have been so prone to make the same mistakes over and over.

George Allen sent someone down to pick us up and take us back to training camp. News of our misfortune arrived before we did. It became a source of embarrassment for us and a big joke for our teammates.

After practice the next day, George dismissed the team, but asked Jones and me to remain on the field. He seemed rather agitated. "I just want to know one thing, who was driving?"

Deacon and I exchanged glances, expecting the other to own up and then, like bad little boys, we looked down to the ground.

"Do you mean that you were so drunk that you don't know who was driving the car?"

We remained silent as George turned and walked muttering to himself toward the locker room.

We broke camp the following Thursday. I only had a few days to find a place to live before our season opener at RFK. Because of the strike, the exhibition season and training camp were significantly shortened.

Redskin Park, the practice facilities and offices were in Herndon, VA, a community about twenty-five miles northwest of D.C.. It was a first class setup. The weight room had every type of exercise machine imaginable, racquetball courts, a training room with all the best equipment and a full size astro-turf field right next to our grass practice field. The joke was that when the Redskins hired George Allen, they gave him an unlimited expense account.

He exceeded it the first two months. I decided to rent a room at the Holiday Inn in Tysons Corner. It was only fifteen minutes from Redskin Park and the English pub downstairs was a popular watering hole among my teammates. The owner and Billy Kilmer had some racehorses together. It would fulfill my needs for the season. Duane Thomas, the former Dallas Cowboy running back, and Maxie Baughan, the ex-Ram, also resided there.

The pub downstairs was like my living room. I never regarded myself as a lady's man, but I never lacked for female companionship during my time there. Even if you looked like Quasimodo, if you were a Redskin, women were willing to jump in bed with you. One night after a game, I walked into the men's room at Franny O'Briens. Right there, in front of God and anyone else that might need to piss, knelt two white girls sucking the dicks of two of my black teammates.

"Hey Walt, you want some of this?"

"No thanks. I don't think my date would appreciate it."

I lied about having a date. Even if I wanted a blowjob, the speed I had taken for the game prevented me from having an erection. I wondered what the girls' parents would think as I made a hasty exit.

Besides George's genius for defense, he was a great motivator. He always had something different in store for our first meeting every week. Once it was the mayor of D.C. telling us that if we won, it would help pull the community together. Washington had one of the highest crime rates in the country. The logic was that if we won, people would stop robbing and killing each other. After the mayor spoke, he asked us to rise and sing "Hail to the Redskins."

I was amazed to see all of these old vets jump up and start belting out the team's fight song.

Another time, George brought a karate instructor to give us a demonstration of mind over matter. After the instructor broke a number of boards and cement blocks, George gave it a try. He got a small cut on his pinky and went running from the room calling for his secretary. We all got a big kick out of that performance and it achieved its purpose. It brought the team a little bit closer; laughter does that, at least temporarily. Another time, he told us that if it took amphetamines to win, he would bring them in "by the truckload." I knew he didn't mean it, but it made us feel pretty good, especially the guys that were using them.

Whatever he did it was working, at the halfway point we were five and two, sitting on top of the NFC East, the toughest division in football. Every game with the Cowboys, the Cardinals, the Giants or Eagles, was a real ball buster. They usually went down to the wire.

Winning is a cure for a lot of things from body aches and pains to depression. I felt I had a new lease on life. I was still the same fuck-up I'd always been, but at least now I was part of a winning team. The fiasco in San Diego seemed like ancient history.

I struck up a conversation one evening with a cute cocktail waitress in a bar not to far from the Holiday Inn. Her name was Donna. She had just started working there. I was looking for some weed and she had some to sell. That night after work, she brought an ounce of some strong grass to my room. After that, I exclusively went out with her for the rest of the season. They say the way to some men's hearts is through their stomachs. I guess the path to my heart was through mind-altering drugs. Of course, it helps if the provider is good-looking and a member of the opposite sex.

The next to last game of the season was a Monday night game against the Rams in Los Angeles. It's the biggest game of the year for us. If we win, we're in the playoffs. Deacon and I had been rooming together on road trips. I guess it was George's way of cutting down surveillance. Deacon was one of the best defensive ends to ever play the game. He starred for a dozen years with the Rams, but had a backup role with the Redskins. This would be his last year.

It was homecoming for Deacon. George was going to start him. The Rams won the toss and elected to receive. The defensive team would be introduced. A thunderous roar came from the crowd when Deacon's name was announced. We were playing at the Coliseum. Deacon sprinted from the visiting team's tunnel entry at one end of the stadium to the fifty-yard line. He must have run full throttle for eighty to a hundred yards. He went straight to the oxygen at the end of the bench and wasn't worth a shit for the rest of the night.

My work was cut out for me, because I had to block Merlin Olsen. I thought Merlin, Bob Lilly, and Joe Green, were the best defensive tackles in football. Fortunately, when we played Dallas, I didn't have to block Lilly. Olsen had gone to the Pro Bowl every year he played in the league and he was currently in his fourteenth season. I was in my twelfth. We had played against each other about four times and I always held my own. He had said some nice things about me when I was with San Diego:

"I'd rather sell used cars than play against Walt Sweeney." At the time, he owned a Volkswagen dealership.

I hoped that it had to do with my ability rather than bad breath or my occasional habit of throwing up on a defensive tackle.

On this Monday night, he was giving me everything I could handle and then some. It was early in the last quarter. I was setting up for a Kilmer pass play when I lost my footing. Falling backwards, I grabbed Merlin's facemask and pulled him down on top of me. I didn't like to do this, because it could cause serious injury. If I got caught, it would negate any yardage gained plus tack on a fifteen-yard penalty. It's very difficult for an official to catch, because it's done so quickly. I didn't get caught. We were in the huddle and Kilmer was about to call the next play when Olsen grabbed the back of my shoulder pads. "If you do that again, Sweeney, I'm going to break your neck."

I'm sure he was big enough to do it, but it caught everyone in our huddle off guard. Merlin was known as a gentleman both on and off the field. He was not one to make idle threats. Two plays later, I slipped again and repeated the infraction. Something I might have done twice in twelve years, I was forced to do twice in one game. I'm happy to say he didn't break my neck, but he probably could have. We won the game and for the first time in years, I was on a playoff team.

A bunch of fools—guys who loved to be called "fools"—had taken a bus up from the Beachcomber in San Diego to watch their favorite football player in action. I visited with them outside the stadium after the game. As we were saying our good-byes, one of them slipped a gram of cocaine in my palm as we shook hands. "Have a nice flight, Walt."

"Thanks, Steve. I will now."

Two weeks later, we would be flying back to Los Angeles to face the Rams in the first round of the playoffs. I wanted to ask George if I should bring my things, which probably amounted to two suitcases of clothes, to LA. In case we lost to the Rams, I could fly to San Diego instead of flying back to Washington and then back to San Diego. I didn't have enough balls to ask him. George would have construed it as a negative approach to the game.

We lost a close game to the Rams. I guess we shot our wad two weeks earlier in the Monday night game. I went back to Washington and caught a flight home to San Diego the next day.

There's No Place Like Home

The minute I arrived in San Diego, I headed for Jean's house for a reunion with my kids. Tears welled up in my eyes when I saw Kris and Rick. I couldn't believe how much they had grown in the short time I was gone.

"What happened to you guys on Sunday?" Rick asked.

I joked, "I didn't get any help from those bums that I play with."

Jean made a nice dinner. We made plans for the kids to come to the beach the following weekend to resume our normal schedule. I also showed them the airline tickets that I had for the three of us to take a trip to Hawaii. In two weeks, we would be leaving for a ten-day stay. The kids could hardly contain themselves. Jean was excited too. It would be a nice break for her.

My next order of business was to reclaim my apartment from a friend living there and overseeing the place for me. I got in my car that had been parked at Jean's and headed for the beach.

Sonny McCrea was the gentleman at my place. He was a sixty-four year old heavy equipment operator who I had befriended several years earlier. He was a big, burly guy who stood about 6'4" and weighed about 240 pounds. He was a dead ringer for Joel McCrea, the movie actor, and Sonny claimed he was his brother. He also boasted that he had been John Wayne's stuntman for a number of years. Sonny had a penchant for Budweiser and an occasional line of coke. One of the most hilarious days of my life was spent with Sonny and Dave Costa. The three of us dropped some windowpane (LSD) and just roared over the stupidest shit for hours. Sonny had a million stories, most of them bullshit, but you couldn't help liking the guy. Like that old Floyd Cramer song, Personality, Sonny had a great one. A few years earlier, I had met him in a bar over by the stadium. I brought him down to the beach and introduced him around. He was a big hit. Although I knew his "Hollywood" stories were a crock, I helped perpetuate the "Legend of Sonny."

Sonny took up residence at the Catamaran Hotel after he left my place. The hotel was about two miles north of my apartment in Pacific Beach. I spent many an afternoon by the pool with Sonny just shooting the shit and drinking beer.

The kids and I had a great time in Hawaii spending three days in Honolulu before going to Maui for a week. We visited Pearl Harbor and a sugar plantation in Lanai, but for the most part, we swam and played in the warm waters of the Pacific. If we didn't get room service, we dined at one of the many restaurants on the beach. Between the sun, salt water and three-hour time difference, we were out like a light by eight-thirty every evening. It was one of the best times of my life.

One night, after I had been back from Hawaii for about two weeks, I was sitting around my apartment feeling particularly lonely. I decided to give Donna a call. It was good to hear her voice. I asked if she would come out for a visit if I sent a plane ticket. She accepted the offer and stayed for the next six years.

I drove to La Jolla every day and worked out at Maylen's Gym. It was only about ten minutes from my place in South Mission. Maylen (he only used one name) used to be the Charger strength coach in the early seventies. He knew his business and I give him a lot of credit for enhancing my career. He was about 5'9" with a stocky build. He always wore a sweat suit. His head was completely shaven and his plucked eyebrows gave him a Spockish look. He was the kind of a guy that would give you the shirt off his back, but alcoholism cost him several marriages, his job with the Chargers, his business, and eventually his beautiful home in Del Mar. When he was with the Chargers, he would show up at banquets half sloshed. That's hardly good for public relations. Usually, after he put me through a good workout, we'd cross the street to the Velvet Hammer for a few cocktails. I should have known he wasn't quite right because he drank vodka and water with no ice.

One night we were at a San Diego Gulls hockey game at the Sports Arena when he stuck a loaded starter pistol to his head and pulled the trigger. I was as shocked as everyone else. I got away as quickly as possible, because I'm the type of guy that doesn't like to bring attention to himself. After this incident, I avoided going out in public with Maylen. I could handle the Velvet Hammer. It was a dark, quiet lounge and one of the few bars that still accepted Maylen's patronage.

He was probably in his fifties when he got married for the fourth or fifth time. No one was sure of his age. He kept it a secret like some sort of aging movie star. Karen, his bride to be, was a twenty-year old rugby player from England. The wedding took place in Maylen's Del Mar home. Sonny, Donna and I were among the many guests. Karen's parents had flown from England for their only daughter's wedding. One of Maylen's old drinking buddies, Judge Robert Cooney, performed the ceremony. Maylen dressed in tails and sneakers for the occasion. Donna and I were on the upstairs porch smoking a joint, but we could still hear Judge Cooney conducting the sacred ritual.

"Does anyone here oppose this union? Speak now or forever hold your peace."

"I do!" A drunken Sonny blurted out. He probably had far more foresight than anyone realized at the time.

"No, Judge, I really dig the fuckin' chick," Maylen said.

As high as I was and as good as I felt, a wave of shame and embarrassment sweep through me. I felt so bad for Karen and her parents who had come such a long way for this freak show. I grabbed Donna and we hightailed it out of there. Needless to say, the marriage lasted less than a year.

I continued to work out at Maylen's and became stronger than ever before. July rolled around and it was time to report to training camp again. Donna, Magee, and I were going to drive to Lorton, Virginia and spend a few days on her folks' farm. Then I would take the two-hour drive to Carlisle, Pennsylvania and camp.

"Deaf Bob," a friend of mine from the beach, was going to make the trip with us and visit his parents who also lived in northern Virginia. As his name infers, he couldn't hear and it was very difficult to understand him when he did speak.

My old pal and one of the "San Diego Eight," Dave Costa, would accompany us to Denver. Taking Costa to Colorado was out of our way, but we had the time. Dave was a funny guy and that leg of the journey would pass quickly.

I got behind the wheel and half a dozen Disoxyn, several joints and twenty-three hours later, we pulled into the Zang Brewing Company in Denver. Zang was a bar owned by Bronco linebacker Freddie Forsberg. Dave had spent five years with the Broncos. He and Freddie were the best of friends. Costa was originally drafted by the Raiders, played twice with the Buffalo Bills and put a year in with the Portland Storm of the short-lived World Football League. He was a good journeyman tackle. I first met him at the Coaches All-America Game in Buffalo. Dave was from a large Italian family in the Bronx. He was a loud, boisterous guy who reminded me of a big Danny Devito. I can't remember exactly what we were talking about, but once as we walked into a crowded restaurant after practice, he blurted out: "Well fat people like to fuck, too."

It wasn't exactly how I like to make an entrance.

Freddie Forsberg was the middle linebacker for the Broncos. I had played against him many times. He, like Costa, was another funny guy. I can remember when we played against each other and I was down in my stance listening for the quarterback's signals, Freddie would call across the line of scrimmage. His eyes were all dilated and sweat rolled down that big white face. "Hey, Walt. How many did you take today?"

He was referring to the number of amphetamines I took for the game. That always made me laugh instead of smashing into the defensive tackle I was playing against.

We had dinner and drinks and took a couple of rooms at the motel next door. The next morning, we would start the long trip to Virginia.

I drove all the way, stopping for only gas, food, beer and to let the dog get some exercise. Toward the end of the trip, Bob was flipping out. He thought I was Jesus Christ one minute and the next he accused me of stealing from him. I had never even asked him for gas money. I was doing speed to stay awake and get the trip over as soon as possible. Bob was trying to stay up instead of catching some shuteye like Donna. One of the side effects of speed is flapping your jaw a lot. Poor Bob had no way of venting his feelings because of the communication problem.

We arrived in one piece. I spent a night at Donna's parents before heading to training camp. Bob stayed on for a few days to unwind and come back to Earth before his parents were called to pick him up.

I've always hated training camp, because it was real hard work. No matter how many weights I lifted in the off-season, I could never quite push myself to get into good running shape. The cigarettes and joints I smoked certainly didn't help my conditioning program.

I was starting my thirteenth season and beginning to think I could play forever. So far I had been lucky and managed to escape serious injury. I was stronger than I had ever been. My speed and reactions were still intact.

As we were preparing for our season opener against the Colts in Baltimore, I developed phlebitis. Three days before the game, my right leg was very sore, swollen and discolored. I was hospitalized until game day and joined the team in Baltimore.

George wasn't going to start me, but he sent me in the second quarter for a few plays to keep my consecutive game streak alive. I hadn't missed a game in thirteen years and was proud of the string. I appreciated what George was doing. We won the game, no thanks to me, and we were off to a good start.

I remember more off-field incidents that year than actual games. After playing for so many years, the games become one big blur unless something extraordinary happened and that rarely occurred.

One night, Donna and I had a shouting match, so I headed down to Frannie O'Brien's for some relief. I wanted to get out of the house, so I started a fight with her. That gave me an excuse to leave and drink by myself. Most people don't like to drink alone, but I did. I found a table in a dark corner of the bar and started pursuing my favorite pastime to get as drunk as I could. The bar was full of women that night and the more I drank, the better they looked. As my friend, Sonny, would say:

"They all look like Lana Turner at two in the morning."

I must have gone into a blackout, because I don't remember leaving the bar. I do recall waking up in a hotel room thinking someone was trying to suffocate me with a giant pillow. As it turned out, it wasn't a giant pillow. It was a rather large woman sitting on my face. That wasn't the worst of it. Two days later, I had an infection in my right eye. I could barely open it. So much for romance.

The eye doctor told me that he would freeze the surface of my eye to scrape the infection off. When he left the room, I examined the bottle of liquid cocaine that would be used to freeze the eye. I was toying with the idea of administering it myself, but I couldn't quite figure it out. Would I catch a buzz? Should I drink it or pour it up my nose? Would it kill me? I decided to pass.

After the procedure, the doctor gave me an eye patch to wear. At my request, he also gave me a prescription for a hundred Quaaludes. I told him they were for sleep. He wasn't familiar with the drug. I had to spell it out and give him the proper dosage. They would help ease the chill around the old homestead. Donna was still pissed at me for staying out all night. When I showed up for practice the next day, my teammates started calling me "Rooster Cogburn."

I do remember the Cowboy game in Dallas on Thanksgiving Day. Jean had called and told me that Rick broke his leg in a bicycle accident. I knew we would have a couple of days off after the game and made arrangements to fly to San Diego from Dallas. I should have cleared it with George. I figured I'd ask him after we beat the Cowboys.

With eleven minutes to go in the game, things were looking good. We had a twenty-point lead and Cowboy coach Tom Landry had just pulled QB Roger Staubach. Clint Longley replaced him and turned into Y.A. Tittle. The backup threw three touchdown passes to beat us. It was very difficult to talk to George after the loss, but I asked him about my trip to California. He consented.

Honest, It Ain't All About the Money

The scene is RFK Stadium in Washington, D.C.. It's the last game of the season between the Redskins and the Philadelphia Eagles. It's a meaningless game as far as the standings are concerned. Since neither team is going to the playoffs, rookies are simply trying to impress the coaches to show them that they can play in this league. Old vets like me are trying to prove that we still have what it takes. It's only a few days before Christmas, so everyone is in a festive mood. Trailing by six in the second quarter, George replaces Billy Kilmer with Joe Theisman. Joe takes the snap from center, drops back and throws a perfect interception. I was about forty yards away from the defensive back that had the ball. I should have headed for our bench, but I was hopped up on speed. I took off in pursuit. The defensive tackle I had been blocking, clipped me. Pain that shot through my left knee like nothing I had ever felt before.

The trainer's put an air cast on my leg and placed me in a golf cart. I went off to the locker room. I was left to my own devices and that was never a good idea. The trainers had to get ready for the rest of the team who would be coming in at half time.

I hobbled over to my locker and grabbed my shaving kit. I headed for the toilet stalls. I'm sitting on the shitter clad in a sweat soaked T-shirt and a jockstrap. My fingers still have grass and blood stained tape as they fumble through the kit feeling for a baggy with a quarter ounce of coke. I'm still speeding from the

Desoxyn that I took before the game. I'm cursing myself for dropping ashes from the dangling cigarette in my mouth into the now open baggy. I use the cover from a book of matches to spoon the coke and ashes up to my nostrils. Somewhere in the dark recesses of my mind is the idea that cocaine is an anesthetic. It might ease the pain. From my reflection in the chrome toilet seat dispenser, I see that I have white powder all over my mustache and beard. I take water from the toilet with my hand and splash it on my face to wash off the evidence. All the players return to the field for the second-half kickoff, but Bubba Tyrer, the head trainer, and Dr. Palumbo, the team physician, remain.

I return the shaving kit to my locker and slowly work my way to the training room. It takes me several minutes to get stretched out on the training table. The hot searing pain has subsided, replaced by a dull constant ache. I can overhear Palumbo and Tyrer huddled across the room.

The doctor spoke first. "The knee is one of the worst I've ever seen. He needs surgery right away."

"Are you kidding? I don't know what he has in his system, but he's cooking on something."

"I know, I know. To be on the safe side, schedule him for Wednesday at Georgetown Hospital. That will give us seventy-two hours."

A ball boy stuck his head in the door and I asked him to get me a cup of coffee. That's all I needed now, caffeine to add to the speed and the coke. It was just something to wet my mouth. It was so dry I could hardly speak. My mind is racing a mile a minute as I lite up a cigarette. I'm cursing Theisman for throwing the interception, cursing myself for running after it and cursing Bill Dunstan, the son-of-bitch who clipped me.

One minute, I'm feeling sorry for myself. The next, I'm thinking how lucky I've been for getting this far in the game without a serious injury. Thirteen years without missing a game. Not bad for an end from Syracuse that the pros converted to a guard. My anger toward Dunstan had even subsided. After all, I had been holding, leg-whipping, tripping, and using facemask pulldowns for years on defensive tackles. Kilmer told me I was the best holder he ever had.

The recent "pay for hurt" scandal reminds me of my days with the Redskins. We didn't have a bounty system. George had a similar arrangement, but it involved good plays. If you intercepted a pass, made an important block or a timely catch, coaches had ways to show some recognition. They never encouraged us to injury the other players. George Allen once named me Blocker of the Week. I had a full beard at the time and my prize from Coach Allen was an electric razor.

It was one of George's many ways to get the team to laugh. I was very fortunate to play for a guy like George Allen. He was a players' coach.

On Wednesday, Christmas Eve, Donna dropped me off at Georgetown Hospital with three or four joints and a couple of cigars. The operation was that evening. The best part of the procedure was the Demerol they administered before and after the knives started flying. I was supposed to be in the hospital five days, but they kicked me out after two for smoking pot. In my infinite wisdom, I figured that if I smoked a cigar and a joint together, no one could smell the marijuana. I was wrong.

The six-month lease expired on the house we were renting in Fairfax. Upon leaving the hospital, I was asked what kind of pain medication I wanted. I told them Quaaludes and was surprised when they gave them to me. According to my Physicians Desk Reference, Quaaludes are classified as a hypnotic drug, not a pain reliever. I think they prescribed them just to get me out of there. It was a drug that made you feel like everything is all right with the world. It was so good that they took it off the market a few years later.

I wore a full cast from my foot to my hip. We decided to spend a little time down on Donna's parent's farm before heading home to San Diego. I vegetated in an upstairs bedroom for about three days or until the ludes were gone. We thought we would stop in Fort Lauderdale for a few days of sun and relaxation before heading west.

I purchased a Smith & Wesson thirty-eight caliber snub nose from Donna's uncle. I don't know if it was the helplessness I felt because of the huge cast I was dragging or the paranoia from the drugs I was taking, but I felt the need for a gun. Donna scored a pound of marijuana, in case there was a shortage in San Diego. Off we went.

In Chapel Hill, North Carolina, I was stopped for speeding. The state troopers didn't see the weed, the gun or assorted pills I had stashed away. If they had, I'd probably still be in North Carolina. I told them how I got hurt during the game and my Christmas Eve operation.

It turned out that they were Redskin fans. They let me go with a warning. It was raining when we got to Fort Lauderdale. The weather was still lousy when we got up the next morning, so we headed for the West Coast.

Because of the cast, the driver's side of the car was the most comfortable for me. I did all the driving which I probably would have done anyway. I still had some Desoxyn left and they enabled me to stay awake for long periods of time. We drove from Florida to Las Cruces, New Mexico. We only stopped for the essentials: beer, smokes, coffee, and gasoline. I drove all night and was so thankful when that old sun came up. By the time we got to New Mexico, I was hallucinating. I was seeing cars backing out of driveways in front of me. Sagebrush appeared to be different animals such as buffalo, deer or moose. I finally pulled off the road and checked into a motel in Las Cruces. Before we went to our room, we wandered into the motel gift shop.

A very dignified looking Indian woman asked us if she could be of assistance. She had on a suede dress and she struck me as one of the neatest and cleanest people I had ever seen. She didn't have a hair out of place. We must have looked like fugitives from skid row after driving non-stop for two days sucking beer and cigarettes. I told her we were just browsing. She probably thought we were going to rob her. She was standing behind me as I bent over a display case to look at some Indian jewelry. That was when I cut what sounded like the loudest beer fart of my life. I was so embarrassed I whipped out a hundred-dollar bill and spent the better part of it on her wares. I can't even remember what I bought. I just knew I couldn't wait to get out of there.

The NFL owners held their annual winter meeting in San Diego in February. George Allen was in town and invited me to join him for breakfast at the Hotel Del Coronado. I was very apprehensive about the meeting. I was thirty-five years old and coming off major knee surgery. Did he hear about the pot incident at the hospital? If he did, was it a big deal to him? It certainly wasn't to me. Was he going to give me my walking papers? I didn't know what to expect. I showed up and exchanged pleasantries. George quickly got down to business.

"You know, Walt, you just can't come back this season for the money."

"Coach, I wouldn't do that." I lied.

At my age and considering the severity of my injury, I wasn't coming back for the glory of old D.C.

"I've played thirteen years and this is probably my last chance to get a (Super Bowl) ring. We have a good nucleus on the team and I think we have a shot." I continued to bullshit and I'm sure George was aware I was bullshitting him.

Somewhat reluctantly, he said, "If you really feel that way and you can pass the physical, I'll see you in training camp." Who was kidding who?

The Chargers were kind enough to let me use their facilities to rehabilitate my knee. Perhaps my eleven years with the team influenced their decision. Whatever the reason, I was very grateful.

I reported to Redskin training camp in Carlisle in mid-July and passed the physical examination. So far, my hard work had paid off. In those days, unless you had a serious injury, which I did, all you needed was a pulse to pass the physical.

The coaches slowly worked me into the drills and after a couple of weeks my knee felt strong. I was quite pleased with the way it was holding up. The team ordered a custom knee brace for me. The day it arrived, I strapped it on and went out to practice. It caused a lot of pain and was very confining. When I took the brace off, my knee was swollen to the size of a soccer ball. George Allen and Bubba Tyrer looked on. All three of us knew I was finished.

The Redskins put me on Injured Reserve. Back in those days, IR was a fuzzy category. At least in my mind, it was fuzzy, but then a lot of things were fuzzy to me. I was told not to step on the practice field and only attend the team meetings. I felt like a complete outcast. I felt more frustrated as each day went by. I kept waiting for someone to tell me that they were going to pay me for the season, but nobody ever did.

Before attending a night meeting, I had to tear my room apart trying to find my playbook. If you lost it, you were fined $1,000. I knew exactly where I had left it. Three things that professional football taught me were that it was better to drop an eyeball than a football, you show up to meetings and practices on time and you guard your playbook. If you were late, you were fined. As a result of this, I am very punctual. I might not know what to do when I show up, but I'll be there on time. Protect your playbook was drilled into me since high school. Even though my personal life was in shambles, I tried to abide by the rules set down by the football establishment. This was my livelihood. In all the years that I played football, I had never even misplaced my playbook. Now it was missing.

I wandered over to the assistant general manager's office to see if maybe it had turned up there. When a player is released or traded, his playbook is turned into the assistant GM's office.

"Hi, Tim. My playbook is missing. Have you seen it?"

"No. It hasn't turned up here."

Then I went to the trunk where they kept the books. There was my playbook. I was enraged! The nerve of this pencil-pushing fuck who didn't know a football from his ass. I held up the book.

"What the fuck is this?"

"One of the coaches must have put it there," he replied timidly.

"You're a liar and you're fucking with the wrong guy."

I stormed out of his office to seek some relief at the local saloon. What were these people trying to do to me? Were they trying to get out of paying me for the season? Were they just trying to get me to leave?

I had never developed any coping skills. I remember throwing a tantrum at the dinner table when I was about ten years old. Every Saturday, my mother would cook a big pot of baked beans. Everyone in the family liked beans except me. She usually cooked me some potatoes and eggs. It wasn't like the poor woman didn't have enough to do. I guess I wasn't in the mood for potatoes and eggs either. I jumped up from the dinner table and shouted the four-letter word. I ran out the door. After that, whenever I had a hissy fit, someone would say, "Well, you know how he is." There were never consequences for my bad behavior. I thought I was "special."

I didn't feel too special the day they commandeered my play-book. As a matter of fact, I felt like a used-up piece of shit. When I got to the bar, I washed four Quaaludes down with a double scotch. Two "ludes" can make you feel great, but four can sometimes make you ornery and mean. I had about three or four more drinks in the hour I was there. I knew enough to get back to the dorm while I could still see. After safely reaching my destination, I grabbed the gun out of my glove compartment and headed for my room. Once inside, I fired six rounds into my empty bed. Don't ask me why I did it. At the time, it seemed like the right thing to do. I guess the two extra Quaaludes put me over the edge.

"That's that crazy bastard Sweeney." I recognized Billy Kilmer's raspy voice.

I thought crazy bastards shoot people. I was only shooting fur-niture. I decided to smoke a joint…perhaps that would mellow me out a bit. I had never smoked weed in the dorm before, well not in my room anyway, maybe in the stairwell a few times. Usually, when the mood hit me, and that was every evening, I would sneak off under the cover of night and toke up. The players had too much respect for Coach Allen to flaunt the use of marijuana. My last couple of years on the Chargers, two thirds of the team would be smoking weed in their rooms during training camp. Our dismal record proved that we had a bunch of dopers on the roster.

After firing my gun in the dorm, smoking a joint in my room didn't seem like such a big deal. I knew I was out of there one way or another. The next morning, one of the trainers came to see me. He said George wanted to see me right away. I bet he did.

"Walt, we can't have guns in training camp."

"Nobody ever told me that." Not only did he think I was nuts, but now he must have thought I was dumb as a box of rocks.

He was about to go on, but I cut him off at the pass.

I lied. "George, I've already got the gun out of camp."

"Good, Walt. We're going to pay you for the season and you will get a share of any playoff money should we go that far. I think it would be best if you went back to San Diego."

There was method in my madness. The next day, I said so long to some of my teammates. John Riggins waved me down to his room. I really didn't know John that well. This was his first year with the team and I had only practiced with them for a couple of weeks. Inside his room, he proceeded to break out a Tai Stick and rolled a big fatty. We didn't say too much as we smoked. Afterwards, we shook hands and wished each other good luck. That was my departure from pro football. It seemed ironic that fourteen years after I signed my first professional contract on national television, now, in my mind anyhow, I had to shoot a gun to collect on my last one.

.

Out of Football and "Ready" For the Game of Life

After the shooting incident in Carlisle, Donna and I returned to San Diego. I was 35 years old and for the first time since I was in the seventh grade, I wasn't playing football. I'd never been one for reflection or self-inspection. Now I had plenty of time to look back on my life and football career. The more I looked and thought about it, the more depressed I became.

Today's athletes, amateurs and professional, are subject to intense scrutiny by the media. Hardly a day goes by when there isn't a story in the papers about some ballplayer arrested for drunk driving, assault, spousal abuse, drug or weapons charges. There seem to be a large number of crimes against the opposite sex these days. I was never one to hit a woman. Scream, yes. Hit, no.

During my time with the Redskins and the Chargers, I was arrested eight times. Looking back, I can't believe I was that stupid. At the time, I thought it was just part of life. Didn't everyone go through this? I was arrested six times for driving under the influence, once for being drunk in public and another time for felonious assault. Except for the felonious assault charge in New York, none of these indiscretions ever made the newspapers. When the police confront some athletes, they try to use their celebrity to get out of trouble. Whenever I got into a jam, I never mentioned that I played ball. I gave my name was Walter Sweeney instead of Walt Sweeney. What a ploy. I always went peacefully, well almost always.

One night, I was giving a girl a ride home from the Beachcomber. The police stopped me a few miles from the bar. They saw a 6'4", 260 pound, fairly well buffed, drunk exit the car. My t-shirt expressed my attitude at the time. Printed in bold letters across the front were the words, Fuck Everything. I usually didn't wear clothing with such outlandish statements, but the owner of the Beachcomber gave it to me before I left the bar. I was drunk enough to put it on. Sometimes when I was drinking, I would think that the dumbest things were a riot. When I sobered up, the humor of the situation escaped me. The cops didn't think my shirt was very funny. When I struggled to avoid being handcuffed, they got downright hostile. They beat the shit out of me.

When I got out of jail the next day, I went straight to my barber. He took photographs of the nightstick wounds on the back of my head. I was going to sue the San Diego Police Department for police brutality. Of course, I never did, but it seemed like a good idea at the time.

It's not like I was all over the road when I was drinking and driving, I did have a certain amount of bad luck. One night, I was driving from the Beachcomber to my place which was only two blocks away. A woman pulled out of a side street and it was impossible to avoid running into her car. She was cited for causing the accident, but I had been drinking. I went directly to jail. A week later, I got my car out of the body shop and was stopped again for an equipment violation. The garage hadn't fixed my headlights properly. Only one was working. I got a ticket for the headlight and was taken to jail for drinking and driving.

One night, three other "fools" and I drove to Ensenada, Mexico for some seafood. The trip would take us about sixty miles south of the border. Nick "The Wheel Man" Rendich was our designated driver. This didn't mean Nick wasn't going to drink. It meant he was the best at drinking and driving. After we crossed the border at

San Ysidro, we headed for one of the many bars that lined Avenida Revolucion in Tijuana. After a few rounds of beers, we got back into my Mercedes and headed south to Ensenada.

Halfway to our destination, we stopped at La Fonda, a charming hotel that sits high on a cliff overlooking the Pacific. We wandered into the bar and someone had the brilliant idea of tequila shooters. No one's arm had to be twisted. Even with the salt and lime, I couldn't handle the first two. I broke out in a cold sweat and barely made it to the men's room before throwing up. (It wasn't easy having all this fun.) Feeling much better, I returned to the bar and drank the next several shooters without any problems. If I were as persistent in other areas of my life as I was about catching a buzz, I'm sure things would have gone smoother for me.

I've had many battles with Jose Cuervo (tequila) and Jose kicked my ass every time. Tonight would be no exception. We reached Felipe's in Ensenada and grabbed a table. The restaurant was nearly empty. We gorged on clams, shrimp, lobster and my own personal favorite, Mexican sea bass. These seafood delights were washed down with countless cervezas (beers).

I decided that I was the most sober of the lot and would drive home. I've made enough bad decisions when I wasn't drinking, but when I hit the sauce, any common sense I might have goes right out the window.

Just south of Tijuana, I failed to negotiate the "curva de la muerte" (curve of death) and slammed into the guardrail going about 70 mph. The car did a couple of full spins, but didn't roll over. Nick said the car frame looked like it had been sprung. My Mercedes was probably totaled. The four of us were outside the car when the policia showed up.

"You're under arrest for drunk driving," the cop said to no one in particular. "

"Who is?" I asked.

"Whoever was driving," he said to all of us.

I gave him $200 and he gave me a dime to make a phone call. I called a friend in South Mission Beach and he picked us up. As far as I know, the car is still there.

Money Well Spent

One of the attorneys who represented me for a drunk driving charge offered this insight.

"See that building across the street?" He pointed to a six-story office building.

"You could have bought that building with all the money you've spent on attorney fees, fines, auto repairs and insurance hikes."

A judge in one of my cases gave me probation and I had to see a probation officer once a month. The PO had to deal with hardened criminals. I was just some guy whose only criminal act was trying to catch a buzz (and drive).

Part of one of my many sentences was to see a psychologist. This wasn't my first trip to a head doctor. Sid had sent me to see a psychiatrist years earlier when I was working for the Chargers during the off-season. My job was to sell group season tickets to bars and restaurants in the greater San Diego area. It was a great job for a practicing alcoholic with an expense account. Gillman, who ran every phase of the Charger operation, noticed that I wouldn't show up to work for days at a time. He sent me to a shrink who dealt with drinking problems. I guess all you get out of these sessions is what you put in them. I didn't put in very much. In the first place, the only reason I went to the doctor was to keep Sid happy. In the second place, I thought he was nuts for even thinking I needed it. I wasn't honest with the shrink. I think that just to get rid of me, he told me it was Jean's fault that I drank. He didn't have to tell me twice. I never went back.

Getting back to this court appointed psychologist that I had to see once a week, I can remember one of the conversations went something like this:

"Well, Doc, I haven't been drinking that much lately."

"That's good, Walt. Have you been using marijuana?"

"Yeah, it cuts down on my drinking."

"That's right and marijuana is a lot better for you. If booze were invented today, the Federal Drug Administration wouldn't legalize it."

I wondered if this was the opinion of the entire medical profession or if it was this quack's personal view? He continued:

"Alcohol is highly toxic. By the way, have you come across any good weed?"

"As a matter of fact a friend of mine at the beach has some Colombian that gets the job done."

"Just between you and me, what are the chances of you getting me some?"

"No problem."

I wasn't a bit surprised by the request. It was the early 1970s. The Viet Nam war was over. It was the era of feeling good. People were tuning in, turning on, and dropping out. Drugs were no longer just a ghetto problem. Coke was being snorted in executive boardrooms and speed was being dropped on the assembly lines.

Marijuana really did cut down on my alcohol consumption, but on one occasion, I had a mighty thirst. After taking the kids home on Sunday evening, I returned to the beach and the Pennant. I was in a dark mood and the International Stingers I was swilling down weren't helping.

I left my car behind the Pennant and walked two blocks to my house. When I arrived, Donna was on the phone with her mother in Virginia. Only God knows why, but I wasn't happy about it. I got my revolver out of the bedroom dresser and returned to the kitchen. I shot the phone off the wall. Apparently, Donna's mother feared for her daughter's life, so she called the San Diego Police Department. I had stumbled back to the Pennant before the police got to the apartment. They were long gone when I got home, but I became incensed when Donna told me that the cops had checked her arms for needle marks. The unmitigated gall!

"There would be lawsuits filed!"

I was very indignant about the whole situation and ran across the alley to a friend who was a San Diego cop. I expressed my displeasure. I was ranting and raving and the poor bastard looked at me like I was completely out of my mind. He was probably right.

Because of my drunk driving violations, my driving privileges were revoked for ten years in Virginia and seven years in California. I continued to drive. You drive very carefully when you don't have a license. I must have been doing it right because I was never stopped once.

Besides losing my license, seeing a probation officer and a psychologist, I also had to attend "bad driver's" school. Later, I progressed to "drunk driving" school. I hoped against hope that the latter was a school where you were taught you how to drive safely while you were drunk. In the first class, I ran into my old pal, Pete Mikolajewski, a backup quarterback for the Chargers and sometime drinking buddy when he came to the beach.

"Hey Whiskey," I greeted Pete. With a nickname like that you know he belonged here.

"Walter Francis, they got you too."

When Jack Murphy wrote in the *San Diego Union*, he always called me by my full name. A handful of people still referred to me as Walter Francis. Pete was one of them.

"Those El Cajon cops must have it in for me," I said. It couldn't have been my fault that I was here.

"You probably screwed one of their old ladies," Pete said.

"Probably," I replied. We both knew that wasn't true, but it seemed like the macho thing to say at the time.

"Yeah, the pricks got me two blocks from my house," Pete bitched.

Both of us agreed that we were victims of bad luck. We didn't belong here.

The meat and potatoes of the drunk-driving course was viewing films from the Ohio State Police. They showed the aftermath of some horrific automobile accidents caused by drunk drivers. I guess the idea was to scare us, but it's difficult to scare a drunk. I know it didn't scare the two guys who went out to their car during a coffee break and sucked on a pint of Jack Daniels.

"Look," Pete said as he pointed to our thirsty classmates. We were outside having a smoke.

"I'm glad we're not that bad," I said.

"Me, too."

Although we probably had eight or more DUI's between us, we knew we were victims of bad luck. Vindictive cops were jealous of our celebrity. We didn't drink like the losers in the parking lot. We just drank to have a good time.

The only jail time I did, besides initial bookings, was for a DUI in 1981. I was sentenced to forty-eight hours in the "Duffy Hotel." John Duffy was the Sheriff of San Diego County. He presented Sam Gruneisen and me with honorary Sheriff badges years earlier when we were involved in some school programs.

I was supposed to check into jail on a Friday evening around 6:00 p.m.. I had a doctor's appointment the previous Wednesday. I was having trouble sleeping because of the pain in my knee. He gave me a prescription for some pain/sleeping pills.

While waiting for check-in with all the other criminals, I started to panic about the eight pills hidden in my pack of cigarettes. The routine at the front of the line was to hand the contents of your pockets to the officers. They return your smokes, but their medical staff administer any prescription drugs you might have. In my case, they were to give me two pills every four hours for the duration of my stay. The closer I got to the check-in window, the more nervous I became. If they found the pills, what would they do to me? I'm already in jail, but they might extend my stay. Realizing that a longer stay would be totally unacceptable, I decide the best course of action would be to eat all of the pills. My original plan was to take half the pills when I got to my cell in case the jailers were slow giving me my medication. I would take the other half as needed. If I were conscious during my stay, I would need them. As things worked out, I almost slept through my entire sentence. I woke up with four hours to go.

I was hung over from the pills when I woke about 2:00 p.m. on Sunday afternoon. I was in a pisser mood.

"Where's my medication?" I yelled. I didn't want to be conscious for the remainder of my stay.

When a guard informed me that I had taken all of my medication, I really became an asshole.

"I want to see Sheriff Duffy!" I continued to raise my voice. "He's a personal friend of mine and he'll be bullshit when he finds out how I've been mistreated!"

I must have been fairly amusing, because everyone within earshot was having a good laugh.

While alcohol was usually the main reason I crossed paths with the law, I almost got into some serious trouble south of the border with marijuana. Five of us were headed to San Felipe which is located on the Baja side of the Sea of Cortez about 120 miles south of Mexicali. We were going to the La Jolla Beach & Tennis Club's annual spring bash. Eating, drinking, dancing and swimming under the hot Mexican sun for three days. Believe it or not, I had been asked by the organizers of the event to help maintain some sort of order during the festivities. The previous year, the number of arrests were unusually high and this year they wanted to keep a lid on things. In return for my services, my room (which was a real scarcity), my food and booze would be gratis. Free booze alone would be a big savings.

I was driving Richard's van. Richard was a longtime beach buddy. Three gals we knew from the beach needed a ride to the party, so they accompanied us.

Once we crossed the border at Tecate, we broke some beers out of the cooler and smoked a little grass. I only had enough for about six joints because I was very paranoid about taking drugs in or out of Mexico. After getting high, I was even more paranoid. I could always tell the quality of marijuana by my paranoia. The stronger the weed, the more paranoid I became. This stuff must have been pretty good, because I buried it under all our clothes and other belongings we'd brought for the trip. No one would ever find it.

I used to get high in my apartment and hide weed in cereal boxes, stereo equipment, etc.. Sometimes I would find it years later while packing to move. I imagine that there was a lot I never found.

About forty miles north of San Felipe, we were waiting in line at a drug and gun checkpoint. The Mexican Army was conducting the searches.

"Richard, I'm going to get the weed out and put it in my wallet."

"It's fine where it is. Leave it there."

"I don't think so."

I follow through with my plan. After what seemed like hours, it was our turn for inspection. We were asked to get out of the van while three soldiers went through our belongings. An officer, I don't know his rank, approached me.

"Senor, your wallet por favor."

When I heard this I thought my bowels were going to cut loose. I handed over my wallet and he immediately pulled out a little crumpled baggy of pot.

"Mota!"

He shouted to one of his comrades who was returning a small vial of marijuana to his shirt pocket. Apparently, they had smelled the pot we had smoked earlier and were going to plant some in the van. Thanks to my stupidity, they didn't have to put on that charade.

They pulled the vehicle over to the side, took the keys and we just sat there while they continued to check other cars. I had heard horror stories about how people were busted in Mexico with small amounts of marijuana and they were never heard from again. Thoughts of making a run for it crossed my mind. We were in a wide-open area and the foothills were about a mile away. After looking at the hills and the soldiers with carbines strapped over their soldiers, I decided against trying to make a break for it.

I had always heard and read about the widespread corruption that pervaded the army, the police and just about all levels of government in Mexico. We pooled our resources and came up with about three hundred dollars. I had credit cards, but didn't think that they were equipped to handle them.

"Mi bueno hombre." I was trying to say my good man, but I might have said that I was a good man. This got the attention of the officer who discovered the marijuana in the first place.

"Dinero. Vaminos." I was trying to say that we would give him money if he would just let us go. My Spanish must have been better than I thought, because he understood perfectly. I gave him the dough and he gave me the car keys.

I thanked God for the way things worked in Mexico.

The Beat Goes On

I knew a couple guys who played for a long time and had to seek psychiatric help when their careers ended. Financially, these guys had prepared for that day by going back to school or learning another trade while still playing football. Even with training and education, the transition from football to the outside world was very difficult for them.

One friend told me he missed the roar of the crowd more than the actual game. I didn't miss the roar of the crowd. The noise I remember most were the boos from 1970s Chargers fans. I definitely didn't miss the game. If I hadn't ended my career with a bad injury, I might have felt differently. I doubt it. I loved football, but after all those years of ramming my body into blocking sleds and other people, I had had enough. I had a good run. It was time to move on. To what, I didn't know. Most guys join the rat race along with everyone else. Some of the lucky ones who can read and speak become sports announcers.

My first year out of football wasn't bad as far as I was concerned. I had enough money to support Jean and the kids. There was even some left over for the drugs that I felt were needed to keep me numb.

Over the years, I had developed an affinity for downers. It started with the Seconal I used to take the night before Charger games. I loved the feeling that swept over me an hour or so before they put me out.

Sometimes I would get a few Placidyl from a psychiatric nurse I knew. They were literally "knockout drops" or "Mickeys." They looked like green vitamin E pills. One night, I cut one in two and gave half to Donna. Within two minutes, her head fell into the potatoes she was mashing.

I don't know why I thought I had to knock myself out at times. I blamed myself for the failure of my marriage and for letting my kids down. I used that as an excuse for blackout drinking and pill popping. I have had bouts with insomnia where I tossed and turned all night, usually thinking of how to avenge all the injustices that had been done to me. Today, I don't keep any kind of sleeping aids around the house. I don't need them. If they were around, I'd take them every night until they are gone.

My second year away from the game, I was broke. As long as I was playing ball, I could get as fucked up as "Hogan's goat" and just be considered a good old boy who liked to catch a buzz once in a while. Now that my career was over and I continued the buzzes, I was considered a drunk and a bum.

Donna was taking the first step of fulfilling her life-long dream of becoming a cosmetologist to the stars. She enrolled in beauty school. I needed to go to work and make some money. I was almost a year behind in my rent. Dora Place was my landlady during the years I was playing ball. Now she was letting me slide until I got on my feet. When I was on my feet, I was usually staggering.

I couldn't get a decent job, because I couldn't hold a thought. Bob Chumsky, another old drinking buddy, had a small paving company and gave me a job as a laborer. There's nothing wrong with being a laborer, but I felt there must be something better out there for me. Anything. I had a BA with a history major. I had a successful NFL career with years of making All-Pro teams and winning numerous awards. You know what? That didn't mean shit in the real world.

I had been on the job a couple of months when I asked Eddie, a fellow paver, to score some heroin for me. Heroin seemed to be the drug of choice among pavers. Eddie, a long time junky, said he would. He promised to bring it by the house that evening. He never made it. He died from an overdose in his trailer. There, but for the grace of God, go I. I never thought about doing heroin again.

About a week after that, one of the truck drivers who delivered asphalt approached me.

"Aren't you Walt Sweeney? Weren't you a big star for the Chargers?"

Right about then, I wanted to climb under the asphalt. I had to get out of San Diego. Maybe I could return to the Boston area and get a fresh start. That evening, I discussed it with Donna. We agreed to leave the end of August. I thought geography would cure my problems. Most alcoholics feel that way. I could run away from San Diego, but I couldn't run away from myself.

First, Magee, Donna, and I drove to see Donna's folks in Lorton, Virginia. I'm sure her parents felt better knowing she would be a little closer to home. I assumed they thought I was a maniac, especially after the shooting incident.

My brother Bernie and his wife, Gloria, lived in Worcester, Massachusetts. We decided to stop for a visit since it was on our route to the Boston area. Bernie was five years older than me. I always liked him. When I was a kid, I used to watch him play football for Cohasset High. He was a halfback and gained most of the team's yardage all by himself. It wasn't easy being a football star for Cohasset back then. During in his four years on the team, they never won a game. A couple of schools were interested in recruiting him to play football for them, but he decided to run off to Florida with Gloria. By the way, Gloria was twenty years his senior. Bernie was a cocky guy with a sarcastic sense of humor. His personality could really turn people off if they didn't know him. He followed sports closely and I had a feeling he did all right gambling on various games. The last time I had seen them was five years earlier when I was still with the Chargers. We were playing the Patriots. My hometown, represented by my high school coach, Evie Dorr, and some former high school teammates, presented me with a portrait of myself at halftime. The entire Sweeney crew was in attendance.

I hadn't told Donna much about my family. Now I was trying to warn her about the dysfunction as we approached Bernie's house. Gloria answered the door. Before I had a chance to introduce Donna, she started in. "Do you know he tried to screw my daughter?"

Gloria had a twenty two-year-old daughter from a previous marriage. I wasn't sure I was ready for this. They must have started cocktailing when they got up that morning, because they both looked shit-faced.

"Your brother tried to fuck my Maureen. Can you believe that?"

Well, yeah. It was easy to believe as I looked at Bernie standing several feet behind Gloria. I could tell by the look on Bernie's face that he couldn't believe Gloria brought up this ugly little escapade. Her behavior didn't surprise me at all. I always knew she was a nut case.

After that grand reception, we settled down for some serious drink and reminiscence. Bernie, Donna, and I were throwing down shots of peppermint schnapps at the kitchen table. Gloria was in the next room, screaming in the phone, telling her mother that my beloved Donna "didn't have a brain in her head."

I didn't know whether to laugh or be offended with this latest news flash. Donna didn't give a shit, so I laughed.

We all laughed. The more we laughed, the more irate Gloria became and the louder she screamed into the phone. I asked Bernie if he wanted to smoke a joint with Donna and me. I surmised from his hand gestures that he wanted to join us, but pot was on Gloria's "just say no," list. There was a vacant bedroom upstairs for Donna and me to spend the night, so we climbed the stairs and broke out the weed.

Even as we got high with our door closed, we could still hear Gloria ranting and raving over the phone. It was one of those deals where you just can't stop laughing no matter how hard you try.

The more we laughed, the more bizarre Gloria's behavior became. It was a vicious cycle.

What happened next seemed right out of an Alfred Hitchcock movie. When we tried to go back downstairs, we discovered she had locked us in the bedroom. The whole scene took on a surreal quality as Bernie begged Glo to set us free. The more he pleaded, the more she screamed at her mother. I wondered how many times her poor mother had to put up with this insane broad and her crazy phone calls. Maybe I brought out the worst in her. She always imagined I had slipped her a Mickey fifteen years earlier and she never forgave me. The broad could sure carry a grudge.

Here is the background story. During the off-season, I had taken my kids to visit my mother while Jean was visiting her parents in New Jersey. We would join Jean and her folks in about a week. Bernie and Glo were also visiting my mother that weekend. One afternoon, my mother and sister took the kids across the street to the beach. Training camp would open in a couple of weeks. Bernie and I were sitting around the kitchen table, talking football, having a beer. Gloria, well aware of my knowledge of pharmaceuticals (a NFL prerequisite), asked if I had anything for a headache.

I told her, "The only thing I have are Seconals."

She asked for a couple and I obliged. Gloria had been a psychiatric nurse for twenty years. I figured she knew what she was doing. She washed them down with a beer and, within twenty minutes, Gloria was out like a light.

"Bernie, lets make a Red Lion run. Let's go. I'll drive."

The Red Lion Inn was in Cohasset, a fifteen-minute drive from Hull where my mother now lived. It was built in 1757 and its motto was "food and lodging for man or beast." It was one of two bars in town, the other being the American Legion. People came from all over the South Shore to dine at the Red Lion. Lobster stew, steaks, pork chops, fried clam rolls, and lobster rolls were the specialties of the house. The Cohen family, Irwin and his mother had owned it for years. I never drank much at the Red Lion Bar, because by the time I was old enough, I was in California. My brothers on the other hand, did their share and mine too.

I hadn't been back to Cohasset for several years. Since then, I had made All-Pro five years in a row. I felt like going down to the Red Lion would give the locals the opportunity to feast their eyes on the hometown hero, at least in my eyes anyway.

Bernie and I bellied our way up to the small crowded bar. We had a good time shooting the shit with each other and the other patrons. After a few hours, we headed back to Hull.

"Where have you two been?" Gloria whined.

"The Red Lion," I answered.

"You drugged me with those pills so I couldn't go!"

"You're supposed to be a nurse. I told you what they were."

Over the years, I heard the story about how I drugged her more times than I can remember. After a while, I took credit for it.

Back to Gloria and our imprisonment, she didn't give a shit about unlocking the bedroom door. Now she was yelling that I was a "fuckin drug addict" and we were all smoking pot upstairs.

Bernie offered a simple solution. "Walt, put your shoulder to the door."

I followed his instructions and we were free. Gloria continued to give her mother a blow-by-blow description. "They just kicked the door down and now they're in the kitchen drinking and laughing like idiots!"

The next thing I know, I'm trying to catch my breath. The crazy bitch hit me in the back with a two by four. That was all she wrote for me. Despite Bernie's objections, Donna and I decided to forego the hospitality and get a motel room.

The following day, we stopped to say goodbye and thank them for a "lovely" evening. As we drove up, I could see the two of them sitting in a couple of rocking chairs. They looked more like Ma and Pa Kettle than Bonnie and Clyde. Nothing was ever said about the previous evening. Everything was hunky dory. What a family.

I had taken $15,000 out of my pension fund, so we weren't exactly starving. We rented a large, older summer type house right at the entrance of Scituate Harbor. Scituate was about thirty miles south of Boston and adjacent to Cohasset. The rent was reasonable because the place was about as warm as a walk-in cooler in wintertime.

Donna went to work for a beauty salon in Scituate. A former New England Patriot helped me get a job as a permanent substitute teacher at Charlestown High School. Charlestown used to be a predominantly Irish neighborhood when I was growing up, but now at least half the student body were Vietnamese and Chinese. Blacks and whites were in the minority. Many of the old brownstone apartment buildings had been converted into million-dollar condos.

I ran an in-house detention center. The kids that got kicked out of class were sent to my room. They would stay with me until the school day was over. They all knew that I used to play football and were fairly well behaved. Most of them were trying to figure out how to catch a buzz, so I started toking up on the way to school. I was on the same level as my students. Summer rolled around and the job ended. The principal was glad to see me go, but the kids weren't.

After that, I got a job as a commercial sword fisherman. I had never fished at this level before, but the owner/captain of the boat and I had been childhood friends. The first day on the job, I became terribly seasick. We were moving the boat from Gloucester about sixty miles south to Scituate. This is where we would fish for the summer. My job was to clean the engine room and I became ill. It appeared my fishing career was over before it started. After that trip, I never went in the engine room again and never became seasick again.

If I had to go fishing, this was the way to do it. It was a brand new ninety-five foot, steel-hulled, air-conditioned boat. We had five crewmembers plus the captain. Everyone had their own cabin.

During the summer, we long-lined and harpooned off Georges Bank, about two hundred miles east of Boston. There were at least a dozen boats within a mile radius and each boat had its own spotter plane. The guys who flew these planes were excellent pilots. It was an aerobatic circus, but I never saw an accident. Sometimes they barely made it back to land before the planes ran out of gas.

Fishing was hard and healthy work. The money was good. We were usually out for two or three weeks at a time. When we hit the beach, we were like drunken sailors.

It was mid-August and I had the weekend off. Donna wanted to see Johnny Cash who was appearing at the Music Circus in Cohasset. A theater-in-the-round, covered by a huge green and white tent, it had been in town for as long as I could remember. Top acts from all over the country played the Music Circus. When I was about fourteen, a couple of buddies and I went to the Music Circus when it was closed. Celeste Holm, the Broadway actress, was appearing and we found her equipment van in the parking lot. The keys were in it. The temptation was too great, so we took it for a little spin around the premises. The cops arrived as we were fishtailing around the parking lot.

Country music wasn't my thing, but I loved Johnny Cash. Otherwise, I wasn't much for "lying, crying, dying or going somewhere." An old friend used to say that listening to too much country music would make you stupid. In the early seventies, I wore out a couple of eight track tapes of Cash's Folsom Prison Blues. Maybe it did make me a bit stupid, but I liked the Man in Black.

Donna and I had a pretty good coke buzz when we arrived for the show. I really wanted to hear him sing Cocaine Blues. I couldn't get the lyrics out of my head.

After Cash performed for an hour or so, he started taking requests from the audience. We were only three rows back from the stage, but he seemed to be ignoring my constant requests for Cocaine Blues. The people seated around me thought I was some kind of freak. I probably was, but Johnny was into spiritual renditions that night and I never got to hear my song.

We were off the last two weeks of November and I was stoked. On the first of December, we would head south for the warm waters of Florida to fish out of Key West. I decided to invite my family over for Thanksgiving. Johnny wouldn't be able to make it as he would be in New Hampshire with his wife and three kids. Jimmy would be in Connecticut with his family.

Regardless, it would still be an interesting gathering of those who could come. My oldest brother, Donald, was a welder at the same shipyard where my father worked. He would bring his long time live-in girlfriend, Mary. They were both hardcore alcoholics. Booze and time had ravished them physically and mentally.

My sister Louise, like so many women from alcoholic environments, married an alcoholic. Her marriage ended when her husband, Charlie, passed away a few years before. Like our mother, Louise never drank and the little joy she found in life was derived from her pets.

The day before Thanksgiving, I drove to Hull and picked up Bobby. He was going to spend a few days with Donna and me. Although he was as soft as puppy shit, he was a good guy. We got along very well. I got to his place early, so I could check him out. Lately his bathing and grooming habits were almost non-existent. I wanted to make sure he was all spiffed up for the family reunion. I had taken him to the Veteran's Administration Hospital for some psychiatric help, but all they did was load him up with useless anti-depressants.

The night before the festivities, Bobby and I were sitting around the fireplace drinking beer while Donna was baking pies. A

Norman Rockwell scene with beer. I had never seen Bobby have anything stronger than beer. No cocktails, no pills, no cigarettes, not even a joint

I had bought two grams of coke from one of my fishing friends. I never really saw the big deal with coke, but once in awhile I did it, just to make sure I wasn't missing anything. It was one of Donna's favorites. I thought a little blow for Thanksgiving would be appropriate and pulled the vial out of my shirt pocket.

"Donna. Bring in a plate and we'll do a couple of lines."

I found a razor blade, chopped and played with the coke until I was satisfied with two huge rails. We snorted them with a straw and Donna returned to the kitchen.

"What's that?" Bobby asked.

"Coke. Do you want to try some?"

"What'll it do? Will it hurt me?"

"I don't know. How's your heart? Do you want some?"

"Sure. Why not?"

Why not? Because it cost a hundred bucks a gram!

After explaining how to inhale and not exhale, we were ready for the big moment. I laid out a big fat line for him. Bobby sucked it up like a big old Hoover, not missing a crystal. After a minute he spoke.

"I liked that. It made me feel pretty good."

"That's why it's so popular," I mused.

"How about a little more?" He asked.

This was great I thought. He would have to like the expensive stuff. I hoped I hadn't created a monster. If I had any left the next day—and at this rate I probably wouldn't—there wouldn't be anything to offer the gang. I figured the food, booze and weed would be plenty for a Sweeney Family Thanksgiving Feast.

The last time these people had seen one another was seven years earlier at our mother's funeral. In our family, holidays like

Thanksgiving, Christmas and the Fourth of July, were good opportunities to get as fucked up as humanly possible.

The whole family was nuts with the exception of my brother,
John, and my sister, Louise. Louise never had a chance being
brought up with a bunch of drunks. Half of them were psycho-
paths; the other half had some sort of psychosis. When I told
Donna that I was the sanest member of the family, she thought
I was joking. Then she met them. I was lucky to be the youngest.
I spent most of my adult life away for them. I wasn't caught up in
their insanity. I had my own demons to fight.

My sister arrived at 10:00 a.m. Thanksgiving morning. Everyone
else got there by early afternoon. I had bought more than enough beer
and liquor. God forbid we should ever run out of booze at a Sweeney
family gathering. I know I wouldn't be happy. Donna, Bobby and I
had been doing lines since 8:00 a.m.. To say we that had "a good buzz
going" would have been an understatement. Bernie and Glo brought
their own brand of poison, some sort of flavored brandy.

Donna wanted to put some weed in the turkey dressing, but I
talked her out of it. I had seen stable people eat brownies laced with
marijuana and have bad trips. In this group, there were too many
candidates for bad trips. I would have enough problems with their
drinking without worrying about introducing a "special stuffing"
to the mix.

Initially, everyone seemed to be on his or her best behavior.
I guess they wanted to make a good impression on Donna, like
she gave a shit. She did a great job with the turkey and everyone
got stuffed. Whenever I interrupted my drinking with a big meal,
I was done with the sauce. Over the years, my significant other
always tried to get me to eat.

There were plenty of turkey leftovers. Being the good host, I
wanted to send everyone home with sandwiches. Mary Livingston,

Donald's dowdy girl friend, reminded me for the umpteenth to put plenty of meat in the sandwiches. I was never too fond of the old sot. She got on my nerves so much that I sent her home with a bag of lettuce sandwiches. Later, Donald told me that she bitched about those sandwiches for months.

Soon after Thanksgiving, I left for Florida. We would fish the south coast and stay in Key West. Key West is one of the strangest places I've ever been. The streets were crawling with bikers, hippies, and dropouts. It seemed to be caught in some sort of time warp. You could score a gram of coke on the street for forty bucks (cheap) as easily as you could ask someone to light your cigarette. When we weren't out fishing, I was usually at one of the many bars that dotted the landscape. Ted, the captain and owner of the boat, owned a condo in Key West. When we were in port, he spent time with his family and left the boat in our capable hands. There were always plenty of women around and we had some pretty good parties on the boat.

The swordfish we caught were half the size of the ones we caught off Georges Bank. They only weighed about two or three hundred pounds. One afternoon, after we had just finished setting out our lines, the crew from a Bahamian gunboat boarded us. They were the equivalent of our Coast Guard. Five huge black guys with machine guns ran around the boat searching for drugs. Their captain, a seven-foot gentleman, held an automatic pistol to Ted's head. Needless to say, Ted shit his pants. I can't say that I blamed him.

We heard a commotion from the hole below where we stored our bait mackerel. They found our loom lights, fluorescent lights we put on the lines to attract the fish. At first, they thought the lights were some kind of dope. When they were satisfied we had no dope, they left.

We would have been up shit creek had they had boarded us a week earlier. We had come across a "square grouper" bobbing up and down in the water. This was a bale of marijuana that had been thrown overboard when smugglers feared they would be boarded by authorities. Because of all the smuggling activity, it was not an uncommon sight to find such treasure in the waters off south Florida. We hauled the bale aboard and stored it down with the fish. I managed to grab a handful and stashed it in my cabin. Other than tasting salty, it was pretty good smoke. A week later, we were back in Key West where we unloaded the fish and the weed. It was decided that our cook, Ralph, would rent a car and take the bail up to Boston. He sold it for $24,000.00 and we split the windfall profit six ways.

We had left Key West and were headed for home the day before the first load of Cuban refugees landed. It seems Castro had pulled a fast one on President Carter. Cuba was emptying their jails and mental institutions and shipping their undesirables to America.

A week after our return to Scituate, I was informed by Ted that my services would no longer be needed. He knew I was drinking and smoking dope on the boat. He wasn't going to put up with it. This put me in a deep funk and I started to drink even more. I was no longer trying to catch a buzz, I was trying to feel normal.

Donna had enough of me sitting around the house, drinking and feeling sorry for myself. She split and I can't say that I blame her. Being around an extremely moody, unemployed drunk and drug addict couldn't have been too much fun for her.

After she went back to Virginia, I had two friends move in to cover the rent. Duncan, a fisherman from another boat, and Mike, a part-time fisherman and full time drug dealer. We never had a shortage of drugs around the house. Mike was a smart guy who could have been successful in legal endeavors, but he chose the quick and easy way to make a buck. His dad was one of JFK's favorite speechwriters. I believe that Boston College named a wing of a building after him.

I was home alone one night listening to Willie Nelson tapes and draining a bottle of Scotch. After knocking off a quart of Cutty, my depression sunk to greater depths than usual. My life was in the shitter. I missed Donna. I just didn't want to go on. I stumbled to the bedroom to find those bright red shiny capsules. Seconal would take me away from all this misery. I threw all thirty in my mouth and washed them down with a fistful of water.

About two hours later, Mike and Duncan pulled into the driveway and found me crawling in a snow bank. They managed to get me to Mass General Hospital in time for the doctors to pump my stomach. They saved my life. I walked out of intensive care two days later knowing one thing for sure. I didn't want to die. I like to think that if I hadn't been drunk, I wouldn't have taken those pills.

While in the hospital, the woman I loved and couldn't live without, returned to Massachusetts and took my brand new pickup back to Virginia. They say there's a thin line between love and hate. I believe them. Love her? I wanted to kill the bitch. What made me even more furious was the fact that I almost took my life because of her.

Brian Anglin, my childhood friend and crime partner (we were kicked out as altar boys together when we were thirteen), and I drove to Virginia to retrieve the truck. We had little resistance from Donna's father and brothers. I think that they realized what she did was wrong.

I stayed in Massachusetts for two weeks. I didn't have much after Donna cleaned me out. I sold my stereo and a few odds and ends, so I had about six hundred bucks in my wallet. I could remember a few times when I would spend that much on a good roll. I was never very frugal with money. It just seemed to just slip through my fingers. The day after Super Bowl XV in January of 1981, Magee and I piled into the truck and began the three thousand mile trip to San Diego.

Doing the Same Things, Expecting Different Results

We pulled into San Diego after a four-day jaunt across America. I headed for Mission Beach and checked into the Mission Beach Motel, about two miles from my old digs. Across the street was a used car lot. I couldn't believe my eyes when I saw my old friend, Sonny McCrea, showing a car to a young couple. I hadn't seen Sonny since I left about a year and a half ago. I went right over to see him. After shaking hands, he motioned me to the back of the lot and pointed to a 30 foot Winnebago.

It was his home. "I'm beating the system," he said. "I bought this about a year ago and I've been running this car lot for the last six months," he explained.

I told him about my situation and he asked if I wanted to sell cars.

"Fuck, no!"

I was hardly in a position to be choosy, but the thought of selling cars didn't do much for me.

Later that same afternoon, I ran into another old friend, Pete Barnes, my old holdout partner. Pete was having a beer at the Beachcomber with his latest girlfriend, a twenty one-year-old coed from San Diego State.

"Walt, the duplex I was buying on Santa Barbara Court is being foreclosed. I moved in there after my divorce, but the downstairs apartment is empty and you're welcome to use it until the bank throws us out." Things were looking up. I'd been in town less than twenty-four hours and already had a rent-free place to live, temporary as it was.

A few nights later, I ran into Bill Fallis at the Surfer Lounge. He was an avid Chargers backer since the team moved from Los Angeles in 1961. Bill owned a number of successful bars in San Diego including the one we were standing in.

"Walter Francis, I have this bar called The Trains in Solana Beach, about a mile north of the Del Mar Racetrack on Pacific Coast Highway. It's actually two old train cars. I'm operating the bar in one of the cars. The front car on the PCH side is empty. With a little bit of remodeling and the right people, I think it could be a gold mine."

Fallis was a hustler from the word go. He made money over the years on various gimmicks, screwing the IRS and anyone else that got in his way. I thought I'd explained my financial situation, but he continued the sales pitch.

"If you and someone like Pat Shea wanted to come in and work it, I'd give each of you a third."

This sounded too good to be true. I knew it was too good to be true and tried to contain my enthusiasm.

"Is Shea still working in North County?" I asked.

Since he left football, Pat had been a bartender, mostly in North County. The Trains was in the North County. My brain was working overtime. He could teach me the bar business. We would have a built-in following.

"Yeah. He's working at the Albatross. Why don't you get in touch with him? If he's agreeable, the three of us will sit down in a couple of days and discuss it."

Fallis excused himself and walked to a booth in the corner of the bar. He started talking with a very attractive woman in her forties. She obviously knew him, because she was all smiles as he approached her table.

Bill was around sixty-five and round like Jackie Gleason. Women liked him a lot, but I couldn't figure out what they saw in the guy. His hair was still mostly black with some graying on the sides. He combed it back into an oily ducktail. I've seen a lot of heavy men who were handsome, but Bill Fallis wasn't one of them. I never saw him without his spectacles hanging from his neck on a gold and pearl chain. He also had a fondness for garish looking pinky rings. Within five minutes, Bill and the woman were out the door. Maybe he had a dick like a baseball bat. It was puzzlement to me.

Pat Shea was a local legend with the beach crowd. He played football at Mission Bay High School in San Diego and the University of Southern California before joining the Chargers in the early sixties. He was a better street fighter than he was a football player. If you ever got into a fight with Shea, you'd have to shoot him to stop him.

Shea, Fallis and I got together and agreed on a three-way partnership. The next couple of months were busy. Solana Beach is twenty-five miles up the coast from Mission Beach. When I wasn't driving back and forth, I was trying to help with the bar as best I could. I'm not the handiest person when it came to carpentry, but, fortunately, Shea had a lot of pals who were. They did a great job fixing up the old railcar. At one end, they built a long straight bar that horse-shoed into a lower bar. We had booths by the large windows on both sides of the car. Tables were in the middle. An entrance on the old Pacific Coast Highway side led into a small office. Across from the office was an old standup piano. Restrooms were at the opposite end of the bar where another entrance and a stairway led down to Bill's other bar.

In the meantime, Donna called Sonny. She told him the truck was in her name and the bank was bugging her about late payments. It might have been in her name, but I put up the down payment and made all the payments until I left Massachusetts. I called her back and told her I didn't have the truck. I said I'd left it at Logan Airport and flew to San Diego.

In early March 1981, we were finished with the work on the bar. We put up dozens and dozens of pictures of former and current NFL players. Behind the bar hung a painting of Shea and me, resplendent in our beards. The painting was done by Bob Clark, an artist friend of ours. Clark was divorced and one of the most cynical men about women that I have ever known. Like everyone I knew, Clark liked the sauce and the weed.

One night, a few years earlier, he was going to have dinner with Donna and me at our place in South Mission. I was cooking a big pot of beef stew and got pissed about something. I can't even remember what it was. I'm sure I had too much to drink and started screaming at Donna. Long story short, the neighbors called the police. Bob split. The cops showed up and I explained that we were just having a little domestic dispute. Convinced that everything was under control, the cops left. Clark had the balls to show up thirty minutes later for dinner. He didn't get any. Other than that, I always had a lot of laughs with him.

The bar was going to be called Sweeney O'Shea's. The grand opening was a week away on St. Patrick's Day. Since Pat and I were both offensive guard teammates on the Chargers, Fallis had some green T-shirts made with Irish Infantry printed on them.

In a celebratory mood, Pat broke out some shrooms (psychedelic mushrooms). I had done my share of psychedelic drugs, but mushrooms were a first for me. Several hours after eating the mushrooms and downing about ten beers later, I decide it was time to get back to my place in Mission Beach. I didn't have any hallucinations, but I had a headache from laughing so much.

Driving south on Interstate 5, just as I was cresting a hill, an 18-wheeler was stopped dead ahead in my lane. Maybe I was hallucinating. I swerved to avoid a crash and lost control of the pickup. It flipped several times before coming to a stop and landed upright on all four wheels on the ice-plant covered embankment. Magee, who had been sitting in the passenger seat, was long gone. Apparently, he jumped out the window when we started to roll. I scurried up the embankment and frantically looked for the dog. He was nowhere to be found. There was a convenience store about a block away. When the Highway Patrol showed up twenty minutes later, I was sitting on the curb smoking a cigarette and drinking a beer. I wasn't arrested for drunk driving because of the time lapse between the accident and the arrival of the cops. "Donna's" truck was totaled. I put an ad in the newspaper and got Magee back in a few days. After that, he watched me very carefully whenever I drove.

As planned, we opened Sweeney O'Shea's on St. Patrick's Day. Bobby Riggs, the tennis player, and Eddie Mathews, the Hall of Fame baseball great, were among the local celebrities in attendance. We received a lot of free publicity from the San Diego newspapers and TV stations. The cameras rolled as Shea and I schmoozed it up.

Three months earlier, I was on my back in Mass General Hospital, not caring if I lived or died, and now I was on top of the world. I was part owner of a bar. If opening day was any indication of things to come, Sweeney O'Shea's was destined to become a big success. I suppose it's the dream of every alcoholic to have his own bar.

The Trains, Bill's other bar in the rear, opened at 6:00 a.m. and attracted an older crowd. There was a trailer park next door and many of the fixed income inhabitants filled his place when it opened at the crack of dawn. We opened at 10:00 a.m. and our clientele was a younger, wilder crowd.

Charger training camp was about 15 minutes away at the University of California at San Diego. Their future Hall of Fame quarterback Dan Fouts and Big Ed White, the great offensive guard, were among the more prominent Charger players who dropped in for a cold one after practice. Ballplayers drinking at our place certainly helped business. They attracted the local girls and good-looking chicks bring in the guys.

Pat and I each pulled four shifts during the week. Since we really didn't trust each other, we pulled double shifts on the weekends. I think all the money we made from those double shifts was spent on coke so we could stay awake to watch each other. What's the difference between a shark and a bartender? Sharks don't steal.

Bob Long was a local piano player who entertained on Friday and Saturday nights. He was a very talented guy and really packed them in. I was behind the bar one night when six girls in a limo sauntered in. I knew most of the girls from the beach. One of them was celebrating her 40th birthday. I was happy they included our humble establishment in their celebration.

I had a crush on one of the women for years. Her name was Nanci. She was the ex-wife of one of my former Charger teammates. The last time I saw her was when Donna and I lived at the beach. I was walking home from The Beachcomber and spotted her painting one of the condos on the way. We made small talk. I think she knew I had a thing for her, because she asked if I would like to go to the Del Mar Fair with her. I told her that I thought that was a great idea and we made plans to hook up later. Donna wasn't home yet, so I headed back to The Beachcomber. I stopped on the way to visit Nanci again.

"You know that I live with someone." Vagueness was one of the things I did best. I didn't want to let on that it was a woman.

"The last I heard was that you and Jean were divorced."

"I've been living with a gal named Donna for awhile."

"Oh, I hadn't heard that."

"I suppose the Fair is out." I already knew the response.

"Yep."

I hung around, ogling her for a few minutes and not really know what to say.

"Go away, Walt," she said. I obeyed.

That was a couple of years before the birthday party at the bar. She looked better than ever. The girls stayed for a while. I got Nanci's number before she left. We started seeing each other and before long, we were living together.

One day, her boss from the Sheraton called and said he needed her to come in early. I informed him that she would no longer be working there. She was pissed to say the least. We rented a beautiful condo overlooking the Pacific, about a mile from Sweeney O'Shea's. Nanci went to work for us.

At times, the bar was an absolute zoo. I was one of the animal trainers. At other times, I was like a kid in a candy store. I tried to drink every cocktail the patrons bought me. Many of my tips came in the form of drugs. One morning, I did some shrooms before I went to work. That turned out to be disastrous. I would take an order for drinks at one end of the bar and, without delivering the drinks, go to the other end of the bar to bullshit with someone else. That was the first of many times Nanci would relieve me of duty.

I tried to conceal my drug use from her and she assumed drinking was part of the bar business. She hadn't been around too many alcoholics. She thought they were all downtown on skid row along with the drug addicts.

Her mom, Lee, was very ill in Sacramento, so she drove back and forth to visit her. Her preoccupation with her mother's health allowed me to slide a lot as far as the drugs were concerned.

One night, Nanci and I got into a heated argument as we were closing the bar. We had two cars. I wanted her to have some breakfast with me.

"I'm not riding with you. You're drunk! You told me you would cut down on your drinking."

"I'm fine. I only had a couple." As usual, I lied about my alcohol consumption.

While I was locking the back door to the bar, she got into her car. Before she had a chance to close the door, I grabbed her arm and pulled her out of the car. I threw her over my shoulder (she only weighed 110 pounds), but I tripped before I got to my car. She hit her head on my fender and screamed in pain.

"Get away from me!"

I got into my car and sped out of the parking lot. One of the local deputies was on me as soon as I hit the street. Lately, they had been hanging around our place to catch drunk drivers. It was great for business. The officer saw that Nanci was hurt and that I was drunk. She went to the hospital; I went to jail.

As always, I was very repentant. I even promised Nanci that I would stop drinking. I quit for a while, but still smoked weed and did an occasional line.

My mother was the only other person I had ever promised to stop drinking. When I was seventeen, I got very sick drinking gin. As I crawled on all fours around my mother's kitchen floor, I promised never to drink again. I kept that promise and never drank gin again.

Jean and Donna just wanted out. I wasn't given the opportunity to prolong those relationships with bullshit promises about abstinence.

One afternoon, Oakland Raiders Hall of Fame receiver Fred Biletnikoff came into the bar. He was with a guy he introduced as Bobby T. They knew each other from Lake Tahoe. Fred was running junkets of high rollers out of the Bay Area to Caesar's Palace. Bobby was staying at Fred's house in Valley Center, about fifteen miles inland from Solana Beach. Bobby became a regular at the bar. He was always very generous with a seemingly endless supply of coke. Nanci was a moderate drinker and had never tried drugs until I talked her into trying a little coke. She liked it. After doing some one evening, we walked on the beach for five or six miles. No wonder they called it Colombian marching powder.

Bobby was well connected in Tahoe. He offered Nanci and me a free vacation. We would stay four nights at the River Ranch, a popular hotel and restaurant. Besides the comped room, any other charges such as food and beverages would also be covered. What a sweet deal. Nanci and I were excited as we drove to Sacramento to visit her mom. We needed a break from the insanity of the bar. It was off to Lake Tahoe.

Bobby told me that a friend would be dropping by River Ranch with a little gift. I knew it would be cocaine. When we got to Sacramento, I searched through Nanci's mom's medicine cabinet for something to enable me to sleep as I came off the coke. I had a bad habit of looking through people's medicine cabinets and reading the warning labels on their prescription bottles. If the label had a warming like "Don't operate heavy equipment" or "Could cause drowsiness", I usually helped myself. Lee had cancer and the cabinet contained a lot of pain medication and sleeping aids. I helped my self to some Phenobarbital and the next day we made the two-hour drive from Sacramento to Lake Tahoe. I would make it a vacation in hell.

We checked into the River Ranch about 6:00 p.m. As the name implies, it was beside the Truckee River in a beautiful setting of huge pines and majestic mountains. Bobby must have told the people who worked there about my football background. Everyone was super cordial and went out of their way to make us feel comfortable. We had dinner at the hotel restaurant and then drove to the Cal Neva Casino for some fun.

After being seated in the lounge, I ordered a screwdriver for Nanci and a soda water for myself. When Nanci went to the lady's room, I told the waitress to switch me to double vodkas and soda. I knew Nanci wouldn't be able to smell the vodka, because she was drinking. We listened to a singer for a while and decided to head back to our hotel. Our waitress brought the bill and Nanci picked it up. "How come this bill is so much?"

I lied and said, "Once the entertainment starts the prices go up." The lounge shows were free.

She believed me, but soon would learn how devious I could be when it came to protecting my mistress: alcohol.

The next day, Bobby's friend showed up with two grams of coke. So far it had been an ideal vacation as far as I was concerned. Free room, food, booze and, now, free drugs.

"Every night I just wanna go out, get out of my head…but tonight I just want to stay in and be with you."

Those old Beatle lyrics reminded me of how I used to be before Nanci came into my life. I still wanted to get out of my head, but not nearly as often. She was everything I wanted in a woman. She was smart, so smart I wondered what she was doing with me. She had to wonder that herself. She was pretty and sexy, but the thing I liked most about her was her great sense of humor. I had never met anyone more genuinely concerned about people and their feelings than Nanci. Watch out if she heard a racial joke. She was bombarded with that type of humor when we lived in Boston. She hated it and always let the "idiot" who told it know how she felt. For the liberal Northeast, Boston was a very bigoted town. Blacks bore the brunt of jokes and prejudice.

The great NBA Hall of Famer, Bill Russell, wrote in his book, "I'd rather be in jail in Sacramento than be mayor of Boston."

When Russell first started playing with the Celtics, a predominantly white team at the time, some morons burned a cross on his lawn. He was a big star in a sports crazy town, so you can imagine what the average black guy went through.

Right now I was on vacation. To me, this meant you altered your mind even more than you do when you're not on vacation. This might be difficult to understand considering I'm talking about me. When I think back, I was always on vacation. I traveled the world and never left my kitchen table.

We did a little coke and went for a roll in the hay. After we showered, we sat out by the river and caught some rays. On the way back to the room, we wandered through the gift shop and into the bar. The two bartenders acted like they had known me forever. Besides telling them about my football past, Bobby must have told them I was a fuckup.

After their insistence that I should have a beer, I finally gave in. Unbeknownst to me, Nanci had been gesturing with her hands and shaking her head at the bartender trying to dissuade him from giving me a beer.

"Nanci, we're on vacation. I won't be drinking when we get home."

Reluctantly, she ordered a drink. I slipped into the men's room and did a little more coke. I was feeling pretty good. What the hell, I was on vacation. I drank about six Heinekens and Nanci had a cocktail. She decided we should go to the restaurant to eat. She had that head him off at the pass mentality.

Since Nanci and I had been together, her need for alcohol had slowly diminished. I must have been a good influence on her. While perusing the wine list that evening, she saw a wine she loved. Nanci had expensive taste and this bottle of wine proved no exception. I knocked back a couple of scotches before dinner and we each had a glass of wine with our meal. She wanted to save the rest of the wine and take it back to the room. Things were looking up.

"A jug of wine, a line of coke and thou," or is it "thee?" Something like that anyway. When we got to our room, the red message light was flashing on the phone. Nanci called the office to check it out.

"They need the room and asked if we would mind moving to another. I told them no problem."

I liked the room and didn't feel like moving. Besides, a change of venue would interfere with my plans for a romantic evening.

"Call them back and tell them we're not moving."

"You call them, but remember, these people have been very nice to us. We haven't had to spend a dime here. That bottle of wine was a hundred dollars!" Her voice was on the rise.

She went to the shower. I called the front desk and acted like the real jerk I was. I gave these poor guys all kinds of shit. After I got that off my chest, I agreed to move to another room.

Over the years, I've said my share of nasty things and have offended my share of people, but this is still an embarrassment to me. I was also embarrassed about finishing Nanci's wine while she was in the shower.

Bobby T's friend showed up again the next morning with two more grams of coke. I guess Bobby hadn't heard that I had been a jerk. That night, we went back to the Cal Neva Casino. It was Frank Sinatra's favorite spot at Lake Tahoe. They even had the showroom named after him.

Since I hadn't spent any money on our vacation, I decided to try my luck at Black Jack. I hadn't played since Jean and I would go to Las Vegas in the sixties. After a few hours of losing a thousand dollars and drinking too many "free" Scotches, I headed for the bar. Nanci was waiting. I couldn't afford to lose that much money, or any money for that matter. I was in a foul mood as I approached the almost empty bar. Nanci and the bartender looked like they were hitting it off. That really infuriated me.

"What the fuck's going on here?" I shouted.

"I turn my back for two minutes and you're flirting with this fucken guy!"

At this point the bartender turns to me and says, "Walt, I'm more interested in you than I am in Nanci, I'm gay."

Now, I'm really humiliated. I can't wait to get the fuck out of there, but my escape route is blocked by two huge gorillas with bulging breast pockets. While they advised that I'm no longer welcome, Nanci brought the car around to the front entrance. By the time I get to the car, I've gone completely ape shit!

"Move over! I'm driving! I'll give you a ride you'll never forget!"

People who were coming and going from the casino were gawking. Who was this mad man? I sped off into the night in the wrong direction. I made a U-turn and found myself in bumper-to-bumper traffic. The same people who witnessed my hasty exit were now hearing me scream at Nanci.

I have no excuse for what happened next. I leaned over and bit Nanci in the small of the back. She let out a scream that attracted even more attention. Later, Nanci said she thought she'd been stabbed. Talk about a mad dog. I had bitten through her leather coat. After twenty years, she still bears the scar. I turned down a side street and drove about another mile. I pulled over and started to walk. Tears streamed down my face as Nanci drove off.

After she realized that she had gone the wrong way, she turned around and came back. She stopped for me. I sniveled about how sorry I was. Believe me, I was sorry and lucky. If she hadn't picked me up, I probably would have froze to death. I was wearing an unlined leather jacket, jeans and a pair of cowboy boots with no socks. A spring storm had dropped about six inches of snow. It was about twenty-five degrees. I had no money. Thank God that Nanci felt sorry for me. The next day on our way home to San Diego, I told Nanci I would try to stop drinking again.

The following weekend, we went camping with Janice Markey and her family. Janice was Nanci's long time friend. Janice and Chris Jordan, another old friend of Nanci's, had expressed concern when we started living together. They were aware of my reputation and were afraid that I would push drugs on her.

The day before we went camping, I had scored a couple of grams of coke at the bar. I gave one to Nanci, but she left it at home. I brought mine on the camping trip. I also brought some Valium to help me sleep. Everyone thought it was wonderful that I wasn't drinking. Surely they realized something was wrong as I stumbled around the campsite all weekend in a cocaine/Valium haze. When we returned home, Nanci flushed her gram of coke down the toilet. She never used it again. She later admitted that she thought about cocaine too much. She was smart enough to realize it could become a problem if it kept her so preoccupied. I was never that smart.

Meanwhile, back at Sweeney O'Shea's, business had taken a downward spiral. Other bars put their best foot forward to attract customers, but we seemed to be doing just the opposite.

One Saturday night, a very drunk customer grabbed our amply bosomed cocktail waitress by her boobs. We served drunks as long as they had money. When they misbehaved, Mr. Shea stepped in. He enjoyed kicking the shit out of assholes. I felt a twinge of sympathy for the poor drunk as Shea come out from behind the bar. He put the guy in a headlock, took a ten-foot run and tried to put his head through the reinforced glass window in the rear door of the rail car. When the cops showed up, the drunk's eye was hanging out of the socket. Granted, the guy was an asshole, but the punishment was downright Biblical.

Another time when it was busy, Nanci came behind the bar to help. She's very sociable and, when I'm under the influence, all kinds of things happen in my alcohol-warped mind. On this particular evening, I thought she was paying too much attention to one of the customers, so I was getting pissed. I started chasing her around the bar. I don't know what I would have done if I caught her. She probably would have punched me in the nose. Anyway, my good buddy Sonny, who was half in the bag himself, pulled out my snub nose revolver and placed it on the bar underneath a cocktail napkin. He took it from me when I shot the phone so Donna

Mrs. Dixon's Fourth Grade Class (1950) Ripley Road School, Cohasset, Mass.
Front Row (lower left) Walt Sweeney, Cub Scout

That's me carrying the ball for the Cohasset High School Skippers in the top photo, but I'm (#1) watching the action in the bottom picture. Our coach, Evie Dorr, made football fun. He was like a father to me.

The top newspaper article meant a lot to me. As a senior, my average touchdown was 35 yards from scrimmage. (Bottom) It was great when my hometown honored me prior to a Patriots game in 1970.

The Kid

The Veteran

Joe Madro taught me everything I needed to know to become a good guard. He chose me to block alongside Ron Mix because we were the two fastest linemen on the team.

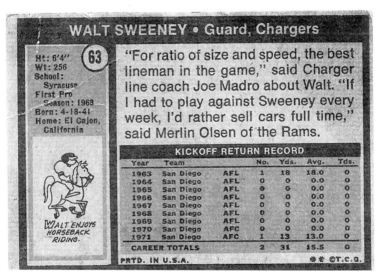

WALT SWEENEY • Guard, Chargers

Ht: 6'4" **63**
Wt: 256
School:
  Syracuse
First Pro
  Season: 1963
Born: 4-18-41
Home: El Cajon,
California

"For ratio of size and speed, the best lineman in the game," said Charger line coach Joe Madro about Walt. "If I had to play against Sweeney every week, I'd rather sell cars full time," said Merlin Olsen of the Rams.

WALT ENJOYS
HORSEBACK
RIDING.

KICKOFF RETURN RECORD

Year	Team		No.	Yds.	Avg.	Tds.
1963	San Diego	AFL	1	18	18.0	0
1964	San Diego	AFL	0	0	0.0	0
1965	San Diego	AFL	0	0	0.0	0
1966	San Diego	AFL	0	0	0.0	0
1967	San Diego	AFL	0	0	0.0	0
1968	San Diego	AFL	0	0	0.0	0
1969	San Diego	AFL	0	0	0.0	0
1970	San Diego	AFC	0	0	0.0	0
1971	San Diego	AFC	1	13	13.0	0
CAREER TOTALS			2	31	15.5	0

PRTD. IN U.S.A. ★ ★ ©T.C.G.

Joe Madro—Joe was the champ to Ron and me. I appreciated his comment on the back of my card. I liked Merlin Olsen's quote, too.

WALT SWEENEY GUARD
SAN DIEGO CHARGERS

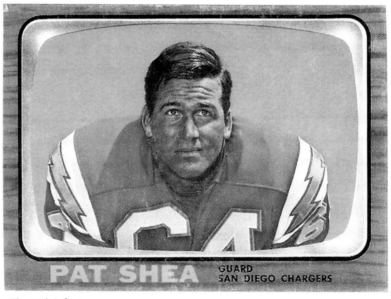

PAT SHEA GUARD
SAN DIEGO CHARGERS

The Irish Infantry

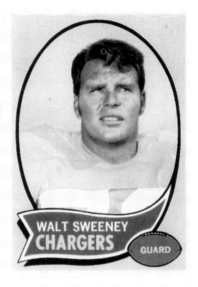

My Chargers cards

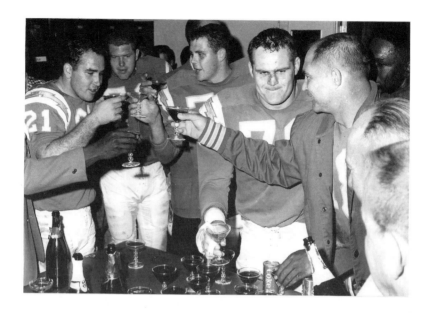

(Top) John Hadl, George Gross, Walt Sweeney, Hank Schmidt and Tobin Rote enjoy champagne after the 1963 AFL Championship Game. (Bottom) Ron Mix, Lance Alworth and Walt Sweeney light John Hadl's cigar. Hadl belongs in the Hall of Fame along with Lance and Ron.

Paul Lowe (#23) said "following Sweeney is like following a flashlight in the dark"

Blocking for #22— Keith Lincoln (top) and Dick Post (bottom).

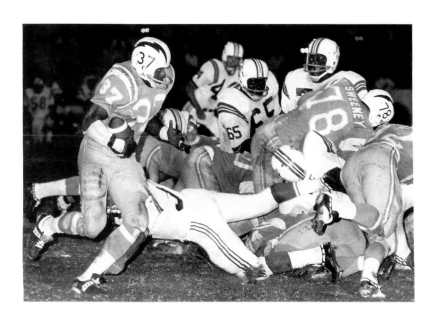

Blocking for Gene Foster (#37)

(Top) Doug Wilkerson (#63) and Walt Sweeney (#78) escort Mike Garrett (#20) on sweeps against the St. Louis Cardinals and Denver Broncos (Bottom).

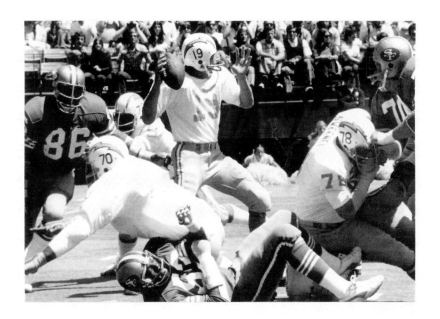

The end of one Hall of Fame career, the beginning of another—
(Top) Russ Washington (#70) and Walt Sweeney (#78) pass block for Johnny Unitas (#19) against the San Francisco 49ers. (Bottom) We line up in the mud with Dan Fouts (#14) against the Oakland Raiders in 1973.

It looks like either I'm winding up for a haymaker or directing traffic.

Analyzing this picture, I don't know what I'm doing with my hands.

ANOTHER WORKDAY FOR WALT SWEENEY

Chargers' All-Star Right Guard Walt Sweeney (78) Pulls Out in Front of Quarterback Johnny Unitas.

Blocking Line Forms for Mike Garrett with Sweeney in Between Doug Wilkerson and Russ Washington.

Sweeney "Swings" Into Action Against Bengals' Sherman White.

CHARGERS ACTION

Photos by
CHARLES AQUA VIVA

View From Sideline for 11-Year Veteran Sweeney.

PICTURE OF WEEK

GARRETT ESCORT
Charger All-Star guard Walter Sweeney
escorts star running back Mike Garrett
on sweep against Oakland. Raiders
won, 21-19.

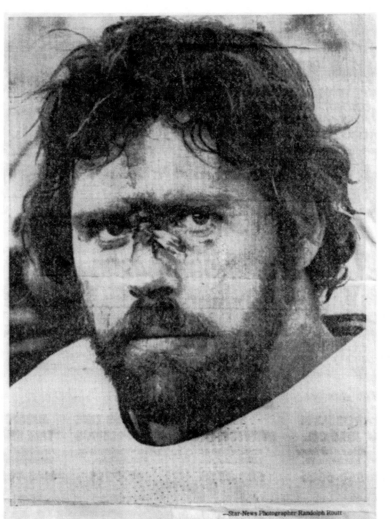

It's not exactly all fun and games when the ball is snapped and the offensive line clashes with the defensive line. People can get hurt. For instance, Walt Sweeney shows the results of quite a few of those meetings. No matter. Just have the trainer put tape over the wound and it's back to the struggle.

Thursday, December 21, 1972

GARY GARRISON   WALT SWEENEY   DEACON JONES

Garrison, Sweeney, Jones
Named To Pro Bowl Team

CHARGERS SET FOR PRO BOWL

Wide receiver Gary Garrison, left, and guard Walt Sweeney, Chargers' contribution to the Ameri- can Conference team in Sunday's Pro Bowl game, pose outside Los Angeles Coliseum, site of game.

126

WALT SWEENEY

GUARD   S. D. CHARGERS

HT: 6'3"   WT: 260
AGE: 25   YRS. IN AFL: 4
COLLEGE: SYRACUSE

Big Walt was the San Diego Chargers' No. 1 draft pick in 1963. The versatile performer can play at tackle, tight end, defensive end, defensive tackle, linebacker or even fullback. Walt has speed, strength, agility and talent!
The American Football League

WALT PLAYED IN THE 1963 COLLEGE ALL-STAR GAME.

Sweeney Voted NFL's Top Blocker

APPLETON, Wis. (AP) — Guard Walt Sweeney of the San Diego Chargers yesterday was named the National Football League's outstanding blocker for 1971 by the National 1,000 Yard Club Foundation.

Sweeney will receive the

eighth annual a... the foundation's a... at the Countryaire here... Others nominated for blocking award were Ed... gan of Detroit, G... of Green Bay, Miami, John... and t...

...o honored will be five NFL ...rs who rushed for 1,000 or ...e yards last season: John ...sion of Green Bay, Lar... ...r of Miami, Willie Elli... ...Angels, Floyd Little ...d Steve Owens of ...tion will be

given Ken Dyer, Cincinnati de...fensive back who was partially paralyzed for several month... after a collision with Broking...ton in a game here last Octo...ber, and Rufus (Road Runner Ferguson, star running back the University of Wisconsin.

Do you like the size of the Coaches All-America Game souvenir? The 1971 NFL Outstanding Blocker trophy is more like it!

I won the coveted Wally the Walrus Award at SeaWorld. Doug Wilkerson, Lionel Aldridge and Deacon Jones are having more fun than Sweeney and the chimpanzees

(Top) Johnny Unitas meets the San Diego media and his "O" line: Doug Wilkerson, Carl Mauck and Walt Sweeney. (Bottom) Our basketball team (front row) Steve Tensi, Ernie Wright, ball boy, Bob Mitinger (back row) Walt Sweeney, Earl Faison, Sam Gruneisen, Speedy Duncan, Jacque MacKinnon

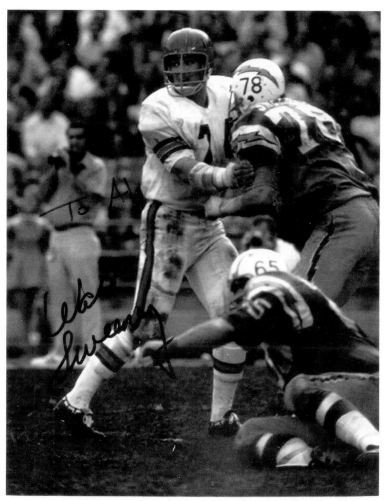

Sam Gruneisen (#65) tries to cut in while Cincinnati Bengals defensive lineman and Grammy-Award-winning musician Mike Reid and Walt Sweeney dance on the gridiron.

"When Alex Karras gave him a bad time, Sweeney picked him up by the face mask, slammed him down, spit on his shoes, then walked nonchalantly back to the huddle."

Sweeney, the rookie, in 1963 (left). The mature, more hirsute Sweeney today.

"The mature, more hirsute Sweeney"—I had to look up "hirsute" in the dictionary.

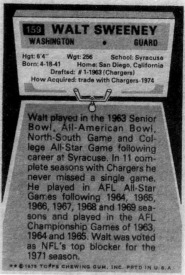

WALT SWEENEY

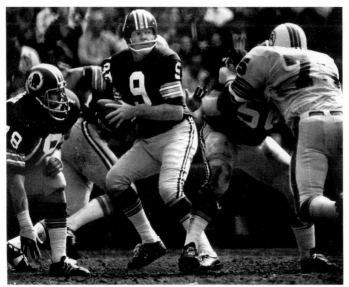

I was traded to the Washington Redskins. (Top) My last football card and (Bottom) Sweeney blocking for another Hall of Fame quarterback, Sonny Jurgensen.

(Top) Ernie Ladd, Mrs. Ladd, Walt Sweeney, my daughter, Kristin, my son, Rick, Bob Breitbard, Warren Jones, Bob Ortman, Jerry Magee at Chargers Hall of Fame Induction.

(Bottom) Sid Gillman, Leslie O'Neal, Paul Lowe, Earl Faison, Junior Seau, Ron Mix, Walt Sweeney, Courtney Hall, Stan Brock, John Carney at Chargers 50th Anniversary Celebration.

Sail Boat—Nanci's dreamboat was named *Touchdown*

Nanci's Favorite Picture—Walt and Nanci at Lake Tahoe

couldn't talk to her mother. Nanci left immediately. For once in my life, good sense kicked in and I left, too.

Once we had two bomb threats in one week. Customers seem to frown on going to a place with so much potential for dangerous activity. People just want to go out, relax and have a good time.

Business became so slow that Shea quit and returned to his old job. Shortly after that, Fallis closed Sweeney O'Shea's. He offered me the day shift at his back bar and I took it. The Trains opened at 6:00 a.m. and when I arrived at 10:00 a.m., the bar was full. Thanks to my recent drunk driving arrest and the ugly scene in Lake Tahoe, I hadn't had any alcoholic beverages in about a month. I toked up on the way to work. I called the bar the "Muppet Show," and I was the head "Muppet".

In October, the Chargers called to inform me that Ernie Ladd and I would be inducted into the Charger Hall of Fame. Ernie was one of the first really big men in professional football. He was a defensive tackle for San Diego in the early and mid-sixties. He was 6'9" and weighed 320-pounds.

He was the first teammate I met at my first Charger practice. I was a little late getting to the practice field and so was Ernie. It was customary to take a warm up lap when coming onto the field. Chuck Knoll, our defensive coordinator, who later went on to take the Pittsburgh Steelers to three Super Bowl victories, was waiting for us as we approached the field:

"Ladd and Sweeney, take a lap!"

"Take a lap around my dick-head!" Ladd shouted back.

I couldn't help laughing as I took the lap by myself.

The PR department of the Chargers informed me that Ernie and I would be their guests at the Hanelei Hotel in Mission Valley for the weekend of the Denver Broncos game. The induction ceremony would take place at half time. Usually they had some sort of banquet or dinner for the inductees, but not this time. I guess they figured I'd be happy with the tab they set up for me at the hotel liquor store. I was. I invited Dave Costa and some other friends from the beach. They provided the cocaine while I provided the booze and the suite. I think we all had a good time. All except Nanci; she just went to bed.

On the day of the game, Nanci was trying to keep me straight enough to get through the half time festivities. Rick and Kris were on the field with Nanci and me. Ernie was with his family. Nanci was introduced as my wife. In reality, her divorce had not been finalized even though she had been separated for eight years. All of the chemicals in me didn't make me feel nearly as good as when I heard the roar of the crowd at my introduction. During my playing days, I was a popular player with the fans. It was nice to know that they remembered me. As I stepped up to the microphone, all I could think of saying was that I was very honored to be selected to the Charger Hall of Fame and that I loved the people of San Diego. It wasn't a very eloquent acceptance or thank you speech.

The next day, I was back at the "Muppet Show." It was tough after basking in such glory. It reminded me of the Thanksgiving Day football game in my junior year between Cohasset and Hull. We beat Hull 20–0. I scored all the points. After the game, I had to go to my dishwasher job at the Red Lion Inn.

My landlord wasn't too impressed with my new status as a Charger Hall of Famer, because we were asked to vacate the premises. Nanci was so excited when we found a condo that I agreed to have Magee stay with a friend down the street. It was a beautiful place with a panoramic view of the Pacific. They didn't allow pets. I figured, much to the dismay of Bill Fallis, that Magee would be with me at the bar most of the time.

Hugh and Helen Marlowe, a nice couple in their early seventies, owned our condo and lived directly below us. They liked Nanci a lot and Nanci liked them. Once in a while, after a hard day at the

"Muppet Show," I would wake Hugh by shouting obscenities at his bedroom window as I climbed the stairs to my place. I was very resentful that I couldn't have my dog with me. These incidents, plus the fact that one of my derelict friends smashed his pickup truck into Hugh's wrought iron fence, caused our eviction. It was no big deal to me. I'd been asked to leave lots of places, but Nanci was mortified.

We had to be out by the middle of January, so we decided to take advantage of the place while we still had it. We were going to have a New Year's Eve party for some of our pals that had no plans for that evening. We had plenty of room for the twenty or so guests who showed up. Rather than risk a drunk driving arrest, I made it clear to everyone that they should spend the night. The whole evening was pretty much of a blur to me. I remember some guy ejaculated on a gal's dress while in the throes of dry humping. Nanci said that around 5:00 a.m., I jumped out of bed bare-assed and dragged her by the leg through the house and told our guests to "get the fuck out!" This was one of the many times I rely on her memory of events, because my drinking caused me to blackout. It was hard for me to defend my actions when I didn't know what they were. I was a little curious about where everyone had gone when I woke for breakfast.

After we left the Marlowe's, we rented a small house in Del Mar for about three months. My old roommate, Mike from Cohasset, showed up and needed a place to stay for a few days. How could I say no? He and Duncan had saved my life when they found me in the snow and took me to the hospital.

Apparently, Mike had been involved in a dope deal that had gone south and people were looking for him. At the time, I didn't even think of the dangerous situation this created for Nanci and me. It all seemed like a game to me.

There were times when Mike was living with me when he'd get so blown away, he'd be unable to find large sums of cash that he had hidden around the house. On one occasion, he misplaced a brief case containing $40,000! No one knew its whereabouts except me. I was pretty desperate at the time. I thought about stealing the money and heading for Mexico. I guess that's what separates me from the real crooks. I think about it and they do it.

Since Magee was still living with a friend, Nanci decided we needed a pet. She bought a rabbit and named it Buckwheat. Being house broken, he was allowed to freely roam the residence, occasionally pausing long enough to snack on the telephone cord.

Our little house was right next to a small park filled with squirrels. One afternoon, Nanci and I were taking a stroll in the park and she spotted a baby squirrel lying helplessly on the ground. She scooped it up and brought it home with us. I'm on a first name basis with the people at the Wildlife Center in San Diego. Over the years, because of Nanci, we'd taken numerous sick or injured birds and animals to them.

One night, Nanci's Land Cruiser was stolen from outside the bar by three illegal aliens. They rolled it over in the Santa Cruz Mountains. The damage was minimal, so Mike went up and retrieved the Cruiser for us.

The day after Nanci's Cruiser was stolen, Buckwheat got out of the apartment and got run over in traffic. I told Nanci that I had seen a little boy and his father put the rabbit in their car and drive off before I could get there. A few days later, when she rubbed me the wrong way, which seemed fairly easy to do at the time, I told her the truth about the rabbit being run over.

A few days after Mike got back from up north with the Cruiser, he headed back to the Boston area. A few months later, I learned he had a fatal dose of heroin and speed. The police said it was an accidental overdose. I knew he wasn't into intravenous drug use. He had a phobic fear of needles. I often wondered if the people who were looking for him while he was in California had found him.

A few months after we moved in, we were told our building was to be razed and replaced with condominiums. Nanci and her ex-husband owned a house in University City, an upscale community just east of La Jolla. When Nanci wasn't living there, it was usually rented. The current tenants were about to leave, so we decided to move in until it was sold.

It was a nice four-bedroom house on a quiet cul-de-sac that sat on the edge of a canyon. One of Nanci's oldest and closest friends, Barbara Caruso, lived only a block away. I can't remember if I quit the "Muppet Show" or was fired. I needed to work someplace closer to University City. Nanci and I knew the manager at Moby Dick's, a harborside establishment in Point Loma. Years before, I had frequented the restaurant when it was called The Rib Cage. I was grateful to be given a job in my new profession: bartender.

Contemplating and Executing More Shrewd Moves

I pulled four shifts a week at Moby's, two days and two nights. Their clientele consisted of business types, fishermen and, at least once a week, a group of fools from South Mission.

Most of the time, I was more busy trying to make a buck than bemoaning my fall from football stardom. Over the years I certainly had times when I felt sorry for myself, but they were usually alcohol or drug induced. Alcohol didn't help me forget my problems; it just magnified them. I'd come to realize that I wasn't a football player who became a drunk. I was a drunk who became a football player. I had a good run in college and then thirteen years in the pros. When it was over, I was just an ordinary drunk again. I had come full circle. I was trying to get off the sauce for Nanci. I was doing it for her and when you do it for someone else, you're doomed for failure.

I did most of my serious thinking in the backyard while I played lawn darts by myself. If lawn darts would ever become a professional sport, I was going to be ready. It was easy to sneak a joint outdoors.

I thought I was doing a good job of controlling my vices, especially since it was so against my nature. The house was full of liquor I'd liberated from Sweeney O'Shea's, but I never touched it. I'm a binge type drinker who could go for weeks without alcohol. A few times over the years, I checked into motels by myself and drank nonstop for days. During those times, I always felt like Ray Milland in *The Lost Weekend*.

More than once, Nanci noted with caustic humor, "If you're going to go that far, you might as well get yourself a woman and try to have some fun anyway." I always hoped she didn't mean it and just didn't understand me. Maybe she understood me all to well.

At first, it was all right to smoke marijuana as long as I didn't drink. What she meant was for me to toke up before we went to a party on Friday or Saturday night. I broadly interpreted this as license to smoke whenever I wanted. I would wake up at 6:00 a.m. and fire up the first of many joints for that day. I didn't even consider marijuana a drug. As far as I was concerned, it was an herb that helped me to relax and feel better. Most of the time, Nanci never knew I was smoking it. Even though she had a nose like a bloodhound, my clandestine use of marijuana was surprisingly successful. I had to sneak around and smoke it in some weird places. I was like a teenager fearing discovery by my parents.

I remember once when we were living in University City, I took a short ride to the market and smoked a joint on the way. Before I made my purchases, I went to the men's room to wash the odor of marijuana out of my mustache. I was feeling pretty good. I vigorously chomped a mouthful of Juicy Fruit as I drove the five blocks back to the house. Before I parked in the driveway, I hid my baggy of weed under the floormat in the back seat.

I always tried not to act silly or stupid around Nanci after smoking a joint. That was a dead giveaway. With all my sneaking, mustache washing, gum chewing and trying not to act stupid, it hardly seemed worthwhile. Oh, yes, and then there was the "eye." Due to my infection incurred while with the Redskins, my right eyelid drooped when I smoked pot. Keeping my "eye" wide open was something else to worry about.

I entered the house wide-eyed, somber-faced, smelling good and, almost immediately, Nanci engaged me in a conversation about my sobriety.

"Walt, I know you haven't had anything to drink lately, but how long has it been since you smoked marijuana?"

"Are you crazy?" is my standard response when I'm guilty.

I continued. "You would know it if I was smoking that garbage."

"How would I know? You always say that I can't tell the difference if you're high or not."

I did feel that way, but I wasn't going to go that route now.

"No, Nanci, I'm not. As a matter of fact, I'm starting to think a little more clearly and I'm getting more honest with myself. You know, I have to get honest with myself before I can get honest with anyone else. Nanci, do you think I've been smoking grass?"

"Your eye is sagging."

"That doesn't mean shit. I'm jumping in the shower." I had let the dreaded eye droop.

I was scrubbing down in the shower and a few minutes later, I got hit in the head with a bag of dope. Nanci couldn't have been more on target if she tried. How did she know? Shame and fear swept over me.

The thing that bothered Nanci the most was the lying. She said if I wanted to drink or use dope, I should tell her so she would make other arrangements for herself. I didn't know what "other arrangements" meant, but I didn't like the sound of it. I wanted my drugs and booze and Nanci regardless whether she participated or not. I just wanted her around. It was a very selfish and unfair attitude on my part.

One night, I brought a couple of bottles of wine home from the bar. I talked Nanci into a little social drinking experiment. We would drink two bottles of wine with dinner and that would be it. She just wanted to share one, but she drank one glass and I drank the rest. The more alcohol I consumed, the more it consumed me. I was out of control like I'd been so many times in the past. I jumped in the car and went to the liquor store for more alcohol. I bought two six packs and chugged one in the parking lot. Nanci was in bed watching TV when I got back. I told her I would join her as soon as I finished the beer.

"Take your time," she said.

She didn't sound to enthusiastic about sleeping with me. I made short work of the beer and was chugging a bottle of Crown Royal when she walked into the kitchen.

I think the thing that embarrassed me the most was the fact that she knew I hated Crown Royal. She knew I just wanted to get out of my mind. It was hard for Nanci to understand why I had to do these things to myself. How could she understand when I couldn't figure it out myself? She certainly wasn't responsible for my chemical abuse. On the contrary, the times I was sober was because of her.

June was a bad month for me. I got fired from Moby's and the time between my drinking bouts were getting shorter and shorter. I caught Nanci off guard one day and asked her to marry me for the umpteenth time. I had finally worn her down. I convinced her I would stop drinking, if she agreed to marriage. We drove to Tijuana. Juan Morales married us.

Unfortunately, the vows of matrimony did not slow me down. As a matter of fact, I started drinking more. A few weeks later, Nanci wanted out of the whole situation. My daughter Kristin was staying with us at the time. She was working at a movie theater in nearby University Town Center. Nanci gave Kristin some cash and told her that she was leaving me.

The straw that broke the camel's back was when I came home drunk one night and mistook Kristin's stereo for a urinal. As a kid, I remember the revulsion I felt when one of my brothers came home drunk and tried to piss in the corner of the room. This happened while my mother and I were watching *The Ed Sullivan Show*.

I drove Nanci up to her mom's in Sacramento, spent the night and flew back to San Diego. My friend Nick picked me up at the airport. I was so drunk at one point that I thought I was driving the car. It reminded me of the accident with Deacon.

I could stay at Nanci's home until I figured out what I was going to do. Even as fouled up as I was, I could see that my drinking was taking over my life. I locked myself in the house and stayed drunk for several days. Barbara Caruso came by to see if I was still alive. I invited her in for cocktails, but she politely refused.

Nanci called her attorney, Dave Nugent. Dave had handled her divorce and it looked like he'd be handling another one. I knew Dave from years ago at the Twenty/Thirty Club. He came by the house and explained the situation.

"Walt, Nanci sounds adamant. She wants you out of here and she wants a divorce."

I was such a mess that none of this made sense to me.

As tactfully as possible, Nugent said, "I'm affiliated with a hospital that treats problems like the ones you have. I asked Nanci if she would stay if you went into the hospital. She said you wouldn't go."

"Why would I go to the hospital?" I really wanted to know.

"For Christ sakes, Walt, look at yourself. You're forty-two years old. You don't have a job. Your wife of thirty days is leaving you. You don't have a place to live and, last, but certainly not least, you're a raging alcoholic."

Besides the part about Nanci leaving, the part about being an alcoholic hurt the most. It sounded so final. Nugent took me to the Chemical Abuse Rehabilitation Program located at Sharp Cabrillo Hospital in Point Loma. I knew it was the only hope I had with Nanci, so I agreed to enter CARP.

I stashed a few joints in case the first few days were a little rocky. God forbid I should suffer any discomfort. I was in detox for the first five days. It was my favorite time, only surpassed by the day I was discharged. The joints lasted about three days. In detox, they gave us a five-milligram Valium three times a day and a Dalmane (non-narcotic sleeping pill) in the evening. Some hardcore alcoholics could go into convulsions and die if all of a sudden when their alcohol supply was cut off. The Valiums brought them down slowly. I did not fall into this category. When the nurse handed out the Valium, I palmed mine and took them all at night with my Dalmane to insure a sound sleep.

After laying around for five days, I was ready to begin rehabilitation. There were 25 or 30 patients in the program. The last thing I wanted to do was go into the nut ward and introduce myself. "Hi, I'm Walt Sweeney. I used to play for the Chargers and the Redskins. I became a drunk and a drug addict and fucked up my life and a bunch of other lives. I'm happy to be here."

I didn't have to do that. One of the patients was a girl that I had dated about ten years earlier. The day after I checked in, they sent her to similar facility in Minnesota. I wondered at the time if there was any connection. I knew another patient as I.W. Harper, Jr. He was the son of Mr. and Mrs. I.W. Harper, nice people and long time Charger fans, who had a penchant for I.W. Harper Whiskey. I didn't know their real names; they were the Harpers to me.

Junior didn't waste any time telling everybody that I used to play ball. I became an instant celebrity in a room of losers. I realized that I was the biggest loser of them all.

I wrote long letters about the program to Nanci. I was learning about my disease. I wasn't a drunk anymore. I had a disease. She saw a spark of hope.

She decided to come down from Sacramento to visit me. Dr. John Milner was the director of the program. He was a white haired gentleman in his sixties and one of the leading experts in the field of recovery. The CARP unit was the first of it's kind in San Diego. I told John that I needed some time with my wife and threatened to leave the hospital if I didn't get it. Ten days sober and I was already making demands and issuing ultimatums. He agreed to let Nanci spend the weekend in my room with me. Of course, he billed my insurance company.

I learned a lot about addiction and, most importantly, learned how to talk a good game. I could tell others how to get sober, but I couldn't do it myself. After twenty-three days, when my insurance ran out, I was given the old "heave ho." The bill was over $17,000.

Wow! Alcohol and drug rehab was an expensive proposition.

These rehab hospitals based their programs on the principles of Alcoholics Anonymous. Every evening, they would take us to different AA meetings all over San Diego. After I was discharged, I continued to attend these meetings. I wasn't the type to sit up front or to volunteer to speak. I sat in the back of the room near the exit. I was usually the first one out when the meeting concluded. One of the philosophies of AA is to support one another and to help a suffering alcoholic when he's in a slippery place. To do this, you hang around after meetings, exchange phone numbers and get to know each other. I felt I didn't really need all that support. After all, I had Nanci at home.

Surprisingly, there was something about the meetings that did make me feel better. Perhaps it was the hope these poor drunks expressed. They were all worse off than me. Initially, their "first they were blind and now they could see" stories were uplifting. If these guys could get sober, maybe I could, too. I'd rather quit through this program now, instead of stopping because I got to old to lift a beer can.

The program encouraged everyone to get a sponsor after you've been around for a while. Preferably a person who had something you needed and one with good sobriety. A sponsor is like a mentor. Someone you can go to when you're having problems relating to sobriety. Hopefully, this person could give you some good direction. I was never very good about confiding in people. I guess I didn't want strangers to know how fucked up I was. It's like keep your mouth shut and they might think you're an idiot; open it and remove all doubt.

Usually new people in AA helped by setting up the meeting room, making coffee, distributing literature. Once, my sponsor asked me to go around the room and empty the ashtrays.

"If I empty ashtrays, I'll be depriving some much needed therapy for someone that's sicker than me," I replied.

That's how my early days of Alcoholic's Anonymous went. I didn't feel I needed help from anyone. I got to these meetings all by myself and I'd work the AA program my own way. One of my problems was a selective memory. I remembered only what I wanted to remember. Nanci, on the other hand, can remember blackout blinds being dropped at a Robert Hall clothing store when she was just a baby during World War II.

I was drug and alcohol free for a few months. Nanci and I were getting along and having some fun again. She thought she heard that the success rate for rehab was 99 out of a 100. With stats like that, she had reason to be optimistic. Unfortunately, the statistic was the exact opposite: 99 out of 100 relapse.

Nanci had some money, so there wasn't a lot of pressure for me to get a job right away. A lot of people relapse because they have to jump right back in the rat race. I was lucky. I was looking around, but I wasn't desperate.

I'd heard about a teen recovery group called Freeway that adhered to many of the principals of Alcoholics Anonymous, but had no connection. The founder and head was a charismatic guy named Bob Meehan. Meehan, a former heroin addict, found sobriety in the basement of a Houston church through AA. He received national exposure by getting Carol Burnett's daughter off drugs. He also took credit for 1950s teen idol Fabian gaining sobriety plus he saved a couple of famous rock bands. He looked like a hippie right of the sixties. What little hair Meehan had was pulled back into a ponytail. He wore jeans, T-shirts and sneakers. Bob had the gift of gab. He was one of those guys who could sell ice to an Eskimo. Dave Nugent introduced me to Bob.

"Walt, I've heard you speak. I'm familiar with your great football career and your fall from grace." Meehan made it sound so glamorous.

I had spoken to a few high school groups about my sports career, my drug and alcohol problems and my subsequent "recovery."

"Walt, I want you to go to work for us and I'll give you $50,000 a year."

I couldn't believe my ears. If I worked with kids, I thought I'd have to stay sober.

"Where's the pay window and when does my vacation start?" I joked.

"Seriously, Bob, what would my responsibilities entail?"

"We would like you to raise money for Freeway. As a matter of fact, you get to keep the first fifty thousand.

Aha. That was the rub. All of a sudden, the job didn't sound that great.

The *San Diego Union* heard that I was speaking at schools and wanted to do an article about me. I figured, why not? Everybody knew I was a drunk and a drug addict. It would be nice to let people know I was trying to straighten out my life. Because I was a football player who went through a drug and alcohol treatment program, all of a sudden, I was an expert on recovery.

As a result of the newspaper story, Merced College in Central California wanted to pay me $500 plus expenses to speak to the athletes at their school. When I spoke previously, it was free. Now that I was going to be paid, I became extremely nervous. Basically, I am a very shy person which probably had a lot to do with my alcoholism.

The night before I was to speak, Nanci and I stayed up until the wee small hours, writing and polishing my speech. It went very smooth. I was talking about the things I knew: football, drugs, and booze. I received a standing ovation. Tears welled up in my eyes. I couldn't remember ever taking a drug that made me feel as good as the cheers from those kids.

Don Newcombe, the former great Brooklyn Dodgers pitcher, was also on the program that night. Don is a recovering alcoholic and, for years, he has been a powerful speaker on the subject. At one point, he was in charge of the Employee Assistance Program for the Los Angeles Dodgers.

"Walt, I like what you had to say tonight. I think you could be a dynamic speaker and could be very effective in spreading the message."

I was overwhelmed by his comments. This was one of my child-hood heroes and he thought I had a future in public speaking.

"How long have you been sober?" He asked.

"Over a year," I lied.

I was always very vague about the length of my sobriety when I was doing speeches. Most recovering alcoholics and addicts know the exact date they had their last drink or drug. This is considered their sobriety birthday. If they don't know it, they usually don't have one. I had stopped so many times, I lost track of my sobriety birthday. Who wants to listen to a guy with two months sobriety?

About two weeks later, I received a call from Don.

"Walt, how would you like to go to Chicago and New York?"

"I would love to, what's the catch?"

"The catch is that I lined up a speaking engagement for you in Chicago for two thousand dollars plus expenses."

"Fantastic."

"That's only the beginning. A week after Chicago, you're going to be interviewed by Nancy Reagan on "Good Morning America" in New York. What do you think?"

"I'm flabbergasted!" To say the least, that was an understatement. I was more than flabbergasted.

Nanci and I would drive to Chicago, because she hated to fly. I would speak before a group called IADDA (Illinois Alcohol and Drug Dependence Association). From there, we would drive to New York and the "Good Morning America" show. John Drew, a NBA player, had recently gone through a treatment center in Texas. We were scheduled to be interviewed by the First Lady. She was kicking off the "Just Say No," campaign.

GMA put us up at the St. Moritz overlooking Central Park. The night before, someone from GMA called and said that I'd be on alone. Apparently, Mr. Drew had suffered a relapse. Since then, he has sobered up and gone on to open his own treatment center in the Houston area.

Now, I was really nervous. I was four months being dry. I couldn't call it sober, because I was thinking about weed all the time. I would be interviewed by the wife of the President of the United States on a nationally televised show.

We decided to take a walk in Central Park to unwind a little bit. About thirty yards inside the park, several teenagers tried to sell us some pot. If Nanci hadn't been with me, I'm sure I would have bought it.

There must have been twenty Secret Service agents when we showed up at the ABC studio. Mrs. Reagan made me feel very comfortable as I told an abbreviated version of "the Walt Sweeney Story." The whole thing came off without a hitch.

With two successful appearances under our belt, we decided to head up to Cohasset before returning to the West Coast. Nanci had never been to New England. I wanted to show the hometown folk that I wasn't the suicidal nut case who skipped town two years ago. Between the breathtaking autumn foliage and Indian summer temperatures, Nanci fell in love with the place.

We stayed with the Chattertons, Clark and Sallyann. Clark and I had been friends since his family moved to town in the fourth grade. He was the quarterback on our high school football team. We also played on the basketball team. He was a good husband and father and had been the Athletic Director at Cohasset High for fifteen years.

While we were at the Chattertons, Nanci's stepfather Cecil called to advise mom had taken a turn for the worse. We immediately headed for Sacramento. As we drove west, Nanci talked about how much she liked Cohasset and the people she had met. I could tell by our conversation that she wouldn't mind moving there. If not there, anywhere just to get out of San Diego.

Nanci had been in San Diego since the early sixties. She loved San Diego. She had many friends and fond memories there. In the short time that we had been together, I had caused her to want to leave the town she loved. She had been embarrassed by my drunken behavior and wanted to seek a fresh start. By the time I reached that embarrassing stage for her, I was in a blackout stage for me and couldn't remember anyway.

"If you don't remember, it doesn't count." Not really, but that was my distorted, self-serving way of rationalizing it. Nanci didn't share my opinion. She remembered everything.

Nanci's mom was in considerable pain. I was embarrassed when Nanci caught me going through Lee's medicine cabinet. "What do you think you're doing, Walt?"

I'm just seeing what your mom's taking." I could feel my face redden.

"Yeah, right," she muttered in disgust.

She really hadn't caught me doing anything except looking. I proceeded as an innocent man. If she had entered the bathroom about five seconds earlier, I wouldn't have been so innocent.

In a few days, we left for San Diego. Nanci's house was in escrow, so we had to move everything and put it into storage.

On November 27th, Lee passed away in Sacramento. Nanci was very distraught. I was on my best behavior, so I could be as much comfort as possible. At the funeral home, we talked with the assistant director, Mr. Simms. He was a thin, somber, little man with rote manners.

"Lee was a wonderful man, respected by all that knew him."

"Lee was my mother," Nanci explained.

Mr. Simms barreled forward. "He's in a better place now."

At this point, I looked at Nanci who was looking at this man in disbelief. We decided Mr. Simms must have been employed to provide comic relief for the bereaved.

In December, after the sale of Nanci's house was finalized, we decided to move to the East Coast. Nanci would drive the new Oldsmobile that Lee had given her the past summer. Our cat would ride with Nanci. I would drive a used VW camper we had purchased. Cricket, Lee's seven-pound Yorkshire Terrier, would ride with me. I promised Nanci's mom on her death bed, that I would take care of her little dog. Cricket and I became fast friends. Magee had died the previous summer. He was thirteen.

The day before we were to leave, I went down to the beach to say so long to some of my old pals. I hadn't been around South Mission since before I went into rehab. I wouldn't have anything to drink, but I did accept a gram of coke and a couple of joints as going away gifts. Without giving it a second thought, I said thanks and stuck them in my pocket. Nanci would be in the other car. I could use the drugs without her knowledge. We had installed CB radios, so we could communicate on the long boring ride. I didn't think she could smell pot through the microphone, but I wasn't sure.

We were well into the second day of our trip and everything was going smooth. The CB's were a great idea. It was like having Nanci in the car along with me. Then about 150 miles east of El Paso, near the town of Van Horn, "black ice" warnings were coming across the airwaves. I thought Nanci was driving too slow and decided to pass her. My car hit a patch of black ice and started sliding sideways. I flipped over a guardrail and rolled three times before landing upright at the bottom of an embankment. I didn't get a scratch. By the time Nanci got to my car, I'd already crawled back in the vehicle to get Cricket out.

Nanci told me that an 18-wheeler missed her by inches as she exited her car. She wasn't sure if I had been killed. She was walking around in a daze until someone kept her from wandering out on the highway.

The camper was packed with everything the moving company didn't take. I think it served as a buffer that protected Cricket and me from serious injury or death. With our belongings scattered all over West Texas, I had my work cut out. I gathered our treasure and stuffed it into Nanci's car. We stayed in Van Horn for a couple of days. After arrangements were made with our insurance company to properly fix the camper, I rented a U-haul trailer. We reloaded everything and continued on our journey.

It was the worst winter Texas experienced in over a hundred years. Moving from San Diego to Boston in December wasn't the smartest thing I've ever done. Because of the bad weather, it took two weeks before we got to the Boston area. We had Christmas dinner at Rick's Cafeteria in Meridian, Mississippi. We rolled into Boston on New Year's Day.

The Marketing Man's Dream

When we finally arrived in Cohasset, its beauty again over-whelmed Nanci. Magnificent homes on stone cliffs overlooking the Atlantic, quaint little shops in the village, scenic harbors and marshes. When I was growing up, the population was about five thousand. It had only increased by about a thousand while Nanci and I lived there.

We stayed our first night at a quaint little cottage on Straight's Pond. It belonged to Chris Ford, my good friend from high school. His mom lived in Arizona and stayed in the cottage when she came east to visit her kids and grandkids in the summer. Chris and his family lived in the main house next door. Nanci and I could stay until we found a place of our own. The first night reminded us of a Christmas card as the full moon glistened off the frozen pond. The cottage wasn't insulated and became quite chilly. We lived there for about a month.

Scott Anderson was a hometown kid who made his living as an Elvis impersonator. He was quite a bit younger than me, but still looked me up whenever he was in San Diego. I caught his act on the West Coast and he was actually pretty good. I bumped into him at the Red Lion one night. Always a popular watering hole for the locals, whenever I dropped in these days, which was seldom, I'd be drinking coffee.

Scott lived with his mom and dad. They wanted to rent an apartment that adjoined their house. It sounded perfect for our needs at the time.

We bought the land where my mother's house used to stand. The house had burned down in the early seventies. It was my Grandfather Jim's house and he left it to my mother when he passed away in 1951. It sat on the edge of Little Harbor with conservation woods across the street. It is one of the most scenic spots you could imagine.

The whole town of Cohasset was built on a ledge. All of the homes have septic tanks. In order for me to build a house on the property, since the three-year rebuild time limit had expired, I would need certain permits issued by the Cohasset Board of Health. When my mother died, the land went to my sister. She sold it to our brother, John, who lived in New Hampshire. Over the years, John had been unsuccessful in obtaining these building permits. I felt optimistic that I could get these permits, so we bought the property from John. Actually, Nanci gave John the money since it was hers. We planned to live at the Anderson's while our house was being built.

The apartment consisted of a living room, which doubled as a bedroom, a small kitchen and a bathroom. The whole place was not more than 120 square feet. We had boxes with our things stuffed into every conceivable spot in the apartment. We thought we could handle the living arrangement, but didn't realize the nightmare the Board of Health was going to put us through. The property with the proper building permits was valuable. Without the permits, we couldn't even live in a mobile home during construction. It would just be a beautiful park.

When we moved into the small apartment, we didn't realize that Scott's father lived in the garage between the main house and our apartment. Unbeknownst to us at the time, Mr. Anderson smoked a little weed. Mrs. Anderson banished him to the garage as long as he persisted in this practice. The arrangement seemed fine with him. He had his weed, a big stuffed chair, a wood burning stove, a small bed, a TV and his *Playboy* magazines to peruse

without interruptions. A door in our apartment was connected to
the garage, but Nanci always made sure it was locked. She wasn't
afraid of Norm (Mr. Anderson), but she always thought it was
strange he preferred the garage to a nice house.

One day while changing the sheets on our bed, she came across
a small bud of marijuana. When she confronted me, I convinced
her that it wasn't mine. It must be Norm's.

"We're moving now!" She was adamant. Although she believed
me, she couldn't figure out what Norm was doing in our bed. She
thought it would be best if she didn't know.

Things with the Cohasset Board of Health weren't going as
smoothly as anticipated. First of all, a former member of the board
was the ex-wife of my cousin, Robert. She hated all Sweeneys,
especially me, and I didn't even know her. She poisoned the Board
against me. Instead of looking at the facts in my case, they were
swayed by a bitter, spiteful woman with an axe to grind. I understood this small town bullshit, so I really wasn't that surprised.
Nanci couldn't believe how they could get away with it. Most of the
people who sit on these small town boards run for these positions
because they are on some kind of power trip. Ninety percent of
them are not qualified. It was like I needed heart surgery and went
before a bunch of hairdressers for an opinion.

We spent thousands on engineering studies to prove that our
septic system wouldn't contaminate the nearby marsh. I didn't
know it was such a big deal. A marsh is just a bunch of shit anyway. They continually put me off and turned me down for the next
three years. The local newspapers even took up my cause. They
said as a person, born and raised in Cohasset, I was being denied
my God given right to build on land where Sweeneys had lived for
over 150 years.

Real estate prices were sky rocketing and Cohasset was the
perfect town for young executives and their families drawn to the

booming computer industry in Boston. Although it was only half an hour to the metropolitan area, it had a country atmosphere with lots of woods and horses. The school system was excellent and it was beautiful.

If I had all of the necessary permits to build, I could have sold the property for $400,000. It seemed an inordinate number of people were worried about me selling and making some money. At the time, we had every intention of building a house and living in it. I spent many sleepless nights thinking about harming various members of the Board.

Three years after our first meeting with the Board, they finally gave us the okay. By then it was too late. After we left the Anderson's, we moved into a first floor apartment in an old house across the street from Cohasset Harbor. It was small, but we weren't going to be there forever. It had a front parlor with lots of windows, a small dining room, a bathroom and a bedroom with a fireplace. Nanci and I almost "bought the farm" the first night we started a fire. The fireplace had a faulty flue and we were almost asphyxiated.

To get to the bathroom, a person had to walk through the kitchen. The house was built in the 1800's and the people were much shorter then. There was a beam that ran the width of the kitchen. When we first moved in, I cut my head on it so many times that my forehead looked like hamburger. I'd become so enraged after these collisions that I'd shout out appropriate expletives like "mother-fucker!" or "cocksucker!" One day, after a head smashing followed by obligatory cursing, I overheard the guy upstairs explain to his guest, "Oh, he's always screaming at her."

Nanci and I ordered some nice furniture. When it was delivered, we couldn't fit it into the house. We had been using some old Danish modern and other assorted pieces of furniture the Chattertons had stashed years before in their cellar. A few years later, when we were moving, I asked Clark if he wanted the furniture back.

"Just put it in the front yard and Skinny Laugelle (the city dump manager) will take them to the dump."

Can you picture this scene? We had a tattered old naugahyde recliner stretched out in a prone position. There was a couch with a hole in the size of a watermelon. Nanci always kept a pillow in the hole with a cover over it. An exercise bike with one pedal missing. An old futon and several other pieces of furniture in various stages of disrepair. This stuff was piled up in front of an old jeep that Nanci used to run back and forth to White's Farm to see her horse. There weren't any floorboards on the driver's side. Nanci could stick her feet through to the street if she wanted.

This is what an IRS agent saw when he knocked on our door. A dozen years before, the government gave me a $10,000.00 refund. Apparently they had been trying to find me ever since. Uncle Sam wanted his money plus fines and interest.

Danny Nardo owned the hair salon next to our place. The IRS agent asked Danny where we lived, so Danny showed him. Danny told me later that he watched this guy as he scratched his head and took inventory of the beat-up furniture scattered on the lawn in front of our place. He looked inside Nanci's jeep and left a note: "Mr. Sweeney, give me a call when you get on your feet."

After we had settled in, my cousin, Billy Morgan, introduced me to the president of Telco Systems. His name was Bob Bowman and we hit it off right away. Telco Systems was one of the leading suppliers of fiber optics in the country at that time. They provided technology and state of the art equipment for various telephone companies.

Bob was a former collegiate hockey player. He was familiar with my sports background and, more recently, my public speaking about alcohol and drug abuse, so he hired me in the hope I might develop a career for myself. The hiring was a weird situation. He gave me a job and then I went for the interviews. The Director of Human Resources, Joanne Warren, wasn't very happy about the entire procedure. Unfortunately for her, she couldn't do much about it.

My title was Employee Relations Representative. My duties included acting as a buffer between the assembly line workers and management. I interviewed and checked references of potential assembly line workers. I was responsible for the development of a drug program within the company. This involved assessing the gravity of the problem and finding proper help and treatment for the individual. I was also slated to give "The Walt Sweeney Talk" to service clubs, high schools and any other interested groups.

It was at one of the high school appearances that I met Mike Dukakis, the Governor of Massachusetts. Mike was in his second term with two years left. Under his leadership, the state's economy did an about face and was flourishing. In 1988, he ran for the Presidency and was defeated by George H.W. Bush.

Although his wife Kitty was a recovering alcoholic and diet pill addict, Mike knew very little about drugs. He was determined to keep them out of schools in the Bay State. He was fascinated by my drunkalog and I accompanied him to about thirty schools after our first meeting. Before Nanci and I returned to San Diego, we had lunch with Mike and Kitty at the State House in Boston. We also joined them on the campaign trail in Southern California during his presidential campaign. Mike Dukakis is one of the kindest men I have ever met. I will always consider him a good friend. We have kept in touch over the years.

The Board of Health would eventually grant permission to build on our land after Dukakis sent a state attorney down to Cohasset to plead our case.

Meanwhile, back at Telco, Bob had hired Nanci as a data entry processor. We would make the forty-minute drive to Norwood to work, lunch together and when the day was done, return to

Cohasset. We usually stopped for dinner along the way. I thought it was a pretty good deal.

My immediate boss was Joanne Warren, a devoutly religious and a go-by-the-book career woman. Since Bob had hired another Sweeney without going through proper channels, there was even more friction between Joanne and me. That was one of the reasons I made myself scarce around the office. The other reason was that I was really bored.

My demeanor is what pissed off Joanne the most. I really didn't give a shit what she thought and she knew it. The president of the company hired me and I was rubbing elbows with the Governor. Every time I spoke before a group, Bowman received complimentary letters. I was perceived as a good guy. Telco was performing a valuable public service, so Joanne couldn't touch me.

Sometimes when I would hear she was looking for me, I would steal away to the men's room with my *New York Times* crossword puzzle. Most of my on-site work regiment was spent on the porcelain throne.

Someone once told me I had a "wet face." I already knew my brain was a little damp, but I wasn't sure what this meant. He explained people were comfortable confiding in me. I just had that type of face. An important element of my job was listening to people's problems. I was supposed to help find solutions or steer them to someone that could.

The guy with the "wet face" theory must have been right on, because I heard many outlandish things. One of the younger women on the assembly line came into my office one afternoon with a non-work related problem. She caught her husband in bed with his brother.

"What do you want me to do about it?" I was in a pisser mood.

She explained, "Well, we got this memo and it said that if we had problems, we can talk to you about them."

You didn't have to be a psychiatrist to see that she had quite a problem.

"The best thing I can do for your situation is to recommend a marriage counselor or a therapist".

Another time, we had a twenty-year old male assembly line worker who killed an eight-year old boy in a traffic accident. I talked with him two days after the incident. He was feeling better; he could smile again. It took everything I had to keep from smashing him.

I had an arrangement with Spofford Hall, one of the best drug and alcohol rehabs in New England. They kept me on retainer. In return, I would give talks and refer patients. I sent a girl from Telco. After she completed the program, she thanked me. "Walt, I'm not a drug addict anymore. I now have mental illness."

I continued to fuel my own addiction by smoking a little weed. It wasn't very often, because I was super paranoid about being caught. Nanci found a joint in the back of her jeep and read me the riot act.

"You hypocrite! How can you do those talks and sneak around smoking that crap?"

"The jeep is wide open all the time and anyone could have put that joint there."

I continued to deny it was mine and insisted "they" were all out to get me.

My brother John was gravely ill in New Hampshire. Johnny was forty-three years old and had developed asthma in his mid-thirties. He was being treated with a steroid called Prednisone. It can be a real wonder drug if taken for short periods of time, but John needed it daily to breathe. He saw all the top specialists in the country and even stayed a few weeks in an experimental hospital in Denver. Nothing worked except this miracle drug with serious side effects.

Over a three-year period taking Prednisone, he developed an enlarged heart, diabetes and osteoporosis. He shrunk from 6'3" to 5'3". His death was a very sad time for me. John was my favorite brother. He was only Sweeney boy who wasn't an alcoholic. John was an extremely hard worker, a loving husband and a good dad to his son and two daughters.

Shortly after John passed away, his teenage son was involved in a murder along with two other kids. He provided the knife and helped bury the victim's body in his mother's backyard. They were all caught and did prison time.

Nanci and I missed San Diego. Every couple of weeks, we'd make a ninety-minute drive into Hyannis to a Mexican restaurant called Sam Diego's. Mexican restaurants were few and far between in the Boston area.

When Bob Bowman lost control of Telco in a power struggle, I knew my days were numbered. I sent a resume to Sharp Cabrillo Hospital in San Diego. It was 1987 and I had "successfully" gone through their rehab program in 1982. Sharp flew me to San Diego for an interview. I was hired to market their alcohol and drug treatment program. Nanci and I sold our property and headed back to the West Coast.

Before we left Boston, we received some shocking news. Nanci had been having some problems with balance and vision. Her cousin, Marsha, worked at Brigham and Women's Hospital for one of the leading neurologists in the country.

We showed up for an appointment with Dr. Taylor's at 10:00 a.m. Several hours later, after a CAT scan, a spinal tap and a battery of other tests, the doctor gave us his findings. Nanci had Multiple Sclerosis. Tears welled up in her eyes when Dr. Taylor gave us the news. When he said she should learn to use a cane, she got pissed.

The bad news was there is no known cure. The good news, if there can be any good news in a situation like this, was that this type of MS is classified as transient. It will come and go.

After the initial shock wore off, Nanci exhibited the same attitude when she beat ovarian cancer 15 years earlier. She's one of the bravest people that I've ever known. She handles her disease with defiance and humor. Over the years, a few attacks sapped all of her strength. She would be in bed for a few days or a few weeks. Other than those episodes, she appears perfectly normal. I know there are times when she has problems, but keeps them to herself. On the other hand, I complain about everything.

Before we left his office, Dr. Taylor took me aside and told me to try to keep as much stress off Nanci as possible. A shrink once said that I thrived on stress, but I didn't believe it.

Nanci had made a few good friends in Cohasset and knew she would miss them. The thing she would miss the most was her daily trip to White's Farm. Richardson White was one of the world's foremost equine sculptors. He had done work for the Olympics and his sculptures are in museums worldwide. As a young man, my father worked for him as a farm hand. White's Farm was about half a mile from my childhood home. I spent a large portion of my childhood romping through the woods and swimming in White's Pond. Mr. White rarely left the farm, but Mrs. White made daily runs to the village. She always gave me a ride when I was walking. When we first moved to Cohasset, Nanci bought Rocky, an Arabian horse, and boarded it at White's Farm. Everyday, hot and humid or freezing cold, Nanci would be mucking out Rocky's stall at six in the morning. Mr. White and Nanci became good friends. We felt honored when he sculpted Rocky. When we moved to San Diego, Nanci gave Rocky to a young girl. We kept the sculpture.

My boss at Sharp Cabrillo was Jim Eppink. He had been there for about a year and a half. His background was insurance. The alcohol and drug program was just one of his responsibilities. Sharp Cabrillo was the first hospital in San Diego to have a chemical abuse unit. By the time I went to work for Sharp, there were probably a dozen different treatment programs in the area. Over the years, Sharp's program had fallen on hard times due to the increased competition.

On Friday mornings, I was part of a team that presented seminars about drugs in the work place. We sent invitations to local businesses and always had a good turnout.

At the start of our seminar, the Director of Sharp's chemical abuse unit welcomed the audience and talked about drug problem drugs in the work place. A doctor, an attorney and an employee assistance representative spoke next. Last, but not least, The Walt Sweeney Story. The first three presenters were usually boring, because they were technical. My talk was interesting. People seemed to eat it up. After my first presentation, I overheard Eppink tell his secretary that I was a "marketing man's dream."

My job was to put "heads in beds" and spread the word about our program. Some days, I would speak before three different groups: a Rotary breakfast, a Lions lunch and an Elks dinner. There must be hundreds of service clubs in the San Diego area. It didn't take long to get sick of talking about myself and my problems with substance abuse. I almost went berserk.

It was also one of my responsibilities to conduct interventions. I had never done an intervention, but I listed it on my resume. It was really basic stuff. You gather the significant others of the chemical abuser in a room and, one by one, they confront the addict. The addict is told that his or her relationship with the drug has deteriorated all other relationships. If they do not seek help, they are on their own. It is a tough love approach. More often than not, the addict will enter into a treatment program.

When we arrived in San Diego, we stayed with Chris and Phil Jordan for a few weeks. Chris was one of Nanci's dearest friends and one of San Diego's top interior designers. She has won numerous awards for her work.

Nanci had a thing about boats. She loved them. She had done a little sailing before we got together and, being an avid scuba diver, she had been around a lot of smaller watercraft. When she suggested we live on a boat, I was all for it. I really didn't care where we lived as long as we were together. We decided to rent one to see if we liked that life style. We found a forty-foot powerboat and moved aboard.

Lee LaRosa owned the boat. It was tied up at the Mission Bay Marina where Lee operated a speedboat rental business. He lived in a boat identical to the one we were renting. They were tied to the same dock. It was comfortable to live on our boat, but the engine didn't work. We couldn't cruise even if we wanted to. It was a white whale, but it was perfect for Nanci, Cricket and me. Sea World was across the street. Every night at nine, we were treated to fireworks.

Besides LaRosa, we were the only people to live aboard a boat in this section of the Marina. The second night we were there, I got home later than usual. I had spoken at a Rotary Club dinner and I stopped at a grocery store about five minutes from the Marina. I phoned Nanci to see if she needed anything from the store.

"Walt, you got to get here as soon as possible. Someone is shooting on the dock!"

I could tell by her voice that she wasn't joking. There was a police car in the parking lot when I arrived. I ran over and told them what had happened. They followed me to the boat. Apparently, they had radioed ahead because there were two huge women police officers on the boat when we arrived. Nanci had mistaken the fireworks for gunfire. The whole incident turned out to be, at least to us, a comical mistake.

Living on a boat seemed like a stress-free way to go. You couldn't ask for a prettier setting and the water seemed to have a calming effect on us. Even Cricket didn't bark that much. We had a good view of the launching ramp. Sometimes on weekends, we would entertain ourselves watching people try to maneuver their boats into the water without submerging their cars.

We lived at the Mission Bay Marina for almost a year until Lee decided to move his operation to a bigger marina. We were towed across the bay to Knight and Carver. John Knight and Hugo Carver leased their waterfront footage from the city and maintained a boat repair yard at this location. They also operated Knight and Carver Custom Boat Builders about a mile east of the marina.

The new marina was like living in a small, tightly compacted community. There were lots of live-aboards and their boats were only a few feet apart. Everybody knew everyone else's business.

Our boat was at the end of "E" dock. It was a well-positioned slip. If we ever could have gotten the whale running, it was a straight shot to the channel and out into the ocean. To get to the marina showers, you had to pass about thirty boats. It was about a quarter of a mile walk to take a shower. At times, the shower stroll could take Nanci an hour. She loved people and loved to talk. On the other hand, I am shy by nature. As my high school yearbook noted aptly, "Silent and tall, he walks through the hall." What a legacy. If I was drinking and doing drugs, I'd stop and rave with the best of them. Nanci could do that naturally.

Our next-door neighbors were the Bittermans on one side and the Kedwards on the other. Pam and Joe Bitterman lived on a 50' Brigantine with their two children, Rigel and Halie. Joe was a pharmacist and Pam taught pre-school. Rigel and Halie were good students and very well-mannered kids. All the Bittermans were very cute and very nice.

Pauline and Rob Kedward lived aboard a 40' sailboat on the other side of us. They were an English couple in their forties. They had a married daughter living in Hawaii and a son living on his own who attended a local college. Rob taught scuba diving and Pauline was an office manager. They were also very nice people and lived on their boat for years. Everyone down at our end of the dock was nice except for me.

At the front of the marina were a deli, a Sea Ray boat dealership and the marina office. Inside the boat yard were the laundry room and the showers for the boat tenants. The marina was one of four horseshoed around Mission Bay. If you had a bird's eye view, we would be at the top left of the horseshoe. The open end would be the channel to the Pacific Ocean. Directly opposite us was the Hyatt Hotel and Marina. At the closed end were two smaller marinas, a seafood market, two restaurants, and a commercial fishing dock. There was a parking lot to the west and the jetty that extended several hundred of yards into the ocean. Cricket and I took walks to the end of the jetty and back. There was a small park between the jetty and the parking lot. In the summer, the San Diego Pops performed there. If the wind was right and the tide high, we could hear a free concert. In October, Knight and Carver held a small "in the water" boat show at the marina. Ever since we had been back from the East Coast, Nanci would drag me to every boat show in Southern California. She wanted her own boat. Living on a boat is a goal for many people. I certainly wasn't going to stand in the way of her dream. The boat we were renting wasn't exactly the Queen Mary, but I did enjoy the scenic beauty and tranquility. It wasn't a bad way to go.

She didn't have to drag me to this boat show. All I had to do was roll out of bed and I was there. As we came around the end of the dock where we lived, a stunning 53' black motor sailor stopped us in our tracks. It looked like it should have been on the cover of Yacht Magazine.

"Come aboard," Pat Sullivan said.

Pat was a boat salesman. He was currently living on this beauty. We introduced ourselves and went down the spiral staircase to the galley. The exterior was remarkable, but it was even nicer inside. Sullivan pulled up a section of the galley floor.

"Check this out. It's a Ford/Lehman 135 horse power diesel."

That didn't mean shit to me. Whenever Nanci and I were look-ing at cars or boats, the salesman would always be talking to me. I know nothing about engines and don't have a mechanical bone in my body. Nanci is much more knowledgeable about such things. Although I'd be standing there with a vacant look in my eyes, these guys wouldn't stop. I'd have to walk away before they would start talking to her.

"What kind of boat is this?" That was my only question, because I knew less about boats than I did engines.

"A Mikelson. There were only twelve of these motorsailers made, and from now on, they're just building powerboats. This is definitely a blue water boat. You can go anywhere in the world with this boat."

Yeah, anywhere in the world as long as I didn't lose sight of land. If I was going to be in the middle of the ocean, I sure didn't want Nanci or myself at the wheel.

"Sounds right up my alley," I bluffed.

From the galley, we went down three more steps to the lower salon. There was a washer/dryer encased in teak next to a teak roll-top desk. Above the desk was a home entertainment center with all the goodies. There was also a booth and dining table in the lower salon. There were two forward cabins and the main cabin was in the stern of the boat. The entire inside of the boat was done in a honey colored teakwood. If the boat were made in this country instead of Taiwan, it would have cost twice as much. The upper salon was also an indoor wheelhouse, galley and additional dining area. It had two showers and slept twelve. Nanci and I were blown away.

I continued to look around as Nanci and Pat talked about boats.

"How much?" I asked.

"Two hundred thousand. Originally it sold for two hundred and fifty to a doctor from El Cajon. He was in Taiwan overseeing construction of the boat when he had a fatal heart attack. The boat was brought over here and the price was reduced to what it is now. They're not going any lower."

Nanci and I returned to the white whale and talked about Sullivan's boat. We got on the phone and called Dave Wolf. Dave was a boat salesman and friend who had been showing us boats for a year. We felt it only fair we buy the boat through him even though it would cost us more money. We agreed to buy it for the asking price and put $70,000 down to get the financing. While we were waiting to hear from the bank, the boat was taken back to its berth in San Diego Bay. About a week later, our loan was approved and we had a new home. Now all we had to do was get it back to Mission Bay. The biggest boat I ever operated was a 12' dory with a small outboard. Now I was faced with the challenge of taking this 53' monster around Point Loma to Knight and Carver. The distance was about six nautical miles whatever that meant. I played the role of "Sinbad the Sailor," but in reality I was "Waldo the Landlubber."

Getting the boat out of the marina was going to be the tough part. The only thing that someone with my limited ability could compare it to would be driving an 18-wheeler on ice through a parking lot filled with Volkswagens. I'd only been on the boat once and it was securely tied to the dock.

I asked Phil Jordan, Chris's husband, to help us move the yacht. Phil had a lot of experience with boats and was looking forward to operating such a beautiful vessel. It was about a two-hour trip. We packed a picnic lunch and planned to make a day of it.

I turned the key in the ignition and the engine started right up. So far so good. Nanci and Chris cast off the lines. I put it in reverse and we started to move. I turned around to make sure nothing was behind us. The steering wheel was still in my hands!

Someone had forgotten to insert the cotter pin. I knew being a skipper was going to be difficult, but this was ridiculous! I threw it in neutral, but the boat was already moving out of the slip. Our life savings was heading for a collision with a smaller craft. Nanci was screaming at the people in those boats to abandon ship. She feared they'd be killed or injured. Chris hid her head under a pillow. We all react differently in a crisis. I raced to the bow or stern, whatever they call it, and somehow managed to push off a piling to avoid disaster. Phil replaced me at the helm. Nanci ran below deck to the wheelhouse to man the other steering wheel. Phil shouted out steering directions. Somehow we got the boat back into the slip to avoid a catastrophe.

The whole incident was very bizarre and very scary. The thought of 30 tons slamming into smaller boats was somewhat unsettling. Other than that, I think our maiden voyage went quite smoothly.

Living La Vida Loca

Cricket was 15 years old and incontinent. Nanci, who wasn't too fond of him in the first place, shuddered at the thought of him pissing all over her beautiful teak decks. I could see that Cricket's days were numbered. Nanci put up the money to buy the land in Cohasset and from the sale of the land, we were able to buy the boat. It was her boat. I was just happy to be there. She did allow me to name the boat *Touchdown*. I wanted to call it *Mr. Touchdown*, but thought it might be a bit too much.

We started transferring our things from the whale onto the new boat. Nanci informed me that Cricket was not welcome. I can't say that I blamed her. Cricket was a yappy, spoiled little dog. He had never been housebroken and liked it that way. On the old boat, Nanci was constantly pulling up the carpet to wash off the messes. Nanci's mom had a housekeeper who handled that chore. I assumed Nanci would do it since Cricket was so important to her mother.

I loved the dog and overlooked just about every nasty thing he did. He wasn't the neatest dog around, but he was one of the bravest. Since Cricket wasn't allowed aboard *Touchdown*, I decided to stay on the old boat with my little dog. The slip rent had already been paid. Nanci was so thrilled to have her new boat, I don't think she noticed when I wasn't there.

The boats were side by side. Nanci and I would spend our day together, but retire to separate quarters in the evening. This little separation enabled me to sneak a pint of vodka into the wee small hours of the morning when I knew Nanci was asleep. If no one was around and I didn't think I'd get caught, the obsession would reappear. I had gone months without alcohol or drugs and didn't miss them one bit.

When I became obsessed, I thought these chemicals would make me feel happy and relaxed. Usually, they made me feel guilty and depressed. That certainly didn't stop me from trying. No one knew about the vodka, but Nanci was pretty sure I was doing something that she wouldn't want me doing aboard *Touchdown* or any place else. By this point in our marriage, due to my history, she really didn't care what I did as long as I didn't do it around her, her friends or cause her any embarrassment. She thought I used all the time and if there were any slips, it was an occasional slip into sobriety.

Every time I stopped using drugs or drinking, I thought that I had succeeded. I really wanted to stop and hoped to stop soon. If the hospital ever discovered what their marketing dream was doing, I would certainly lose my job.

Nanci couldn't stand the hypocrisy of my situation. During the day, I was a crusader for sobriety. For the past two weeks, I was a sneak drinker. I had adjusted the "Walt Sweeney Story". I was still saying drugs and alcohol screwed up my life, which was true, but I was vague about the length of my sobriety. When people asked how long I'd been sober, I felt it would be best if I lied. I really felt like saying something like, "What time is it?"

One night while Cricket and I were on the old boat, the late news on TV had a story about a prostitution ring that had just been busted. It reminded me of some business opportunities I actually had the good sense to decline.

I had a drinking buddy from the Surfer Lounge named Tom Shaw. Tom was from Cleveland. He had been stationed in San Diego while in the Navy. After his discharge, he returned to Ohio. Six months later, he was back to San Diego. Once you've been exposed to the Southern California lifestyle and the great weather, it's tough to take the snow and cold. Tom had made a good living in the tire business, but he drank his way through a couple of marriages.

The last time I saw him, he was living across the street from the Del Mar Racetrack. He had just lost his job with the tire company. He motioned me over to discuss a business proposition.

"Walt, I think we could make a lot of money if we got a string of hookers and put them to work during the track season."

My first thought was where would one get a string of hookers? I didn't think the Yellow Pages would work, but I wasn't sure.

Instead I remarked, "Are you crazy?"

"No. I'm dead serious. I know a couple of girls who are working the track now and they're making thousands of dollars a night."

They say alcoholics have wet brains, but Noah could have floated his Ark inside Tom's head.

"What about Nanci?" I couldn't wait to hear his answer. It was bad enough that she was married to a drunk. Throwing a pimp into the mix would be a little more than she could handle.

"She wouldn't have to know," he continued.

I had a hard enough time sneaking a joint from this woman. If I was in the next room and farted, she knew about it.

Even as delusional as I was back then, this seemed like a real bad idea. I have a bad habit of not saying "no" to people. I told him I'd think about it. I never saw him again, but he called when I was living in Boston. He had moved back to Cleveland and found sobriety. I don't recall what he did for his livelihood.

Ron V. was a coke dealer I knew from the beach. When I first met him, he was a house painter who sold a little weed on the side. He once asked if I wanted to become a "mule". A "mule" is a person who tapes bags of coke to his or her body and tries to pass through customs. It would be a "piece of cake." As long Nanci was with me, I'd never be checked. I couldn't wait for him to ask Nanci.

Fortunately for him, he never did. The hooker idea was brilliant compared to this one.

Back to the boat... After the first week on the old boat, I decided a pint wasn't getting the job done. I was not getting enough buzz. I never could. I went to the store for cigarettes and a quart of 100 proof vodka. I stuck the bottle down the front of my pants and covered the top of it with my windbreaker. Had I ran into anybody on the dock, they probably would have thought I had the biggest hardon they've ever seen. Fortunately, I didn't run into anyone.

After Nanci and I had dinner on *Touchdown*, we watched TV for a couple of hours before I retired to my quarters. When I was sure Nanci was asleep, I broke out the vodka and drank the bottle in about ninety minutes. I passed out and woke up around 4:00 a.m. in a pool of piss. Even Cricket had jumped out of bed and was asleep in a chair.

Not only was the dog incontinent, so was I. Fortunately, I slept on a bare mattress and didn't have to worry about sheets and blankets. I flipped the mattress, but a small stain had seeped through to the other side. Nanci popped in about 8:00 a.m..

"What's that smell?" She asked.

"You're right about Cricket. He pissed the bed."

When the second week was over, I moved aboard *Touchdown*. I took Cricket on lots of walks, so he wouldn't make a mess on the boat. About a year later, Nanci announced the dog had to go.

I said, "If the dog isn't going to live on the boat, then I'm not either."

Nanci just smiled and I packed. For the first couple of nights, Cricket and I slept in my van in the parking lot. Vodka and marijuana acted as my sedatives. How else was I going to get some sleep? During the day, I would occasionally join Nanci on the boat. Cricket would play on the dock. I hoped my neighbors didn't know I was sleeping in my van, but I was getting some strange looks. I'm sure they thought I wasn't playing with a full deck. What would you think if you saw a guy with a beautiful yacht sleeping in his car?

After a few nights, I moved just over the bridge to South Mission and stayed with a friend of mine, Dave Moore. I first met Dave when I moved to the marina. He had a business called Charger Marine that sold speedboats. Dave claimed to have been a defensive back for the St. Louis Cardinals. He was about ten years younger than me and had a lot of the same bad habits. After about a week at his house, Cricket and I wore out our welcome. Fortunately, I ran into Merle, an old friend from Alcoholics Anonymous. She was about seventy with twenty years of sobriety under her belt. I didn't meet Merle until I got involved in AA, but I knew her deceased husband. He was another beach alcoholic. We hung out at the same bars. Occasionally, I would give him a ride home.

Merle's dog had just died and she instantly fell in love with Cricket. Cricket's grandfather had been a champion, Jiminy Cricket. Nanci's mom had paid big bucks for him. He was a beautiful Yorkie. When Merle asked me his age, I lied and said he was ten. Who was going to take a fifteen-year-old dog? He looked and acted much younger than ten. Merle took Cricket and allowed me visitation rights. It was time to get home while I still had a home where I was welcome. I went back to the boat.

Because of my work at the hospital, I had to be very discreet to say the least, whenever I did mind-altering chemicals. I never smoked a joint, did a line or had a drink with anyone who knew who I was.

Who was I? An ex-jock with a bum knee dependent on alcohol and drugs who was trying to sell sobriety. I had a college degree, but so what? That and a buck and a half could get me a cup of coffee!

Regarding my discreet use of drugs, Nanci once asked about my source.

"Don't you think that he'll tell your pals at the beach?"

"No. He promised he wouldn't."

She looked at me like I was the biggest idiot in the world. Looking back, I guess I was the biggest idiot in the world.

Most drunks have a tough time around the holidays. I was no exception. It seemed like everyone else was getting fucked up. I was supposed to sit around and be high on life or, at least, abstain from the goodies that gave me some kind of relief. Just exactly what did I need relief from? I had all the trappings of a successful person. I loved a great woman. A good paying job for the amount of actual work that I put into it. I lived on a beautiful yacht in the best climate in the world.

I don't have the brain of a normal human being. I don't know if it was my upbringing, genetics or the ambiguous social norms of the era. Nanci often said that she would hate to live inside my head. I can't say that I blame her. It's no picnic.

On the Fourth of July, we were supposed to meet the Bittermans and their friends in the park next to the marina. Although we had two showers on the boat, we continued to use the facilities in the boatyard. Nanci had just finished showering and was walking through the boatyard on her way back to *Touchdown*. I happened to be hiding under a tarp draped over a large sailboat in the yard. I was smoking a joint, getting primed for the day's activities. A swirl of wind blew the tarp off the boat as Nanci walked past. My dastardly deed was exposed. It was embarrassing and humiliating.

Here I was, a man in his mid-forties, hiding in the dark under a boat, smoking a joint. I felt like a teenager whose mother had caught him masturbating.

After incidents such as this, I'd stop using for a while, but never long enough. I would forget how miserable I felt or how miserable I made Nanci feel. Next thing I knew, I would drift back into it.

The San Diego Racquetball and Fitness Center was about two blocks from the hospital. I signed us up when they had a two-for-one membership drive. The only time Nanci entered the place was when she picked me up a couple of times. She's one of those people with a high metabolism rate. She stays lean as a rail without lifting a finger. Even when I was in the depths of alcoholism and drug addiction, I still worked out. My priorities were backwards. My brain could be scrambled. As long as I looked good, I thought I was all right.

When we lived in Cohasset, I would get up at five in the morning in the middle of winter, put on my wet suit top and sweat pants and jog five miles. As cold as it was outside, I'd still work up a good sweat. I don't think it was the best thing for my knee. When we first got back to San Diego, Cricket and I would go to Mission Bay High School and jog around the track several times a week. Eventually, the pain in my knee became so intense that I had to hang up the old jogging sneakers.

I had two surgeries on my left knee while I worked at Sharp. The first was arthroscopic which was no big deal. The second was knee realignment and I wore a full cast for three months. Dr. John Milner, clinical head of Sharp's rehab, wanted me to detox from the pain medication following the operation. He wanted me to be a resident in the unit I was marketing. I opted to take my Vicodan (pain pills) and go home. Instead of taking one every four hours as prescribed, I took four every hour. I've always been a pig with drugs or booze. Pain medication was no exception. Dr. Schwabb, my surgeron, was familiar with my history of drug problems. I had to lie to get more pills. I convinced him they dropped overboard as I struggled to get on the boat my first day home from the hospital.

My main job at the hospital was to try and get patients. I was good at it. Although I wasn't "Joe Sobriety," I had a certain amount of compassion for drunks and addicts because I was one of them. When accessing the severity of an individual's problem, you try to determine what level of care that is needed. The worst-case scenario is that someone has to get off the street and into a residential treatment center. Some people can get by with out-patient service where they spend the day at the hospital and go home at night. Then again, some of the worst cases who couldn't afford hospitalization or didn't have the insurance, got sober in AA. A person can go through a hundred rehabs, but they will never work unless the patient wants to stop.

At Sharp Cabrillo, rehab cost $20,000 for a twenty eight-day stay. It was rare that anyone graduated in twenty-eight days. If a patient left on his or her own before being medically discharged, most insurance companies would not pay the bill. In other words, once they get you in the door, they've got you by the shorthairs. If the patient has money or good insurance that provides for extended care, the staff recommends a longer stay. In my case, they kicked me out after seventeen days when my insurance ran out.

The rate of relapse for people who work in the drug and alcohol counseling is quite high. After three years, I was getting burned out. My initial compassion was long gone. If a potential patient had the proper insurance, I would insist they enter our residential program. I knew that wasn't right. Sharp didn't have a program for teenagers, so we sent kids to a rehab in Arizona. I had a lot of success with teenagers, probably because I was on the same maturity level with them.

When a patient checked into the CARP unit, the first thing they did in the admissions process was talk with a counselor. The counselor would take a history of the patient's chemical use and check their vitals. The patient register was kept in that office. The register contained the patient's name and referral source. We got a lot of business from the Yellow Pages. My last six months at Sharp, I would sneak into the office during lunchtime. I'd erase the name of the referral and substitute my own. It reminded me of high school when Stuart Pratt and I would slide into our Spanish teacher's classroom at lunchtime. We would find the grade book in her desk and change our "D's" to "B's." That's probably why the only Spanish I know is, "Uno mas cerveza, por favor" (One more beer, please). I had come a long way since high school.

Dr. Milner left Sharp during my second year. He had opened his own treatment center in Dulzura, a small community about thirty-five miles east of San Diego. Rose Jones, who had been the Admittance Director at Sharp since 1972, left with him. The new operation was called Rancho L'Abri. It offered the most reasonable rates of any treatment center in the area. A one month stay cost $5,000 cash payment or $7,000 with insurance.

I had known Dr. Milner and Rose since 1982 when I went through Sharp's program. I liked them and they liked me. They offered me a deal if I made referrals, because many people couldn't afford the Sharp program. When I brought a patient to the Ranch, they paid me a fee. As far as I was concerned, there was no conflict of interest, but I kept the arrangement to myself anyway. Rancho L'Abri was out in the country in a beautiful setting with rolling hills. The grounds were well manicured. Flowers grew in abundance. It had a swimming pool and a small workout area. If you needed rehab, this was the place to go! Almost exactly three years after I was hired, I lost my job at Sharp Cabrillo. Nanci kept telling me that I'd get fired if I didn't conform. I kept telling her they couldn't get along without me. As usual, she was right.

I collected unemployment for a while, but that hardly made up for the salary the hospital was paying me. I missed the money, but I was glad to be out of the rehab business. Nanci was really glad. She couldn't stand the hypocrisy of the situation. It really didn't bother me. Believe it or not, whether I was sober or not, I helped a lot of people get sober. When I gave my talks on behalf of the hospital, I spoke about how drugs had dragged me down. I would say that I was sober today. I was sober the day of the presentation, but they didn't know what I had done the day before. Technically, I wasn't lying. Drug addicts and alcoholics can rationalize just about anything.

Sound New Plans

I liked to fly until I got together with Nanci. As long as the booze was flowing, flying was no problem. Flying across the country was like sitting in a bar for four or five hours. The 1973 Charger team used to smoke grass on home flights after road games. We would open the drain of the bathroom sink and the smoke was sucked right out.

I can't remember the last time Nanci got on an airplane. When we were at Telco, we would drive to and from San Diego for our three-week vacation. When I was on Good Morning America, we had another cross-country drive. Six months after we moved back to San Diego, I had to return to Boston for a speaking engagement. Nanci was going with me, sort of. I flew. She took the train.

She made me very nervous the few times we did fly together. The plane would be cruising and hit some turbulence. I'd feel her nails dig into my arm and then I would start to worry about how safe we were. Of course, I didn't have alcohol to bolster my courage. She's tried alcohol, Valium, and Ativan. None of them eased her fear. One time while flying, I took a couple of her Ativan. I didn't give a shit if the plane crashed or not. Nanci even went to a hypnotist. This guy claimed he could cure her problem after a two-hour visit. A week before her scheduled appointment, she heard on the radio that fear of flying had been removed from the list of phobias. It was now considered good common sense. After hearing that, she cancelled her appointment with the hypnotist.

Two weeks after I left Sharp, I received a call from Boston. The School Board wanted me to come back and speak at five schools. I would be compensated. Being unemployed, I accepted their offer. I would fly to Dallas with a three-hour layover before catching a flight to Boston. I took a couple of Ativan and drank about six Scotches between San Diego and Dallas. At the Dallas airport, I swilled some more booze. On the final lap to Boston, I drank some more. I was so loaded when I got off the plane, I had to go to three different car rentals before I found an agent dumb enough to rent me a car. The plane landed at 8:00 p.m.. I was going to stay at with my sister in Quincy, about twenty minutes from Logan Airport. I showed up at Mary's at 1:00 a.m.. Nanci had called several times. She was in a panic because I was so late. The only thing I remember was making a U-turn in downtown Boston and hitting a parked car. I didn't stop. I had a four-hour blackout and couldn't account for the time between the accident and my arrival at my sister's. This really scared me. I made a vow to myself that I would stop the booze.

Jim Brill owned the Deli at the marina. I got to know Jim and liked him. Nanci wasn't too fond of him. He drank too much and drove while under the influence. Sometimes he would give jobs to his out-of-work drinking buddies. They were known as the "deli bums."

One of these "bums" was Jim Callahan, an old friend of his from Los Angeles. Callahan, at one time, had made a lot of money in the clothing business. He got into cocaine and lost everything. When Brill introduced him to me, Callahan had just completed a six-month drug rehab program and another few months at a half-way house. He was a likeable guy with a good sense of humor. I could see that he probably was prosperous at one time, because he was a natural born salesman. He sold me into going into business.

The pitch began. "Brill and I started a silk screen operation and we would like you to be part of it. You know everybody in town and we think you could be a big asset to us. We'll give you ten percent of the company plus commissions on everything you sell."

Sobriety was a hard sell. I was good at that, so this would be easy. The smartest thing they did was to name the company A-1 Silkscreen. It appeared first in the Yellow Pages. Apparently everybody with a garage was in the silkscreen business. Other than the Yellow Pages idea, I wasn't too thrilled with the way they were doing things. After a few months, I switched to a more established company.

Custom Logos was an up-and-coming enterprise owned by two young guys from Boston. They had carved a nice little niche in the San Diego silkscreen market. I had nabbed a couple of their accounts when I was with Brill and Callahan, so they were more than happy to see me. I dropped by their office and explained my situation. I was hired on the spot. We all took our wives out to dinner to celebrate. After dinner, Jeff and Alan (the owners of Custom Logos) went outside. Jeff broke out some high-grade weed and the three of us got high. I thought they were my kind of guys. I worked for them about six months. Although I was pulling down my share of the sales, these guys didn't like my style. I wasn't particularly fond of them either. They were organized. I wasn't. They liked the business I was bringing in; they just didn't like how I did it. My orders were often written on cocktail napkins, business cards, anything except the proper form. I quit before they could fire me.

Organized or not, I liked this type of selling. I was a popular player when I was with Chargers. Most of the old fans remembered me and that helped a lot. The average t-shirt salesman didn't have that going for him. I mostly sold to bars and restaurants and very seldom did I have a drink in any of them. Ever since the Sharp's treatment program I had been taking Antabuse off and on. Antabuse is a drug that prevents your liver from metabolizing alcohol. Mixing Antabuse and alcohol makes a person very ill. Nanci made sure that I took it everyday. I complied for the most part, because ninety-five percent of the time I didn't want to drink anyhow. If it made her happy for me to take Antabuse, I took it. It was no big deal to me. Most drunks won't take it, claiming that it's bad for their health. If you have a bad heart and drink while on Antabuse, it could be fatal. I tried it once and would never would do it again. I hadn't had an Antause in two days and drank a half can of beer. I became violently ill. It literally knocked me to the ground. I repeatedly vomited and my head felt like it was going to explode. I have heard there are some hard-core drunks who can take this drug and still drink. I'm not one of them.

If Nanci was going out of town and I'd have a day or two to myself, I would attempt to stop taking it. That wasn't always easy under her watchful eye. I'd either spit it back in my coffee and hope it would sink or tuck it under my upper lip. Having a mustache made it difficult to determine if I was hiding my Antabuse.

I knew I could do what Brill and Callahan were doing. I could broker the shirts and hats to a good silk-screener and embroiderer. I would handle the sales and make more money.

I needed some start up money. One of my customers was my old teammate and good friend, Lance Alworth. Lance was the first player from the American Football League to go into the Football Hall of Fame. He was a successful businessman in the San Diego area. His company builds and maintains self-storage units all over the country. He's also an avid fisherman who enjoys his spare time aboard his boat in Cabo San Lucas in pursuit of marlin. I had been doing shirts and hats for Lance's company and boat since I got involved in the business. I explained my situation and Lance wrote a check for $15,000. It was agreed he'd be a silent partner. He wasn't going to be that silent, because I put his name with mine on the business card. I called the company "Touchdown Ink."

Lance was beloved in San Diego. I was notorious. What a combination. His name on our business cards would open doors that might have been closed to me. The only thing Lance wanted out of the deal was for me to do a good job on his shirts.

I learned there was very little loyalty in the silk-screening business. Most of the restaurants are interested in selling food and drinks, not clothing. For the most part, silk-screeners do the same caliber of work. The guy who charges a nickel less, gets the business. In the beginning, I had some pretty good accounts. I was doing shirts for the Chargers, Padres and the local hockey team, the San Diego Gulls. I also sold to a number of popular bars and restaurants.

Our boat payment was $1,600 a month and another $400 went for the car. I was looking at two grand a month before I made an insurance payment or put a hot dog in my mouth. I needed more cash.

I met a guy named Jerry who had just started working at the San Diego Hall of Champions in Balboa Park. He was promoting an anti-drug program for kids. Touchdown Ink would do the shirts and hats. Jerry told me how he had lost his job in the past when he got into crack cocaine. He pulled everything together shortly after that and had been sober for years. I remembered a conversation about how he drove a cab for a short time. It stuck in my mind.

I went down to Yellow Cab and signed up. When I first started, I drove four nights a week. I was a t-shirt guy by day and a cabbie at night. With Nanci picking up and delivering the shirts, at least we were getting by financially. One evening while waiting in line to turn in receipts with the rest of the cabbies, the hack in front of me dropped a small hash pipe. We became fast friends. He turned me on to another option the cab company offered.

"You can rent a cab for twenty-four hours, one day a week and make more money than you're making now."

After that, I'd pick the cab up at 4:00 a.m. Saturday, and drive until 4:00 a.m. Sunday. Nanci hated the whole cab scene. A couple of drivers had been murdered during this period. It wouldn't have eased her mind to know that I drove around with a small automatic pistol in my sock. She would have been more terrified knowing I had a weapon. I went into some of the highest crime sections of San Diego and felt more comfortable being armed. The bad guys had guns, why shouldn't I? It was every junkie's dream. Find a drug dealer, shoot him and take his cash.

I liked driving cab for the short time I did it. One day a week, it was living on the edge. I'd pick up people that nobody in their right mind would allow in their cab. Of course, they were also taking a chance riding with me. One night, I picked up five drunken sailors in downtown San Diego. I drove them to the 32nd Street Naval Base. As they were getting out of the cab, the Shore Patrol approached with a drug-sniffing dog.

"Would you please… open your trunk and glove compartment, please?"

I nearly shit my pants! I had a little bag of weed stashed under some things in the glove compartment.

"Not at all," I replied trying to stay as calm as possible under the circumstances. My head was spinning. I could imagine the headlines in the newspaper:

"Former All-Pro Arrested for Possession of Marijuana While Driving a Cab."

The strange thing was that I was more concerned about people learning I drove a cab than that I was about being in possession of marijuana.

I breathed a sigh of relief when, somehow, the dog didn't pick up the scent of marijuana. As soon as I got off the base, I pulled into the first parking lot. I twisted and smoked a big fatty. My professional driving career lasted about four months until Nanci talked me into hanging it up.

I wasn't a bad shirt salesman and could usually close the deal, but my organizational skills left a lot to be desired. I continued to write orders on cocktail napkins. Sometimes I would lose them and sometimes I would unwittingly blow my nose with them. Sometimes I'd get the printing wrong on the shirts. That pissed the customer off and it cost me money to redo the shirts. These things drove Nanci up a wall. She decided to take more of an interest in Touchdown Ink. I guess it was called self-preservation. She's not the most organized person in the world, but she's a lot better organized than I am.

Even though I was out of the alcohol and drug rehab business, I was still getting calls from people asking for advice. I usually tried to refer them to someone who knew what they were talking about. Bob Estrada gave me such a call. Bob was an old friend who owned and operated some of the finest and most successful restaurants in San Diego. Years before, Nanci had worked in one of his places. Occasionally, we would take in a movie or go out to dinner with Bob and his wife, Diane.

"Walter, Bob here."

"Bob who?" I waited for his usual response.

"Bob up and kiss my ass. What are you and Nanci doing for Easter?"

"Why? Do you want to take me to church?"

"No, seriously, do you remember Chipp?"

"The football player?"

"No, asshole, Dr. Chipp."

Actually, I did remember Chipper. Twenty years ago, we used to work out together at Maylen's Gym. He was serving his residency at a local hospital.

"Yeah, I remember Chipp. What's he up to?"

"About three-eighty. He and his wife just moved back to town from Boston. They're coming over for dinner on Sunday and we'd like you and Nanci to join us."

When we showed up at Estrada's, I realized Bob wasn't kidding about the 380 pounds. Chipp was huge! When we worked out at Maylen's, he weighed a svelte 240. I remembered him as a fun loving guy. He was ready to embark on what hopefully would be a successful career as a doctor.

On this day, Chipp seemed very subdued. Considering we hadn't seen one another in twenty years, I guess I expected a little more animation or something. Later that evening, after the Chipps went home, Bob explained that Chipper was having some drug problems. For the past two years, Dr. Chip had been self-medicating with morphine. No wonder he was subdued.

When the Chipps moved back to San Diego, Chipp's wife, Maxine, filled them in. Because I had so much success dealing with my own drug problems, they wanted me to give him some guidance to Chipp. Dr. Sweeney to the rescue.

I hadn't been to an Alcoholics Anonymous meeting since I my employment at Sharp/Cabrillo, but agreed to participate if Chipp wanted help. He worked nights at a local hospital as an emergency room doctor, so we decided to get together for morning meetings in Pacific Beach. This might even be a good opportunity for me to get my act together.

"Keep bringing the body and the mind will follow," is one of the AA sayings. It really doesn't matter what gets you there as long as you show up. Every time I told Nanci I was going to quit using, I meant it. I was always optimistic.

Chipp and I went to meetings for about a month and were getting along quite well. We had things in common besides a penchant for mind-altering chemicals. He was also from Massachusetts and had played football for Harvard. Chipp joined my gym and we started working out together. One day after a workout he came up with a brilliant proposal.

"I'll write you a prescription for sixty super-strength Vicodin and we'll split them."

Without blinking an eye, I said, "Sure."

Not only was I not going to help Chipp get sober, I was going to participate in his drug usage. It showed how much spine I had when confronted with the opportunity to get certain drugs. Besides, I had a legitimate need for a painkiller.

The chronic degenerative disorder in my knee was getting worse. When I wore shorts, people couldn't help but stare. It was really ugly. I had a bad limp and was eating Motrin by the handful. The cartilage in the knee was gone. It was bone on bone.

If I was riding in a car and we hit the slightest bump, the pain was excruciating. At night, I would sleep on my side with a pillow between my knees. Lying on my stomach was impossible. I could only lie on my back for short periods of time. My knee looked like a grapefruit was growing on top of it. Later, after replacement surgery, the doctor said it was completely out of the socket.

Nanci reminded me, "You took some serious falls on the boat when you were drunk."

I had no recall of these incidents. After some of those bouts with demon rum, I do recall it felt like I played in a football game.

Vicodin is a strong painkiller. It is one of the most widely abused prescription drugs. Junkies melt it down and shoot it up.

Thus began my Vicodin Summer. Over the years, I became infatuated with different drugs. I did acid for about a year and a half. I got into Quaaludes for about six months. Cocaine came on the scene a couple of years before I got out of football. I was never strung out and it wasn't a big deal to me. When I was with the Redskins, Donna and I stayed up all night after a game. We snorted seven grams. That was the exception rather than the rule.

The two drugs that have remained constant have been alcohol and marijuana. I've had long periods of abstinence from alcohol, but not weed.

A lot of people don't get off on drugs. Drugs make them sick, paranoid or they just don't work. They worked just fine for me. I guess I wasn't happy with the way I felt inside. It was like I was broken. The drugs helped mask the pain or maybe I just liked catching a buzz.

There were some drugs I didn't like. Speed was fine when I was playing football, but I didn't fool with it otherwise. When it wore off, I became deeply depressed. It kept me from sleeping. It also kept me from getting an erection.

I had a friend who was a former professional hockey player. He liked crystal meth. One Friday morning, at his insistence, I snorted a very thin line, about half an inch long. I wasn't drinking or partying. I left his house and went back to the boat. The drug had no effect on me. That night, I lay in bed next to Nanci with my eyes wide open. I never slept until I went to bed Saturday night.

I only tried PCP once. Tim Rossovich, one of the notorious San Diego Eight, bought what he thought was coke. It turned out to be PCP. I snorted some at a party at his house and thought I was going to die. The worst part was that I didn't really care if I lived or died. That was a new feeling, because I was still playing football. That by itself was reason for living.

Vicodin, on the other hand, worked just fine. Besides the euphoric feeling it gave me, my knee didn't hurt. I could scoot around like a jackrabbit, but you can quickly build up a tolerance to this drug. In the beginning, I was taking six or seven a day. Before long, I was up to twenty. Chipp was doing forty. We were cracking three prescriptions a week, 60 Vikes a script. I was using different pharmacies all over San Diego County. The AA meetings served as a rendezvous to either pick up a prescription from Chipp or deliver the Vikes to him.

I got to know Chipp very well and liked him a lot. However, I don't think I'd want him working on me if I had to go to the emergency room. He told me horror stories about ER doctors allowing patients die because they didn't like their ethnic background. He said some doctors just didn't give a shit. Hippocrates must have rolled over in his grave.

The few times that I wasn't on Vicodin that summer, I could feel the pain in my knee become more acute. I called Jim Otto, the Raiders Hall of Fame center. I had played in a several all-star games with Jim. He owned a couple of Burger King franchises in Northern California. I think at that time, Jim had fourteen operations on his knees. He was collecting disability from the National Football League Player's Association Pension Fund. I was seeking his advice.

I called the National Football League Players Association (NFLPA) and told them about my plight. I talked to a secretary in Gene Upshaw's office. The former Oakland Raiders great was president of the NFLPA.

"Hi, this is Walt Sweeney. I use to play way back when."

Her reply was cold. "I know who you are, Mr. Sweeney."

Most people like me until they get to know me. This person didn't like me and she didn't even know me.

"I injured my knee in 1975 and I've had several surgeries since then. I can't walk without a lot of pain and, basically, I'm a cripple."

"That's very unfortunate, Mr. Sweeney."

I could tell by the tone in her voice that she really give a shit.

"Yeah it is. What I'm trying to do is get some sort of partial disability for my injury."

"Oh, Mr. Sweeney, I'm sorry. We don't have anything like that."

She reminded me of the Lily Tomlin character on Laugh In who worked for the phone company.

"I talked to Jim Otto. He said that he was collecting money for his injured knees."

"Jim Otto has done very well for himself. I think you ought to be talking to someone in legal."

I told her to forget it and hung up. I couldn't believe the attitude this woman displayed. I had never met or even called anyone in the NFLPA before. The only NFLPA person I knew was Gene Upshaw. I gave everything I had to football. I had been recognized as one of the best players of my era. I had taken all the drugs the NFL gave me and now my union was treating me like shit. I had paid dues since 1963. I was still paying dues when I called them in 1992.

The next day, I was delivering some promo sweatshirts to a local radio station. I got their business because Paul Menard, a popular local radio personality, was a good friend and he worked at the station. I hadn't seen Paul in quite a while. He was surprised to see how bad my limp was.

I asked, "Do you know any good lawyers?"

He laughed. "The only good lawyer is a dead one."

"Seriously, I do know of one," he continued.

"Mike Thorsnes. Charlie and I tried to get him to represent us when KCBQ fired us, but he wouldn't take the case."

Paul was half of a very funny DJ team known as Charlie and Harrigan. Paul's radio name was Irv Harrigan.

I explained that I was trying to get disability benefits from the NFLPA.

"He usually doesn't do anything under 50 million, but he's a big sports fan. He might be interested."

Paul gave me Mike's phone number. I called and made an appointment for the following Friday.

Mike Thorsnes was a partner in the law firm of Thorsnes, Bartolotta, McGuire and Padilla. His firm represented some big clients and won some huge settlements. Nanci and I showed up at his office and to say we were impressed would have been an understatement. Thorsnes and company occupied the top three floors of the prestigious Fifth Avenue Financial Center. His office overlooked downtown San Diego and San Diego Bay.

I thought the initial meeting went very well. We talked about the condition of my knee and the callous response from the NFLPA. We talked about the drugs the team provided for the players.

"I've been following the Chargers for years and remember back in the seventies there was some sort of drug scandal. Tell me about that."

"Long story short, Mike, they used to pass out speed to the players. It was going on when I got there and went on for the eleven years I played for the Chargers."

"Was the policy of passing out drugs to its players an isolated incident in San Diego?" Mike asked.

"No. All the teams were doing it. We even forgot ours once and borrowed some from the Raiders."

Nanci got up and excused herself. She had heard this story before and, obviously, didn't want to hear it again. When she closed the door, I reached into my pants pocket and pulled out a fist full of Vikes. I placed them on Mike's desk.

"I need these just to walk around."

He looked at me, looked at the pills, got out of his chair and left the room. As I was putting the pills in my pocket, he returned with Nanci.

"What are those pills? You told me they were Motrin." She was pissed!

The three of us talked for another hour. It was determined that I had more problems than a bad knee. Almost everyone either knows a drug addict or has one in their family. Mike was sympathetic to the issues. He agreed to take my case pro-bono.

On the ride home, Nanci and I talked about how lucky we were that Mike was taking the case.

Then she lowered the boom. "Where did you get the pills? I know you got them from that son of a bitch, Chipp!"

Nanci didn't care for Chipp, because his wife told her about his infidelities and the mental pain he had caused her.

"He was doing me a favor. You know my pain."

"He's going to kill you! He doesn't give a damn about you or your leg! You're just a vehicle he uses so he can get drugs for himself."

"What are you going to do?" I asked.

I was stating to panic. I didn't want Chipp to get in trouble. He had two daughters in college and a son in high school. I knew that because drugs were involved, she didn't care if Chipp had a family or not. She felt he didn't care about her family.

After we returned to the boat, I took my remaining pills and went over the bridge to South Mission. I started drinking at the Beachcomber. That's really the last thing I remembered.

Later, I heard that I borrowed a bike and nearly killed myself when I crashed into the cement wall along the boardwalk. Somehow I managed to get to Dave Costa's house. I couldn't remember the bike accident. I thought I had been beaten up because of the abrasions. Dave gave me a ride to the boat. When Nanci got home, she found me unconscious. She called our neighbor, Joe Bitterman, and he came over to make sure I wasn't dead or dying. She then told him about the Vicodin and Dr. Chipp.

"Nanci, it's my duty as an ethical pharmacist to notify the DEA," Joe said.

"I don't care if you call the FBI, that's why I came to you! He's a doctor and he has to be stopped before he kills someone." Nanci was angry.

I stayed on the boat and detoxed myself off the Vicodin. My whole body and face seemed to hurt. Nanci stayed with her friend, Chris, for about a week. During this time, she called to check if I was dead or alive. She really didn't give a shit anymore. If I was dead, she wanted me off the boat before I started to smell. I would sneak up to the deli after dark to get a six pack or a bottle of wine to help with my own personal detoxification process.

By now, all the neighbors knew I wasn't playing with a full deck. I don't know why I cared, but I didn't want them to see me bringing alcohol to the boat. Although Nanci didn't call me that often, I knew she was in constant contact with the neighbors to make sure her boat was all right.

I let the answering machine pick up the calls. I only answered the phone if it was Nanci. I kept getting messages from a DEA agent. I never returned any of his calls. I wondered what would happen if they ever located all the prescriptions Chipp had written for me.

Nanci finally returned to her boat. Chipp called once and Nanci answered the phone. "If you ever call Walt again I'll leave him for good!"

I never did figure out that threat. My future of my marital status depended on the actions of someone else. At the time, I thought it best to not ask Nanci for a logical explanation.

Apparently, the DEA got in touch with Chipp, because I received a call from his attorney, Paul Pfingst. He wanted to see me and I obliged.

"Dr. Chipp has filled us in on what you two have been up to these past three months. We would like to know what your testimony would be if you are called by the DEA?"

"I'm going to say that I was having a lot of pain and Chipper provided medication for it."

"Good, we would appreciate that."

"You know that's a bunch of bullshit, right? I mean, I do have the pain, but we were splitting the Vicodins."

"Yes, we know that."

Six months later, Pfingst became the District Attorney of San Diego County. He must have done a good job for Chipp, because I never heard another word about it.

I never heard from Chipp again. His best pal, Bob Estrada, has never heard from him either.

NFL Means "No Free Lunch"

The NFLPA Retirement Board consists of six people: three former players and three representatives of the owners. These six people determine the merit of disability applications presented by former players. The Board is very tough. They think NFL stands for No Free Lunch. Many of the guys who seek disability benefits cannot afford an attorney. The Retirement Board, out of the goodness of their hearts, offers these players the use of one of the many lawyers the NFLPA keeps on retainer. Can you imagine how successful you'd be if you sued someone and used an attorney suggested by the person you were suing? I think you get the picture. These poor souls didn't have a snowball's chance in hell.

One former player told me that when his case went before the Board, a secretary from the NFLPA office represented him. She omitted pertinent information. Needless to say, he lost.

That's just one of the many horror stories former players have told me about their dealings with the NFLPA Retirement Board. Owners have been screwing the players forever. One would think that former players on the Board would have a little more compassion. I guess not.

I was very fortunate to be represented by one of the best attorneys in the country. On December 12, 1993, Mike Thorsnes submitted my claim to the Board. Simply stated, we claimed I was permanently and totally disabled because of all the drugs the Chargers had given to me. I became an addict and could not hold a job. This claim was not a very popular position and I certainly didn't come up with it. Nanci and my neighbors would agree it was true. In my mind, I didn't know if we would be successful or not. In my mind, I was just trying to catch a buzz.

Under the rules of the NFLPA, the Retirement Board must act on a claim for benefits within a reasonable time. The time period "will be deemed unreasonable" if it exceeds ninety days. If "special circumstances" require an extension, ninety more days are allowed, but in no event shall such an extension exceed ninety days. On a failure to act within ninety or one hundred eighty days, the claim is "deemed denied."

You can't knock an organization for trying to put its best foot forward, but, in my day, at least half the players were "high for the game." They were either on speed, painkillers or a combination of the two. They didn't care. Perhaps the game wouldn't be as much fun to watch if there weren't a bunch of hyped up guys smashing into each other.

The Board wanted me to be seen by a second shrink for another neutral opinion. Initially, they sent me to Dr. Jen Ken in Long Beach. He agreed with my psychiatrist, Dr. Calvin Calarusso, that the drugs given to me by the Chargers caused me to become an addict. He recommended that I was totally disabled.

Next the Board referred me to Dr. Gary Eaton. Was this a coincidence or a devious plot? Dr. Eaton and I had worked together at Sharp Cabrillo. He became director of the alcohol and drug rehab program (CARP) after Dr. John Milner left to open Rancho L'Abri.

I was somewhat apprehensive about my meeting with Dr. Eaton.

I asked Nanci, "Do you think I ought to act a little crazy for Dr. Eaton?"

"Just act the way you always do and everything will be fine."

Dr. Eaton and I talked about the days we were at Sharp. He asked what I had done with my life since then. He concurred with Dr. Calarusso and Dr. Jen Ken, but the Board continued to delay and stonewall.

I had done everything the Board requested. They wasted almost a year in a futile search for an opinion that would defeat my claim. On August 12, 1994, we filed suit against the NFLPA Retirement Plan

In December, I was waiting to hear from Dr. James St. Ville in Phoenix. He was an orthopedic surgeon who replaced deteriorated joints of former players who couldn't afford surgery or insurance. The doctor had been a halfback at the University of Oklahoma in the early 1980s. He donated his surgical skill and service. Phoenix General Hospital donated the facility. The company that made artificial joints donated their product. I don't know how many guys Dr. St. Ville helped, but I know it was quite a few.

I had sent all my records and X-rays about a year earlier. I was becoming very frustrated because I hadn't heard from him. I knew he worked closely with Gene Upshaw and the NFLPA. I worried that he wouldn't call me because of the lawsuit. I thought he, like everyone else connected to the NFL or NFLPA, was against me. One day, when I was in one of my many foul moods, I called St. Ville to get my records back.

"Dr. St. Ville's office, Sandy speaking."

"Hi Sandy. This is Walt Sweeney. Is the doctor in?"

"No, Mr. Sweeney, but I'm glad you called. Dr. St. Ville has an opening next Tuesday and I was going to call you. Do you think you can make it?"

I was stoked. For the last six years, I had put off getting my knee fixed. Nanci and I packed the car and headed for Phoenix. We planned to stay a while after the operation to participate in the rehab process. We rented a small apartment in Scottsdale on a week-to-week basis. Dr. St. Ville and Dr. Tom Carisis, who would assist in the operation, conducted a preliminary examination. They both agreed it was the worst case of knee trauma that they had ever seen.

While I was dressing, Nanci took St. Ville aside. She told him I was an addict. I never knew why this information seemed so pertinent to her. What would they do? Operate without anesthetic? I don't think so. I always thought getting a buzz was one of the benefits of surgery. I hoped Nanci hadn't ruined that for me.

The operation took longer than anticipated. I had been walking on a knee that was permanently out of joint. It disintegrated into dozens of pieces as the doctors removed it.

For the first time since I could remember, I woke up without pain. I felt great. There was no cast. I could walk, but they told me to use crutches for the next six weeks.

After three days, I was released from the hospital. There was a 14-inch scar from the middle of my thigh to below my new knee. Nanci asked if we could return to San Diego by Christmas. It was a couple of weeks away. Dr. St. Ville thought I would be ready to go home by then.

Even though my wife advised my doctor that I was a drug addict, he gave me a prescription for Percocet. This drug is similar to Vicodin, only better. I could tell Nanci was uncomfortable, because of my affinity for painkillers. I told her that she could hold and administer them if she wanted. I knew I could get them back, because she didn't want to be burdened with that responsibility. She was sure I would use them quickly and confident that I wouldn't be able to get a refill.

It was Sunday and the NFL teams were fighting for playoff spots. Nanci, the football hater, was bored to tears as I watched a game on TV. She decided to go to the Scottsdale Mall for some Christmas shopping.

As soon as she was out the door, I popped half a dozen Percocets. I had no pain, but I believed in preventive medication. In about twenty minutes, I felt good enough for a dip in the pool. Between the Percocet and the 100-degree heat, my brain must have taken the day off. It's one of those times that still embarrasses me. I carefully worked my way down the ladder and into the water. How many kids pissed in that pool? God only knows what else was in that water. I'm one day out of the hospital with a quarter inch wide, foot long wound on my leg. I didn't think germs could penetrate my incision during a thirty-second dip. Put another way, I just didn't think.

Actually, I wasn't smart enough to consider infection. After my short dip, I headed for the shower. By the time I got out of the shower, the Percs were really cooking. I walked across the street to a little bar for a couple of cold ones. It was a depressing little dump. I felt too good to stay there. I gave a guy five bucks to give me a ride to another bar that was about a mile down the road. It was more of an upscale joint. I had noticed it when Nanci and I were driving around.

I must have been quite a sight when I walked into Philly's Sport's Bar. I wore an old t-shirt, shorts, and white panty hose to keep my legs from getting blood clots. As usual, I thought I looked pretty good. I washed down about four more Percs with a cold beer. The place had a yuppie clientele who seemed to be having a good time. It reminded me of a TV beer commercial. After about three more beers, I went into my cleanup mode. This is when I stop drinking, eat some food, chew some gum and prepare myself for Nanci. Hopefully, she wouldn't return from shopping until a few hours after my last drink.

I was sitting at the bar. I had just finished a brick of onions and started nibbling on some lemon peels when Nanci walked in. How the hell did she know I was here? Although I was quite confident the onions disguised the odor of alcohol, I braced myself as she approached

"How did you know I was here?" I asked.

"When you weren't at the apartment, I went to the bar across the street. They told me you were here."

"I got hungry and they didn't have any food at the first place, so I came here."

"You're full of shit, Walt. There's a refrigerator full of food at the apartment. Have you been drinking?"

With the most indignant attitude I could muster up, I replied, "Are you crazy? Of course not!"

I thought I pulled it off, because there were no drinks or beer bottles in front of me, just a few traces of onion rings.

The bartender came over. "Could I get you a drink?"

Nanci nodded toward me. "I'll have the same thing he's having."

When he returned with a Budweiser, she walked out. I drank her beer and walked back to the apartment without my crutches. The Percocet, beers and onion rings must have caught up with me. I barely made it home before I started vomiting. Nanci told me later that she had a good chuckle while I was puking my guts out.

The next day, Nanci took off again. This time I stayed home and thought about what an idiot I had been. Then Nanci noticed a black spot on my incision. I was scheduled to see Dr. St. Ville once more before returning to San Diego. We went to his office the day before Christmas. He took one look at my leg and it was back to the operating room. Imagine how angry the doctors were. Instead of being home on Christmas Eve with their families, they had to operate on me again. After surgery, Nanci was waiting in the hallway when the doctors came out. Dr. St. Ville started to take his anger with me out on her. She would have none of it. She yelled at him about the Percocet prescription.

"He won't get a chance to screw this one up! I'm keeping him in the hospital until he's completely healed!"

Two weeks later, I was released from Phoenix General. We remained in the area for another week and a half and to begin rehab on my knee. We got back to San Diego a week before the Super Bowl.

I'm forever grateful to Dr. St Ville, the staff at Phoenix General and the company that provided the artificial knee joint. I no longer had pain or a limp. Actually, I didn't limp as bad as I had. Dr. St. Ville is a great guy and an outstanding surgeon. We have kept in touch since the surgery. Ben Davidson and I have been his guests at the Del Mar Track.

The first thing that we did upon our return to San Diego was call Mike Thorsnes. He wanted me to check into Scripps Alcohol and Drug Rehab Program. He probably thought it would help my case, but I'm sure he also thought I desperately need it. My own feeling was this would be a complete waste of time. Mike was representing me pro bono. I kept my mouth shut.

Rehab: The New Frontier

I called Scripps and arranged for an interview. The young woman I met would access my problem and determine my treatment. It reminded me of my days at Sharp when Scripps was our biggest competitor. I was on the other side of the desk evaluating people about their chemical abuse problems. I didn't tell her half of my problems, but she insisted I immediately needed to enter their residential program.

I was familiar with that game. As I exited her office, I said, "Thanks for your opinion and I will give it some thought."

I called Mike and promised to check into Rancho L'Abri the day after the Super Bowl. The NFLPA Board still had not acted on our suit, but the court took the initiative to remand. A deadline for Board action was set and the Board was ordered to pay for my rehab.

Twelve miles from downtown San Diego, Highway 94, the Martin Luther King Freeway, narrows down to a winding two-lane country road. Campo Road was dangerous. Many cars had bumper stickers that read, "Pray for me. I drive Highway 94."

I made the trip many times taking clients to the "Ranch" in Dulzura. The population of Dulzura was about 200 and they were hard to find. The only buildings were an old post office, an antique store and the Dulzura Cafe. A mile past the cafe on the right side of the road were a half-dozen mailboxes that mark the Community Building Road turnoff. To get to the Ranch, you took a right on that dirt road and drove another mile or so.

The Ranch consisted of five buildings for reception/intake, offices, group therapy, detox, and residency. Probably the most important building was an old barn with a ping-pong table and a pool table. Situated in the middle of the buildings was a thirty-foot swimming pool. This was in a beautiful setting not far from the Mexican border. Often we would see illegal aliens walking across the property. Border Patrol vehicles roamed the countryside.

The day after the Super Bowl, I packed my gear. Nanci and I headed out Highway 94. We rode in silence until turning onto Community Building Road.

Nanci finally spoke. "I hope you get your shit together here."

"I hope so, too."

I wasn't really in the mood to discuss my affliction. Then again, I never was. The only time I wanted to talk about drugs was when there was a possibility of getting some. Right now I was in a dark place. I really didn't feel like talking about anything. The idea of leaving a beautiful yacht in Mission Bay to waste time in Bumfuck, Egypt with a bunch of loons was disturbing. I had been clean for almost a month since the Phoenix incident. If it hadn't been for Thorsnes and Nanci, I wouldn't be putting myself through all this bullshit.

Nanci pulled up in front of the main building. As I was getting out of the car, Les came out of the office to greet me. He was a former biker who had worked at the Ranch for about five years. He had been sober for seven. Most rehabs had recovering addicts and alcoholics working for them: the head guy to the guy who scrubbed the floors. I had known Les from my dealings with the Ranch. He was a good guy.

"Hi, Walt. What did you think of the Super Bowl?"

"I thought it sucked."

The 49ers had just beat the dog shit out of the Chargers. Thorsnes had wanted me to check in a week earlier, but I wanted to make sure I saw my old team in their first Super Bowl appearance. I should have listened to Mike.

"Did you see it out here?"

"Yeah, Rose brought out a satellite dish."

The Ranch was so far out in the sticks there was barely any TV reception. There wasn't any cable.

"Les, could you give me a hand with some of this stuff?"

In addition to my clothes, I had an electric knee machine that worked the range of motion on my new titanium knee joint. I also had a stationary bike and a pair of 40 pound dumb bells. Rose had allowed me to bring the bike and the knee machine. The weights were my idea.

After we put everything in my room, we went back into his office. He went through my luggage and shaving kit looking for any mind-altering chemicals.

"I've got to keep your aftershave lotion. You can come in here and use it."

I gave him an incredulous look.

"Hey, you'd be surprised what these people drink if they get their hands on it. I caught one gal drinking hairspray. You don't have any hairspray, do you?"

"I'll tell you something, Les. If I'm going to drink anything, it's not going to be any hairspray or cologne."

I had heard about people doing this, but I would never sink that low.

There were about twenty addicts in residence when I arrived. They were people of all ages from all walks of life. There were alcoholics, coke addicts, heroin junkies, crystal meth freaks and prescription abusers. There were a couple of gals that weren't into chemicals. One was a self-mutilator. The other was bulimic. The Ranch could cure everything.

Smoking was not permitted in the main building, so people hung around the front entrance to get their nicotine fix. After I got squared away with Les, I went out front for a smoke. One of the first people I saw was a guy I knew from the 20/30 Club back in the early 1960s. For the sake of anonymity, I'll call him Ralph. He was from a wealthy San Diego family. He had a problem with the sauce.

Ralph had tickets for the Super Bowl. He was going to Miami to root for the Chargers. He even sent $400 to a Palm Beach Country Club to secure a tee time for golf. The night before he was to leave for Florida, he ran out of booze. That's a simple problem. You drive down to the liquor store to replenish your supply. Ralph was driving too fast and misjudged a corner. He smashed into a parked car and kept driving. The police stopped him a few blocks from the incident. He attempted to give the policeman some money to let him go. They got him for drunk driving, hit and run and attempted bribery. He had several priors and had wrecked a bunch of nice cars. While his case was pending, his family insisted that he entered rehab before he killed himself or someone else.

I don't think I ever knew anyone who entered rehab on his or her own volition. I'm sure they're out there, but I've never come across them. There's usually pressure from a spouse, an employer or, in my case, a lawyer.

Although I hadn't used in a while, I was still treated as a detox patient and could not participate in the normal schedule. After detox, the men would move out of the main building and into male quarters. My assigned room was known as the Eric Show Suite. Show had been a successful pitcher with the San Diego Padres. He was a highly intelligent guy, an accomplished classical guitarist and a heroin addict.

One night, he slipped out of the Ranch and crossed the border at nearby Tecate. He bought several grams of heroin, put it in balloons and swallowed them. His intention was to return to the

Ranch, defecate and recover the heroin. The balloons burst in his stomach. He died in the room that would be my home. He should have put the heroin in his pocket or underwear and just walked back across the border. I had walked across that border many times. I had never been searched or saw anyone else get searched.

The extra bed in my room was removed so I would have room for the exercise equipment. Instead of moving up to the men's lodgings, it looked like I'd be staying in this room because of all of my equipment. There was a relatively low number of patients. I liked the idea of not sharing a room with anybody. January was usually a good month for rehabs because of New Year's resolutions. This was the time of year when people with bad habits vowed to kick them, but 1995 was an unusually slow month. In past years, the Ranch was always maxed in January which was about a dozen more residents than we currently had.

I was more than happy to stay in the Show Suite. I was close to the kitchen and got to know the cook. When I was in my first rehab, I became friendly with the cook. He would bonus me with extra food.

Caffeine was taboo at the Ranch. The thinking was that patients, especially speed freaks, would sit up all night drinking coffee and shooting the shit. I used to get a kick out of people who would sneak in real coffee. Family or friends would bring it on visiting day. You would think that they were smuggling hash across the Turkish border. I couldn't tell the difference between the real stuff and the decaf. I had done some powerful stimulants during my football days. Caffeine wasn't going to do it for me.

The Ranch had several counselors besides the therapists. They were recovering people and "wannabe" therapists who kept an eye on the inmates. If someone wanted to take a walk around the grounds, they would accompany them. They were wet nurses who drove us to outside AA meetings, did bed checks, conducted exercise sessions. These people had been sober for a couple of years. That was something I hadn't been able to put together. They were usually Rancho L'Abri alumni. I liked all of them except one asshole named Greg.

Because of the proximity of my room to the kitchen, I would slip in during the morning for a cup of real coffee with the cook. I wasn't after the caffeine. It was just a lot closer than the coffee pot in the dining room. One day Greg busted me and reported it to Rose. No one said anything to me, but my friend, the cook, got called on the carpet. Greg was always doing little chicken-shit things that got on my nerves. Because of my surgery and prior business relationship with Dr. Milner and Rose, I was allowed a certain amount of latitude. When I checked in, I told Rose I needed to walk two miles a day for my knee. She allowed me to do this by myself. I think it irritated Greg that I was able to slide, so I guess that made us even.

Detox consists of laying around and eating for five days. I remember laying in bed one morning, hooked up to my knee machine and wondering how I ever got into this spot. Alcohol and drugs had sure fucked up my life. In turn, I had done a number on all the people I had ever cared about and some I didn't care about.

Remember in the movie, *On the Waterfront*, when Marlon Brando says, "I coulda been a contender?" As I lay in bed, I thought about what could have been.

A lot of people, including Al Davis and Sid Gillman, said I should be in the Hall of Fame. The closest I ever got was in 1992 when Al Davis invited me to his induction in Canton, Ohio. The plane was full of former Raiders. I think I was the only ex-player who never played for Al's team. In my eleven years with the Chargers, I played against the Raiders twenty-two times during regular season games. I must have made an impression for Al to include me in the festivities. Among some of his other guests, to name a few, were John Madden, Jim Otto, Ben Davidson and George Blanda.

Al Davis was truly a remarkable man. When I first met him, he was an assistant coach under Gillman with the Chargers. After that, he became head coach of the Raiders, Commissioner of the American Football League, and finally, president and owner of the Oakland-Los Angeles-Oakland Raiders. He's a renegade owner. He took on the NFL in court; won some and lost some. Ask most of his former players and they will tell you that he is very loyal to the guys who gave it their all. I have always admired Al Davis.

Back to my coulda, shoulda, woulda mode, as the machine worked my knee, I felt overcome by a wave of depression. I usually didn't engage in this retrospective-type thinking. I believed in Satchel Paige's philosophy: "Don't look back. Someone might be gaining on you."

Perhaps, had I looked back and examined my life, I wouldn't have made the same mistakes over and over. Then again, probably not.

Not all the counselors were a pain. Gary was a good guy and my favorite member of the staff. He was a recovering crystal meth addict who gained 200 pounds after he kicked the habit.

Gary confided in me, "Walt, when I was using, my ultimate goal was to knock off an armored car." He had a great sense of humor, but was a walking heart attack because he weighed almost 400 pounds. He was an outspoken proponent of AA. Whenever he preached the program to me, I jumped all over him about his weight. That would usually shut him up. They say once you're addicted to something, you're always addicted. Most addicts have compulsive personalities. When they get off drugs, they can turn that compulsion into a positive addiction such as exercise. Gary switched from speed to food.

This was the Monday to Friday routine at the Ranch:

7:00 a.m.	breakfast
8:00 a.m.	meditation (dining room)
9:00 a.m.	lecture (therapy building)
10:00–12:00 a.m.	group therapy
12:00 a.m	lunch and free time
2:00–3:00 p.m.	lecture
3:00–4:00 p.m.	group therapy
4:00–6:00 p.m.	free time
6:00 p.m.	dinner
7:00 p.m.	AA meeting (in house or outside meetings) five or six people would be chosen to go to San Diego for a meeting.
11:00 p.m.	lights out

The counselors would come around to everyone's room and remind them of the various meetings. One morning, when I first got to the Ranch, I was laying in bed hooked up to the knee machine and someone knocked on the door.

"Come on in," I responded.

"Walt, there's a lecture in five minutes." It was Greg, my favorite staff member.

"I've got another 45 minutes on this." I grimaced and pointed to the machine.

Greg walked away shaking his head. That excuse was good for a couple of missed lectures a week during my early stay.

One morning, I heard someone yelling outside my door. "God damn it! There's no soap in these rooms! I'm calling Master Card and canceling!"

I thought to myself that we had a disgruntled newcomer. I grabbed an extra bar of soap and went out to meet the unhappy customer. He was in the room across from mine. I knocked on the door and walked in. A gentleman in his early seventies was standing in front of the mirror trying to comb his disheveled hair.

"Hi, I've got some extra soap."

"I've been here half a dozen times and it's always the same old shit. There're several basic, common-sense things these idiots fail to provide and soap is one of them."

I liked the old fart already.

I held out my hand and introduced myself. "My name's Walt Sweeney."

"The football player?"

"The ex-football player," I replied. He smiled as we shook hands.

"You probably don't remember me, but I was your next door neighbor when you had an apartment out by State College. You had a cute baby girl and you two were in the swimming pool all the time."

"Wow. That was a while back. That was my rookie year with the Chargers."

"That's right and I was young lawyer who had just moved here from Boston."

I didn't remember him, but said I did. Bob was a retired municipal court judge who had visited the Ranch more than once. He was definitely a member of the CIA (Catholic Irish Alcoholic). The judge had long periods of sobriety (14, 10 and 6 years), but he went on a good toot and his friends shanghaied him during the middle of the night. They brought him to the Ranch.

During one of his sober stretches, he helped draw up the charter for Ranch L'Abri. Bob had a bad ticker and shouldn't have been drinking at all. Of all the people I met at the Ranch—and I met quite a few during my seven-month stay—the Judge was my favorite. I took all my meals with him. He stayed about a month, which was about average, but he checked back in before I got out of there. He had a condo about five minutes from my boat. When we were both on the outside, we attended AA meetings together.

The Judge and I had different therapists, but our group therapy rooms were side by side. Because of his hearing problem and his rather vocal way of asserting himself, my group would have a good laugh when we heard him on a roll.

One day at the swimming pool, he embarrassed the shit out of me. I had just gotten out of the pool and was lying down. The Judge was sitting in a chair next to me. Right next to him were two gay guys from his group. In what seemed to be his louder than usual voice, he gestured toward the gays and said, "I don't know what they see in hairy assholes."

I felt like diving under the water and staying there.

The Ranch was like Betty Ford without the celebrities. We had relatives of celebrities. When I first got there, Ross, a ne'er-do-well brother of a rock and roll icon, had been there for several months. He was always asked to speak at AA meetings because he knew just what to say. He could cite passages from the Big Book of Alcoholics Anonymous. I wasn't surprised to learn that he was banging this cute little blond patient on top of the washer in the laundry room.

During my time at the Ranch, I saw several trust fund kids come and go. There was Nick, the son of a TV and movie star. He was getting blowjobs on a regular basis from some of our young lady patients. Ron was the son of a best selling author. Like the Judge, he had been at the Ranch many times. He was always looking for chicks to take care of his "hog." Then there was Joe, whose father was one of the greatest boxing champions of all time. So much for celebrity relatives.

I think everybody is a little crazy in their own way, but I think alcoholics and addicts are crazier than most. The Ranch had their share of crazies. One gal, a long-term resident, carried a Teddy bear everywhere she went. She insisted that everybody call the bear by its name. Bear Woman told me she had once got it on with a German Shepard. She complained that the dog got off, but she didn't.

While riding in the ranch van as we approached downtown San Diego for an AA meeting, she said, "Walt, do you see that green house on the side of the hill over there?"

"Yeah."

"I pulled a seven-man train there." She thought I would be impressed.

"You've given me much more information about yourself than I ever needed to know," I said seriously.

Another patient, Laura, was a pretty girl in her early twenties from Los Angeles. She was tall and slender, a model type. Her arms were covered with scars where she cut herself with knives and razor blades. I guess self-mutilation is an addiction, too.

Sometimes, I thought I was the only sane person in the whole place. My therapist was Edwin, a black gentleman from the West Indies. He was the best therapist at the Ranch. The tough nuts were assigned for him to crack. He had a lot of insight about alcohol and drug problems. Edwin helped many people get on the road to recovery.

Twenty-eight days was the usual stay at the Ranch, but I was going to be there much longer. After a month, Rose agreed to let me go home one night a weekend. Nanci would pick me up after the Saturday morning AA meeting and bring me back on Sunday evening for dinner. This usually wasn't allowed and Edwin was opposed to it. I went anyway. They always tested for drugs when I returned. I passed all the tests, because, at that point, I was obeying all the rules. I did everything I was told to do.

After for four months, I was pronounced "cured" and discharged.

The day after my return to the boat, I talked with Rhonda Thompson, one of my attorneys. From the beginning, Thorsnes assigned my case to Rhonda and she did all of the research and legwork. You've heard of beauty and brains. Rhonda had both. She was very passionate about my case. Professionally and personally, she knew what she was talking about because she was married to Denver Bronco offensive tackle, Broderick Thompson. She was going to be well versed in my case because someday, Broderick might have to deal with the NFLPA.

One of the lawyers for the NFLPA, in a very convoluted conversation, told her that I wouldn't be eligible for any benefits if I was sober. This was very disturbing.

Around 11:00 p.m. that evening, I got out of bed and left the boat. I walked down to South Mission Beach and stopped at several bars along the way. I went to a drug dealer's house to snort coke and drink for the rest of night. I became nasty and psychologically abusive, so she called Nanci and pleaded with her to come and get me out of there. Nanci and the Judge picked me up and took me back to the Ranch.

When she pulled up, Les came out of his office. "What do you want us to do with him?" Nanci said, "For all I care, you can take him out back and shoot him."

Thus began three more months of rehabilitation. I was in pretty bad shape and they sent me to Grossmont Hospital. I stayed for three days and have no recall of going to the Ranch or the hospital. While in the hospital, I had a brain scan. It confirmed a brain was in my head. Actually, the machine showed some old scar tissue on my brain. The doctor said it indicated that I had a stroke, probably during my football playing days.

I thought about my dealings with the NFL while I was in the hospital and realized it was a big mistake. My wife and lawyers were extremely pissed at me. Before I left the boat that night, I had been laying in bed thinking about my situation and the conversation with Rhonda. In the first place, asking the NFL for disability benefits on the basis that they made me a drug addict wasn't my idea. Originally, I was trying to get some sort of compensation for my injured knee. Whether I agreed with the premise that I became a drug addict wasn't important. We filed the lawsuit and that was that. It seemed the NFL would pay me if I used drugs. If I didn't use drugs, I wouldn't get paid. Some might say my thinking didn't make any sense. It made perfect sense to me.

When I returned to the Ranch, I was given my old room. This time there was somebody in it. My roommate was Jose, an ex-con in his early thirties from the LA area. He'd spent ten years in the slammer and it looked like he pumped iron for his entire sentence. Jose was about 5'7" and all the girls thought he was really handsome. Crack was his drug of choice. He was at the Ranch to kick the habit. I liked all the residents at the Ranch and Jose was no exception. I guess as addicts, we all had a common bond.

Confusion best described my state of mind when I returned to the Ranch. I had been clean and sober for five months. I was actually enjoying it, but now I was back at ground zero. I couldn't get the lawsuit out of my mind. Was it true the NFL wouldn't pay me if I was clean? If so, why was Mike Thorsnes so adamant about keeping me in treatment?

After a couple of days, Jose broke out some weed. Before smoking any, I emptied three small shampoo bottles, the kind hotels provide with conditioner and soap. I filled them with my clean urine. If you smoke marijuana on a regular basis, it can stay in your system for a couple of months. If you only smoke it once in a while, residue will only last for a few days. I did a lot of coke the night I left the boat, but that's out of your system in 72 hours. The marijuana would have been gone, too.

So with a small bottle of urine stuffed in my jockey shorts under my nuts, I was ready. We didn't have any rolling papers, so we improvised. Every morning, I'd twist a huge joint with a piece of the wrapper from the toilet paper. Jose said that's what they used in prison. We would get up at 6:00 a.m. and toke up as we walked out to the end of Community Building Road to pick up the morning newspapers. The lady who cleaned our room must have thought we had major bowel problems, because we used toilet paper up the wazzoo.

I enjoyed these morning walks. They helped prepare me mentally to face the daily rigors of the Ranch. It was a great way to start the day: an invigorating two-mile walk, a big fatty, a big breakfast, sometimes two breakfasts.

Once, a coed named Kate joined us, She had a thing for Jose. I was pissed, but tried not to show it. Her presence meant I had to get through the morning without getting high.

Jose had a business partner named Casey who drove down every Sunday from LA to visit him. I never did ask what their business was. I figured that if he wanted me to know, he would have told. One afternoon, Jose got a call from Casey. I could tell he was upset when he returned to the room.

"What's the matter?" I asked.

"Somebody is trying to extort money from my partner."

"What can you do about it? You're stuck here."

"Tonight, after twelve, Casey is picking me up and I'll be back before sunrise."

"Are you sure you want to do this?"

"I don't have a choice. These people have been fucking with us for a long time. We have to take care of them."

This sounded ominous to me. I didn't pursue it further. The less I knew, the better I'd be. When Casey showed up, Jose and I shook hands. I wished him luck. I never saw him again.

The next morning I twisted up the last of the weed and headed out to get the newspapers. I was about a hundred yards down the road when Kate came running toward me. "Walt! Walt! Wait for me."

What the fuck did this broad want? I told her, "Jose's gone."

"I know. He called me this morning. Do you mind if I walk with you?"

"I guess not. I've got this joint I'm going to smoke and if you say anything about it, I'll tell everybody you were sucking Jose's dick."

She started to cry and promised not to mention the weed.

Once a week, all the residents and therapists attended a community meeting to discuss various problems at the Ranch. Kate blurted out that she and Jose were having sex. I lost my leverage, but fortunately, she kept her mouth shut about the marijuana. I wasn't too crazy about this broad, but went out of my way to be nice to her. You never knew when one of these loons would fall apart and take you down with them.

Shortly after that, I moved to the men's quarters. My new roomie was Jack, a 42-year old attorney from Newport Beach, who was addicted to coke and hookers. Jack had been at the Ranch for two months and was about to be going home. I liked living there better than the main building. It offered more privacy and I got to know the guys better in our off hours. I didn't have to contend with all the counselors who hung out in the main building.

I now had a new therapist. Edwin retired and moved to Puerto Rico where his wife was supervising the construction of their new home. I was going to miss him. He seemed to have the ability to cut through my bullshit and get to the root of things that were bothering me. I could bullshit most people, but not Edwin.

Dave Katz was his replacement. He had a Jewish name, but looked like an American Indian. Dave had worked at the Ranch before, but left to go into private practice. He was a nice guy and we got along fairly well. He was into sports and had dealt with athletes in the past. The Chargers sent one of their star linebackers to the Ranch during the eighties. I'll call him "Buck." He lived in Atlanta during the off-season where he was repeatedly busted by the Georgia cops for possession of crack cocaine. Buck spent several months at the Ranch. Katz had done a good enough job with him that he was able to resume his career and play for a couple of more years. The last I heard, Buck was serving a life sentence in a Georgia prison for vehicular homicide.

Rehabs are a good way to get started on the road to recovery. It's the easiest way, actually. You're in a controlled environment. You are told what to do and when to do it. It's difficult to use alcohol or drugs around a bunch of drunks and addicts without being detected. The true test comes when you're released.

I had been through their twenty-eight day program six times and hadn't learned shit. I knew what they were going to say before they said it. The first four months, I was, more or less, interested in getting sober. When I was sober, I enjoyed it. My wife has always said that I have the "brain of a piss clam." I always seem to prove her right. I had been there for four months, went home for a couple of days, and had to come back.

At this point, I had completed my second month since returning. I felt that you had to use drugs just to stay there that long. Once in a while, Dave Katz would push my buttons. I'd scream at him and walk out of group. I'd be back at the next session like nothing ever happened.

The forty-minute drive to San Diego for the AA meetings was cutting in on my ping-pong time. As a matter of fact, I was the ping-pong champ of Rancho L'Abri. Usually the person who was there the longest was the best. I'd been there so long, there wasn't any competition for me.

I got another new roommate. He was a thirty-year-old guy named Jerry. When his father died, he left Jerry with a half million dollars and several houses. The kid had too much money. He blew it on crystal meth and old Ford Mustangs.

At this point, a recent graduate of the Ranch was bringing marijuana from San Diego on a regular basis. He saw Dr. Milner once a week for therapy. Don was his name and rock and roll was his game. He was a guitarist in a local band. It paid to have good relations with the other patients.

I started to think of the Ranch as my permanent home. I'd see people come and I'd see them go, but I never left. I became the unofficial greeter. Of course, I was stoned most of the time, but no one ever knew it. Maybe everyone knew it.

My roommate Jerry was an obnoxious little prick. He loved to talk about all his money. When Don brought the weed, I made sure that Jerry paid for it. One time, I tipped Don a hundred bucks. No problem.

Tuesday night was alumni night at the Ranch. Some of the former patients, usually the recent graduates, would join us for an AA meeting. They shared how they managed in the outside world. One of the alums returned, not for the meeting, but to see a girl he'd been boinking while in residence. There was an old abandoned wooden sauna beside the swimming pool. This guy and his girlfriend romanced in the sauna and left a pipe can with some remnants of marijuana.

The next morning at our 9:00 a.m. lecture, it was announced everyone would be tested. One of the counselors found the can and assumed it belonged to one of us. Of all the nerve! I wasn't worried, because I never went anywhere without my little bottle of urine stuffed into my crotch.

The tests were being done in alphabetical order. A name was called. The men went into the restroom with a male therapist. A female therapist accompanied the women. Only one restroom was used for testing.

While waiting my name to be called, I perused the morning paper. I looked down and saw a huge piss stain in my tan shorts. Apparently, my bottle cap wasn't screwed on tightly. Most of the urine leaked out.

"Son of a bitch!"

I stood up, covered the stain with my newspaper and beat feet to my room. I quickly changed shorts, replaced the leaky bottle with a full one and grabbed an extra for my roommate. I was making a cup of instant coffee when Dave Katz came barging into my room.

"I was wondering why you took off so quickly."

He looked relieved when he saw it was coffee that I was after.

I joked, "I was having caffeine withdrawals."

I returned to the testing area with Dave and slipped the extra bottle of urine to my roommate. Tom Kennedy entered the restroom with me. Tom was my favorite therapist. He had a great sense of humor. I had known him for years and remembered a story he told us about when he was still drinking. Apparently he got so loaded one night, he showed up at home wearing his underwear over his trousers. How do you explain something like that? His wife wasn't too happy. With my back to Tom, I poured some of the urine from my shampoo bottle into the vial. Jerry and I passed with flying colors.

Unlike Jerry, I was always very cautious when I smoked weed at the Ranch. I had to threaten Jerry with bodily harm to get him to stop smoking marijuana in our room. There were acres and acres of woods and the stupid shit didn't have enough sense to go outside to smoke. I took charge of the "bag." I wouldn't let him smoke any unless he was with me. Jerry took Jose's place on the morning paper route. He was in my group and, more often than not, he was still high at 10:00 a.m. when our therapy session began. He would sit there with a shit-eating grin on his face and start giggling.

One day, I had to go to San Diego to see my attorney. I left the "bag" with Jerry. There was an old, dilapidated barn about a hundred yards east of the Ranch property toward the Mexican border. Jerry went out there to smoke a joint and was followed by one of the counselors. I had warned him about this place, because there were no windows on the side facing the Ranch. You were unable to see if anyone approached from that direction. Sure enough, a counselor walked in while he was sucking on a joint. By the time I got back, he had been shipped to another rehab in Newport Beach. I lost my roommate, but more importantly, the "bag" in one fell swoop.

A guy named Leo was a technical engineer at a local TV station. His boss gave him an ultimatum to either do something about his drug problem or lose his job. One Saturday afternoon, when most of the inmates were poolside, Leo made the short drive across the border to Tecate. He bought some "soamers" at a farmacia. So-called Somas, sold over the counter in Mexico, are like a poor man's Quaalude, a downer type pill. When he returned, he took a few. Then he grew paranoid and buried the rest of the pills in the vegetable garden. He came up to me after lunch that day.

"Walt, I'm just terrified that I'll get caught with these soamers. Will you hold them for me?"

"I'd be more than delighted." I was being truthful.

That evening, a woman named Jill who had been there for about three weeks was threatening to leave. She was in my group. Jill was addicted to prescription pills, mostly downers. She had a string of doctors all over San Diego who wrote prescriptions for her. Her husband and parents were at the Ranch, trying to dissuade her from leaving. They weren't having much success. Jill was adamant. I was having a smoke in front of the main building when she carried her bags to her parent's car.

To nobody in particular, I asked, "Could I try talking to her?" Her parents, her husband and a couple of counselors looked at me.

Her mother responded, "Yes, by all means, please,".

"Jill, could I talk to you for a minute?"

"You might as well, everyone else has put their two cents in."

"Let's go into your room." I followed her into her room.

"I'll give you a couple of "soamers" if you don't go."

I could tell by the way her eyes lit up that she knew what they were.

"This has to be kept between you and me," I confided.

"Okay, I promise." She was like a little kid getting her favorite candy bar.

I gave her the pills. She went out, got her bags and returned to the room. She gave me a big hug and I told her I'd see her in-group in the morning.

When I went back out front, her parents and husband treated me like some kind of hero.

"What did you say to her?" her mother asked.

"Sometimes, addicts can relate to each other on a gut level. They can help each other in certain situations that doctors, spouses or even parents cannot"—especially if they have a pocketful of pills.

With those words of wisdom, I made a hasty retreat before my story could be subjected to further scrutiny. Wisely, Jill's family took off before she could change her mind.

Who Wants To Be a Millionaire?

In August 1995, we won the first round in our legal battle with the NFLPA. The following is a news release from Associated Press:

San Diego (Aug 16) The NFL was ordered to pay 1.8 million in disability payments to former San Diego Chargers guard Walt Sweeney, who contended the league pushed drugs on him and helped turn him into an addict.

Lawyers for the Bert Bell/Pete Rozelle NFL Retirement Plan indicated they would appeal the decision by U.S. District Court Judge Rudi M. Brewster.

"If this ruling stands, it could open the door to other suits against pro football's $400 million pension and disability fund," legal experts said.

"This could affect every retired player who has a disability or may have one," Sweeney's lawyer Michael Thorsnes said after the ruling was announced.

The NFL player's union has been paying Sweeney $1,827.00 a month since 1990, doctors determined his drug use, and alcohol use made him incapable of holding a job. The sum is the minimum benefit allowed for disability unrelated to football.

Sweeney, 55, claims his drug addiction was directly related to the game because coaches and trainers for the San Diego Chargers gave him amphetamines before games and sedatives to bring him down afterwards.

The former All-Pro guard played in the NFL from 1963 to 1976.

"I have accepted my responsibility in all this, I hope they (NFL) will accept theirs," Sweeney said from Rancho L'Abri Rehabilitation Clinic where he has been a resident for the last six months.

"There are a lot of guys like me out there, that they did this to. If I win, besides helping myself, I'd be helping a lot of other people."

In his ruling Tuesday, Brewster said the NFL was responsible, contributing to Sweeney's drug problem and that he should receive the highest payment for football related disabilities. "That amount will climb to $12,670.00 a month", said Rhonda Thompson, another lawyer for Sweeney.

Sweeney's lawyers sued for the higher benefits after Thompson learned of them from reading her husband's collective bargaining agreement with the NFL. She is married to Denver Bronco's tackle Broderick Thompson, who played with the Chargers from 1987–1992.

Thompson was a premier offensive tackle and an excellent pass blocker when the Broncos released him after the 1996 season. Since I knew Rhonda, I watched him play on TV a couple of times and thought he was pretty good. After the season, Broderick was told he'd be retained for the 1997 campaign.

On Valentine's Day, Rhonda was driving to work and heard on the radio that Denver had released her husband. That was the only notification they received. Some people, including myself, think he was cut because Rhonda was my lawyer. When a player is waived, he's notified before the press or anyone else. In Thompson's case, they didn't have the common decency to let him know at all. You be the judge.

After we won the first round, the media jumped all over it. I became the poster boy for old screwed-up players. *The Real Sports* TV show with Bryant Gumbel came out to the Ranch. They were doing a show about Dr. St. Ville and interviewing some of the guys he helped. When we won in court, the focus of the show shifted from the good works of Dr. St. Ville to my case.

My old pal, Billy Lenkaitis, called from Boston. After a long successful career with the Patriots, he had become a dentist and invested in a couple of bars in the Boston area.

"Hey, Walt, remember getting shot at in Kansas City?"

"That's the only thing I can remember about KC."

"We've all been following your case and I have a favor to ask of you. My daughter, Jamie, is engaged to John Tully, a sportscaster for Channel 7 in Boston. Is there anyway he can fly out there and interview you?"

"If it's okay with the people that run this place, then it's fine with me."

I liked Bill and his wife Donna, so did Nanci. When we lived in Cohasset, we saw a lot of them.

With Rose's permission, John the sportscaster, came to the Ranch and interviewed me for the folks back home.

Nanci rode out from San Diego with Jamie and John. The girls had lunch at the Dulzura Cafe while John came to the Ranch for the interview. After it was over and John left, I was headed toward my room when Dave Katz intercepted me.

"Greg (pain-in-the-ass counselor) said he was driving past the Dulzura Cafe and saw Nanci out back hiding in the bushes."

I wasn't sure if this was a joke or what. As I was waiting for the punch line, I realized he was serious.

He continued, "She's undermining your sobriety."

He was pushing the right buttons. "Are you out of your mind?"

I was irate to say the least. Nanci was the last person to ever hide from anyone and why should she? The nerve of him to say something like that to me.

"Just stay the fuck away from me!" I stormed off to my room.

Seven months at the Ranch had done me a lot of good. I was still the same raving maniac I had always been.

A producer from *60 Minutes* called and said Mike Wallace wanted to do a segment about my lawsuit with the NFL. He told me that now Mr. Wallace only did six investigative reports a year and he selected mine to be one of them. They wanted to come to the Ranch to tape the story. Wow! I finally made the big time, even if it was in rather dubious fashion.

I told him that I would have to talk with the head honchos, Dr. Milner and Rose. The decision would be theirs to make. It turned out they were fed up with the interviews and felt the coming and going of the radio and TV people was too much of a distraction to their program. They did not want *60 Minutes* at the Ranch.

I thanked them for their consideration and called CBS to advise that I could not grant the interview. Actually, I really was glad it didn't come off. There's a big difference between doing a magazine or newspaper article or even a local TV show, but *60 Minutes* is the most widely watched program on national television. There was just something about telling so many people at one time that I was a screw up that didn't appeal to me.

Besides the distraction issue, Rose and Dr. Milner apparently thought I was having too much fun as a media darling. Maybe I was, but it did give me the opportunity to expose the injustice and indifference of the National Football League Players Association. This might help other guys who found themselves in a situation similar to mine.

Dr. Milner thought my calm and cool reaction to their rejection of the Wallace interview was a sign that I was on the road to recovery. I knew there would be a few more detours along the way.

I had one more task at the Ranch. I had to find some clean urine from somebody that I hoped was sober. I thought I was one of the very few dope smokers, but what did I know? Everyone could have been doing it. I wasn't really paying that much attention.

My next step in the pursuit of sobriety would be to move to a halfway house or a sober living environment. I opted for Bethesda House which was owned by Dr. Bob MacFarland, my friend and co-worker at Sharp Cabrillo. He was also involved with the Ranch. Now that I was working my way back into the real world, I would try to quit smoking weed. They had spot drug checks at Bethesda and I would need at least thirty days to get my system clean. I wanted to be prepared which explains the need for clean urine before I left the Ranch.

As things turned out, I was able to spend a week aboard *Touchdown* with Nanci. I really didn't want to go to Bethesda. Nanci and I were getting along better than we had in a long time and I felt I had a better chance to remain sober on the boat than in a house in the ghetto. Well, it wasn't exactly in the ghetto, but it was as close as I wanted to get. Nanci, Dr. Milner, Dr. MacFarland and my legal team all agreed that I should be in residential treatment.

Bethesda consisted of ten cottages located a few blocks east of downtown San Diego. My cottage already had two residents: Irish and Tom. I had known Irish since my Sharp Cabrillo days when he was in the alcohol rehab outreach program. He was in his late sixties, but looked a lot older. The ravages of alcohol had taken their toll. He was sober now and had been living at Bethesda for six years. The average stay at one of these places ranged from a month to a year. Irish was the resident assistant manager.

He was an ardent Notre Dame football fan and traveled once a year to South Bend to watch "The Fighting Irish" play. He was a funny guy with a good sense of humor, but a terrible bigot. He didn't like me watching Seinfeld on TV, because most of the cast was Jewish. He didn't like Howard Stern either, but that didn't make him all bad.

Irish and I shared a large room in the front of the cottage. Our beds were on opposite sides of the room with a couch, stuffed chair and coffee table in the middle in front of the TV set. There was a tiny kitchen and a bedroom in the rear where Tom slept. Tom was in his forties. I liked him. He had been there for about six months and was thinking about moving in with his girlfriend.

Irish was on a fixed income. Once a week, he would open up "Rosie O'Grady's" and tend bar from 6:00 a.m. until 10:00 a.m. on the morning shift. Rosie's was one of my old t-shirt customers. Tom worked at a super market and had to be there at 4:00 a.m. every morning.

Nanci usually picked me up for lunch and we'd spend the afternoon together. Every evening, there was a mandatory meeting at Bethesda. The only excuse for absence was work. I didn't have a job, so Nanci would return me in time for the meeting. This wasn't a bad setup as long as I could spend some time with my wife, but there were days when she had other things to do. On those days, I'd put on my Walkman and hit the road for a long walk.

The manager of Bethesda was a Mexican gentleman named Ignacio. He went by the nickname of Nacho. I could tell from the first time I met him that we were going to have problems. He was about 5'4" and wished he was a foot taller. Bethesda was his realm. I got the impression that he thought that I was some sort of a threat to him.

There was a small workout room in the back and sometimes I would get stuck in there with him. The little motherfucker rubbed me the wrong way. I was a former professional athlete who had been working out for my entire adult life. He had the audacity to tell me how to lift weights. After Nacho lifted, the little rooster would pull off his shirt and strut around the courtyard like he was "Mr. Universe." It used to piss me off, because I knew I was "Mr. Universe." Oh, to see ourselves as others do.

Nacho had been a high school teacher for a long time, but lost his job when he developed a crystal meth habit. Nacho had been sober for several years, but he was always in a pisser mood. If that was how sobriety was supposed to be, I didn't want any part of it. As I look back on it now, managing a houseful of drunks and addicts would probably put anyone in a bad mood.

One day, he told me to come to his office for a drug test. I went by my room and picked up a small bottle of urine from my shaving kit. I'm glad Irish hadn't gone through my kit looking for shampoo.

A week later, Nacho called me to his office when the results came back from the lab.

"Your test shows that you've been drinking."

"Impossible. They've made a mistake."

"There is no mistake. I've been following you when you go for your walks. I've seen you go into bars in the neighborhood."

"Have you ever heard of coffee, asshole?"

I was fuming! I was pissed at the guy at the Ranch who gave me the alcohol-laced urine. I was pissed at Ignacio for confronting me.

He told Dr. Bob, but the doctor told him that if I had been drinking, he wouldn't need a test to confirm it. That was the end of it. I'm not sure Bob really believed that, but I was glad He didn't bounce me from Bethesda. Bob and I were friends when we were at Sharp Cabrillo Hospital. He had even asked me to be on the Board of Directors at Bethesda. During that same period, I also sat on the Board of the San Diego Mental Health Association. The five-member board met at 7:00 a.m. on the first Tuesday of every month. Half the time, I didn't know what they were talking about. The other half, I thought about whatever could have possessed them to ask me to be on their board. I had absolutely nothing to contribute.

When asked why I was interested in being a board member, I think I said something like, "I have a brother who's mentally ill and I think my main reason for being here is to find out what's available out there for people that don't have the means for psychotherapy or analysis."

That was more or less all I had to say. Fortunately no one asked for anything more.

While at Bethesda House, I did have a few days when I would walk about two miles to the Office Lounge bar. There were at least a half a dozen bars in the neighborhood. No one knew me from Adam. I'd drink about six beers. During my walk back to Bethesda, I'd stop at Jack in the Box to scoff down some grease. I loved fast food hamburger joints. By the time I got back to Bethesda, no one was the wiser. Sometimes I would sneak a pint of vodka in the house. It wasn't an urge for alcohol, but more an act of defiance. No one was going to tell me what to do, especially some guy called Nacho. The lights had to be out by 11:00 p.m., but TV was OK. While watching the eleven o'clock news, I'd take my first swigs of the vodka. Irish needed a nose like Nanci to smell it from across the room. I didn't do these things very often, but as I look back, I'm amazed I did them at all.

Rob, who was my last roommate at the Ranch, came by Bethesda and picked me up. We went to one of the nearby bars for a reunion of sorts. For some unknown reason, we started drinking something called Jägermeister. I don't even know how this stuff was classified. At any rate, I was busted when I returned to Bethesda.

Ignacio told me that I would have to leave the premises at once. If I detoxed for three days, I could return. Actually, it sounded like a pretty good deal at the time. I'd take the weekend off, return for another two weeks and then leave of my own accord. Around 1:00 p.m., I called Nanci to tell her of my misfortune. I asked her to pick me up.

"I'm not going to pick you up and please don't come to the boat."

What the fuck did she think I was going to do? I had very little money and no car. I left Bethesda and walked about a mile and a half to an all-night diner. After a hearty breakfast of bacon and eggs and several cups of coffee, I was ready to start the eight-mile trek to the boat. Four hours later, sweating like a pig, I climbed aboard *Touchdown*. At 4:00 a.m., Nanci was sleeping quite soundly.

I grabbed her ankle and announced, "Life as you know it, is about to change!"

I sat on the floor and passed out. The next morning she drove me to a cheap motel on Midway Drive, about ten minutes from the boat. She gave me enough money for the weekend and told me to go back to Bethesda on Monday. This was even better than I could have hoped. I could drink for a couple of days without restrictions, sober up Sunday night and return to Bethesda on Monday.

I called Rob. He picked me up at the motel and I spent the weekend at his house in Coronado. It was a nice way to go. We ate well, drank a lot of beer and watched football in some very comfortable digs.

On Monday, I returned to Bethesda and stayed a few more weeks. Nanci took me back. Between my stays at the Ranch and Bethesda, I had been gone almost a year.

Rocking the NFL World

Nanci wasn't quite as happy as I was. As a matter of fact, she was downright hostile. She was still upset about me being bounced from Bethesda a few weeks ago. Besides, she had been living by herself and doing things her way for almost a year.

Once or twice a week, I would go to Bethesda to visit Irish and take in an AA Meeting. I knew it was time to move on when Irish asked if I wanted my name on his Christmas cards: Irish and Walt.

Time heals and Nanci and I began getting along. We always got along if I wasn't drinking, drugging or lying. I'd go for three months and, just like clockwork, I'd lift a cup or smoke some weed. She'd be pissed for a couple of days. I'd repent. I must have said "I'm sorry" to that woman a thousand times. If the *Guinness Book of World Records* had a category for the sorriest "sorry sons of bitches," I'm sure my name would be right up there near the top.

Nanci has stuck by me through thick and thin and it's been mostly thin. She's one of the most loyal people I have ever known. I'd like to think that I'd be all right if she was gone, but the truth to the matter is I probably wouldn't. I know I would miss her with all my heart and I'd probably start drinking and wallow in my own self-pity.

In January 1997, three days before the Super Bowl, Federal Judge Rudi M. Brewster granted us a second Summary Judgment. The following comprehensive article by Luke Cyphers appeared in the February 3, 1997 issue of the *New York Daily News*.

AWARDED WITH A FUTURE RULING
FOR SWEENEY PUTS BLAME ON NFL

SAN DIEGO Walt Sweeney is asked to recall the low point in his drug-fogged life, and before he can say anything, his wife, Nanci, interjects, "Low point? Which one?"

It might have been his last day in professional football in 1976. The 6-4, 255-pound, all-pro guard, paranoid about his imminent release from the Washington Redskins, emptied six shots from a revolver into his bunk at training camp.

Or it could have been the suicide attempt a few years after his 14-season career ended. He was found crawling in a snowbank after downing a quart of Scotch and 30 Seconals sleeping pills that had been constant companions since his rookie year with the San Diego Chargers in 1963.

His lawyers think the worst came later, in the early 1990s, when Sweeney, during his shift as a cab driver, combed San Diego's worst neighborhoods with a pistol and a plan. "It was the ultimate junkie's dream, I guess," Sweeney says, in his gravelly, somewhat nasal voice. "I was gonna come across a guy who'd just done a dope deal, with a lotta money, and I was gonna shoot him and get the money and the drugs."

Drugs drove Sweeney, now 55, to the edge of oblivion, like so many other 1960s casualties. But Sweeney's woeful tale is different. Pro football, he says, put him on the path to addiction, joblessness and near-helplessness. Two weeks ago, a federal judge agreed.

In a case that has rocked pro football and once again dredged up one of the most sordid chapters in the sport's history, Sweeney was awarded $1.8 million in benefits and attorney's fees from the NFL's pension fund. Southern California federal district court judge Rudi Brewster ruled that drugs given to Sweeney by Chargers employees in the '60s led to a lifelong habit that has left him "unemployable" and "totally and permanently disabled."

Brewster's ruling stated that the NFL's "practice of furnishing drugs to players to maximize their performance and resistance to pain caught a player who may have been unusually susceptible to chemical dependency," and that "when (the league) creates a tragedy such as that shown by substantial evidence in this case, the Retirement Board may not turn its back on the player who is injured by the practice."

The response of the league and the NFL Players Association was immediate and vehement. The Retirement Board plans to appeal, and league and union officials are telling anyone who will listen that Sweeney deserved the partial pension of roughly $1,800 a month that he had been receiving, but no more. Certainly not the $16,670 a month he will receive beginning in March.

"Substance abuse unrelated to football is being characterized the same as a player being paralyzed during a game," said Doug Allen, assistant deputy director for the NFLPA. "This ruling is insulting to a player like Darryl Stingley."

Thus has the debate been framed for talk radio and tabloid TV. Sweeney, who admittedly contributed to his own demise by continuing his "poly-drug habit" after his playing days, is set off against Stingley, who in 1978 was rendered a quadriplegic after being rammed head-on by Oakland Raiders safety Jack Tatum in an exhibition game.

But the Sweeney story goes deeper than that. His case has resurrected the tawdry 1973 Chargers drug scandal, when it was learned that coaches, trainers and physicians dispensed steroids and speed like M&M's.

The revelations led to bans on the use of stimulants and steroids, new rules for team doctors and the NFL's current drug-testing policy.

But in Sweeney's eyes, the scandal didn't end there. He couldn't break the pattern of his team-aided drug use, and wandered through the aftermath of his playing days an addled shell of a man, a casualty of the NFL's Sunday warfare.

He feels betrayed by the Players Association, which fought against his receiving additional benefits. "The NFLPA is all for the modern-day player," he said. "They forgot about the old guys who paved the way for free agency and the way it is today."

The story laid out in his lawsuit, unchallenged by the Retirement Board, is the stuff of an Oliver Stone movie. And in fact, "Oliver Stone came out last Friday and talked with us," Sweeney said. "He's interested in doing a movie about the drug problems in the NFL."

Sweeney grew up in Cohasset, Mass., part of a family with a history of alcoholism. A court document states: "There was a history of alcoholism in his father's family and all his brothers save one were or are alcoholics."

Sweeney's father was killed by a drunk driver when Sweeney was 2 years old and "every coach I ever had I looked up to as a father figure. I would do anything for these guys."

That determination, and his size and agility, earned him stardom in high school and a scholarship to Syracuse, where he became an All-American playing with stars such as Ernie Davis and John Mackey. He was the Chargers' top pick in the 1963 draft, beginning a career as one of the best offensive linemen of his era. He also began a career as a drug user.

During his first training camp, the Chargers strength coach, Alvin Roy, demanded players take "special vitamins," or face a fine. The pills turned out to be Dianabol, a steroid.

Also readily available were amphetamines, sitting in lockers and in training kits. Wanting to fit in, Sweeney took 20 of the little orange capsules before his first preseason game, made a bunch of tackles on kickoff teams, and got sick. But he never again played a game without the benefit of speed.

"They masked pain, gave you a little extra juice in the fourth quarter, and made you feel good," Sweeney said. "I broke a shoulder during a game and didn't know it until 20 years later."

But coming down after games grew difficult. Of course, the trainers had an answer: Seconal, or "reds," a sleeping pill. Gradually, it took more amphetamines to get up before a game, and more Seconals to relax.

By the early 1970s, the Chargers team psychiatrist, Arnold Mandell, told Sweeney to smoke marijuana to take the edge off the speed leading the then-30-year-old into the world of illegal drugs for the first time.

When the Chargers scandal broke in 1973, Sweeney was fined by the NFL for using drugs, and was traded to Washington. There was a drug culture there, too. Sweeney says Redskins coach George Allen once told the team, "If it takes amphetamines to win, I will bring it in by the truckload."

The beginning of the end came in 1975, when Sweeney blew out his knee. Not surprisingly, drugs played a part.

"Joe Theismann threw an interception, and I was so hopped up on speed, I took off running after the guy with the ball. I got clipped and got hurt," Sweeney said. "I needed surgery that night, but because of all the drugs in my system, they couldn't operate for three days."

He missed the rest of the season, tried to rehab in San Diego, and came back to training camp the following year. But the knee wasn't right. He could barely run, and Allen placed him on injured reserve status, "which was very fuzzy at the time in my mind anyway. A lotta things were fuzzy about then. They didn't tell me they were gonna pay me for the season, and I was worried about money. One night, I was just in a state of confusion. I took this gun I had in the car up to my room and put the six rounds into my bed."

The Redskins turned him loose the next day. His career over, Sweeney was on his own, with nowhere to go. "I couldn't get a decent job because I couldn't hold a thought," he said. His first marriage ended.

For three years, he hung around a San Diego beach, living off a worker's compensation award. "I'd get up and fire up a joint around 6 in the morning, watch cartoons and wonder about what I'd do the rest of the day."

He moved to Boston in 1980, but things soon fell apart. He taught school, and was let go. He worked a fishing boat, and was fired. He tried to kill himself.

He moved again, opening a bar in San Diego. It failed. A second marriage, to Nanci, nearly failed, too. Her mother was dying of cancer, "and when we'd go to visit her, it was a race to the medicine cabinet" for her mother's painkiller prescriptions.

He tried rehab, but left after 23 days when the insurance ran out. Still, his exit was greeted as a success. A news story about his release generated work as an anti-drug speaker. The fact that he was still using didn't deter him.

His only "successful" period was 1984–90, when he held two jobs given to him by Chargers fans. He was fired from both.

The '90s were even worse. His debt reached six figures. His career as a cabbie never netted that hoped-for drug dealer.

Desperate, he tried filing for an NFL disability benefit for his knee. But when he went into lawyer Mike Thorsnes' office and pulled a handful of Vicodins from his pocket, Thorsnes said, "I told Walt he had bigger problems than just his knee."

Examined by physicians and psychiatrists, Sweeney was found to suffer from "impairments in his cognition, memory and spatial orientation" and was "unable to sustain employment."

Based on those evaluations, he filed for a total and permanent disability benefit stemming from his football-related drug abuse.

The Retirement Board comprised of three owners and three ex-players maintained Sweeney's drug abuse wasn't covered under the highest benefit classification. The board denied Sweeney a chance for new disability benefits worked out in the 1993 collective bargaining.

The board said Sweeney's condition deserved a partial benefit. The case went to federal court, and Sweeney's attorneys, including Rhonda Thompson, the wife of Denver Broncos lineman Broderick Thompson, mounted a convincing case that Sweeney's current addictions stemmed from the Chargers' introduction of drugs into his system, and that his disability was "total."

During a final hearing, NFL attorneys argued that Sweeney's addiction wasn't football-related. "There's no blow," the NFL's William Hanrahan told the court. "There's no trauma."

Brewster, a Republican appointee known as a conservative, countered: "There is a blow…

It's still an intrusion into his body by the narcotics. And they put that into him."

Curiously, the NFL lawyers provided very little evidence of their own before the court, and challenged none of Sweeney's. The league probably could have isolated Sweeney by showing dozens of ex-Chargers who didn't end up unemployable.

And not every Charger took amphetamines. Ron Mix, a friend and former teammate of Sweeney's, said he never took speed. "I thought it was cheating," he said.

But the decision went Sweeney's way, perhaps indicating that his tough times are changing.

After an extensive rehab program, he's been clean and sober for nine months, and he hopes the award can help pay his considerable debts.

Since the decision, Sweeney says he's heard from dozens of other ex-players who've had problems similar to his. So the fallout from the NFL's bad old days may continue.

"In my day there wasn't drug testing," Sweeney says. "Back then, they tested the drugs on us."

A similar article appeared in the October 1997 issue of *ICON* magazine and is excerpted below:

Two years ago, Walt Sweeney, who was the former first round pick, and who in fourteen seasons with the San Diego Chargers and Washington Redskins started in 154 consecutive games and appeared in nine Pro-Bowls, stepped forward to claim in a land-mark lawsuit that the NFL made him a disabled drug addict, the first such suit ever filed by a player. Originally, he only wanted money promised him by the NFL›s Pension Plan for his surgi-cally replaced knee. But he grew to believe he was entitled to more. Sweeney sued the NFL and the NFL›s Player›s Association, which jointly administer the National Football League pension fund, charging that his thirty plus years of drug addiction was a direct consequence of playing professional football and for his pains he was due compensation.

"There are hundreds of guys out here like Walt," says Hall of Fame wide receiver Lance Alworth. "There is a wide spread addic-tion problem among retired players. If it's not pills then it's booze. Walt's the first guy to step forward and say that the league did this to him."

Rhonda Thompson looked at the NFL's disability plan, and it appeared to her that along with payments for his knee, he was eli-gible for additional disability benefits because his drug addiction was football related.

The league didn't agree, insisting that Sweeney's addiction was not the result of a collision during a game or practice, he was ineligible for the Supplemental Disability Plan, which would have paid him $156 thousand a year. The NFL and the NFL Player's

Association did not dispute that Sweeney was given copious amounts of addictive substances. During the various hearings and motions, the league's lawyers instead argued that Sweeney's injury was mental illness and the pension fund did not address mental injury. When the Judge didn't buy that, the league's lawyers took a different tact, asserting that because drug addiction is a disease, it is a pre-existing condition and is therefore not covered by the Supplemental Disability Plan.

"The NFL Player's Association is primarily concerned about active player," says former Pittsburgh Steeler, Steve Coursen. "They don't want to hear about problems retired players are having. NFLPA Executive Director Gene Upshaw has a good deal, a two million-dollar salary, and who voted him in? It's not retired players like Walt. It's active players, that's who. Ask them and they will tell you the union's great. Ask them again in twenty years and see what they say."

Retired players' claims are routinely denied, often without explanation.

"They use what's called the pencil test," says Thompson.

"If a player can stand on the corner and sell pencils he's not disabled."

Sweeney had asked the union several times for benefits, only to be dismissed on each occasion. Call after call went unreturned.

"You just get fed up after a while," Sweeney says.

"I wanted some money for my knee, not the addiction, and the secretaries over there treated me like some sort of pest."

"We're in the business of granting benefits to players who deserve them, not the players who do not, Upshaw (whose office didn't respond to interview requests for this story) has said several times that Sweeney's law suit threatens the existence of the pension fund.

"That's ridiculous," says Thompson. "That's a half a billion dollar fund."

The irony is that if the league had offered Sweeney payments for his knee, he would never have thought to sue.

"All I've been asking for all along is fair treatment," Sweeney says shaking his head.

"All my lawyers asked for was benefits I was due, prejudgment interest on that, and attorney's fees. I didn't seek punitive or compensatory damages. I wanted what was fair. The league did this to me, so the league has to bear responsibility."

"They never argued the drug issue," Thompson says of the NFL's defense. "They never disputed that the drugs were highly addictive, that they made Walt take them, and he is addicted now as a result of that."

Other contemporaries of Sweeney, including Upshaw, who played in the same era, point out though the drugs were available, not everyone took them and not everyone got hooked.

"The average guy didn't have a choice," says Alworth. "He had to take them. But not everyone you give drugs to will become an addict. Walt's just unlucky."

'He was exactly what you wanted if you wanted a football player: a lunatic. He wasn't good for anything else. They should have shot him when he came off the field that last time,' Nanci Sweeney says bitterly."

The law firm of Thorsnes, Bartolotta, McGuire and Padilla would reap a million dollars worth of publicity from the ensuing media blitz.

Rhonda and I were scheduled to appear on *Good Morning America*. Our segment would be done from the Thompson's house, which was a huge mansion. Broderick had bought it for an investment. On one side of the house was a small movie theater, on the other was a well-equipped gym. The cameras were rolling when they asked Nanci and me to walk down a few steps. I felt like I was descending the staircase of Tara. Mike said that the next time we did an interview, it should be in less elaborate digs.

Shortly after that, Rhonda and I appeared on "Court TV" with Johnny Cochran. We never saw Johnny or his co-host Nancy Grace. They were in a studio in New York and we were in a room at San Diego State. Rhonda was doing most of the talking and doing a great job as usual. Then Nancy Grace started on me. I could see Cochran and Grace on TV monitors. Grace, somewhat sarcastically, said, "Mr. Sweeney, do you expect us to believe that you are the innocent victim in all this?"

"My family is the victim. I have taken responsibility for taking the drugs, but the NFL has to take responsibility for providing them."

Then I went into a diatribe about how the drugs the NFL gave caused me to lose my family, my self-respect and drove me to a suicide attempt.

I guess my outburst caught Ms. Grace off guard, because she was temporarily speechless. Applause could be heard in the control room from the New York feed. Apparently they rarely saw Miss Grace at a loss for words.

For the first couple of months following Judge Brewster's decision, Rhonda and I made the rounds. All of the evening network newscasts, *Hard Copy, Good Morning America, Hello, San Diego.* There was no way we could do every interview requested. There were authors who wanted to write my life story.

The headline of a *New York Times* article (April 13, 1997) was emphatic, "Painkillers in N.F.L. Are Part of the Game." The story addressed current drug dependency and withdrawal symptoms including Green Bay Packers quarterback Brett Favre's seizures from Vicodin. It was estimated that ten percent of the players in the NFL were addicted to painkillers. Of course, the league claimed it was dealing with the issue.

It was my fifteen minutes of fame. After a few months, my story became old news. Nanci and I resumed our somewhat unexciting life aboard the boat.

We decided to sell *Touchdown*. This was an easy decision for me, but real tough for Nanci. It was her boat and her dream. I was happy to get off the boat and into a house or apartment with cable TV. I wouldn't have to walk a half-mile to the shower. I hid my enthusiasm. I put the boat for sale with Argo Yacht Sales, a company that just moved into the marina.

When Nanci was growing up, she spent many of her summers at Lake Tahoe. Her friend, Barbara Caruso, had recently moved to Reno. She bought a house and also bought a cabin at Lake Tahoe. Nanci had visited Barbara several times and had rekindled a fondness for the Lake. The few times I accompanied her to Tahoe, I was blown away with the incredible beauty of the place. We loved San Diego, but felt it was time to move on. Lake Tahoe seemed very inviting.

The sale of the boat was emotional for Nanci. She agreed to let me handle it, because she didn't want to be around potential buyers or boat brokers as they discussed the sale. One a weekend, when a "live one" was coming back for a second look, Nanci headed north to visit Barbara. I was left to my own devices. My only commitment was to show the boat on Sunday afternoon. I called Linda, Dave Costa's ex-girlfriend. After Dave moved out, she dabbled in drug sales to make a little extra money. Once in a while, I scored a little weed from her. She liked to play golf, so I met her at Mission Bay Golf Course, a par three course not far from the marina. I really didn't want to play golf. I was only interested in the weed in her pocket.

We had a beer at the outdoor cafe and, unbeknownst to me, our boat neighbor, Pam Bitterman, was there with her kids for a golf lesson. She saw me having a beer with Linda and called Nanci in

Nevada. Nanci had asked her to call if she saw anything suspicious happening on *Touchdown*.

"Hi, Nanci. This is Pam."

"Is everything alright?"

"I was picking the kids up at Mission Bay Golf Course and I saw Walt with another woman."

"Was he drinking?" (Didn't she care that I was seen with another woman?)

"He was drinking beer."

I shot the breeze with Linda for about thirty minutes and returned to *Touchdown*. Nanci called and told me about her conversation with Pam. We had a huge argument and she hung up on me. I went up to the deli and started pouring the beers. The more I drank, the madder I became. For Nanci to learn about me having some beers was no big deal, but the implication that I might be fooling around drove me up a wall. I had been a real asshole at times and a lousy husband, but I never cheated on her.

By the time I worked my way back to the boat, I had completely lost it. As I approached the Bitterman's boat I started screaming.

"I'm going to kill you, you nosey motherfuckers!"

I was beside myself. At the time I couldn't comprehend why anyone would call someone 700 miles away to relate what they perceived as bad news. I continued to rant and rave for the next few minutes. Before I knew it, the cops were there. Instead of arresting me, they took me to detox. I was very grateful.

Detox was about twenty cots in half of a large downtown building. The other half was small offices and meeting rooms where the Volunteers of America conducted their seven-day alcohol rehab program. It is one of the only free rehabs in San Diego. A few years ago, I was taking drunks to the same place. Some of them even remained sober.

I had to stay there for at least four hours. I tried to catch some shuteye, but was still full of rage. At 6:00 A.M., I was allowed to leave. I took a cab to the marina and picked up where I left off by screaming at Bitterman's boat. The cops were there in a matter of minutes and escorted me off the dock.

"Listen Walt, (we were now on a first name basis) do you think you can stay away from here for a couple of days or until everything cools down?"

"Absolutely officer. You won't hear another peep from me." I was grateful these guys gave me another break and my anger subsided.

Now I realize that Pam acted out of concern. I'll be forever sorry for the way I behaved on the docks that night.

I got in the car and made a five-minute drive to the Ocean Beach Motel where I resided for the next several days. My car didn't move. The room had everything I needed: TV, bed, shower and a small refrigerator to keep the beer cold. When I got tired of being with myself - which usually didn't take long - I'd go on a walking tour of the three or four bars in the neighborhood. After three days, I was running out of money and checked out. Nanci made sure she took the checkbook and credit cards with her.

I was on an alcoholic binge and not ready to cut it loose yet. I figured I had about two more days in me and drove down to South Mission which was just ten minutes away. I parked my car in the amusement park lot and walked to The Beachcomber. My old pal Ponto was behind the bar.

"Ponto, is Steve around?"

Steve Billings owned The Beachcomber. We had been friends for years.

"He's in the office. He should be down in a minute. Jesus Christ! You look like you've been on a good roll."

"Just having a few beers and taking a little break from the boat."

"I heard that," Steve said as he entered the bar.

"Do you need a place to stay? The penthouse is available."

The penthouse was a three-bedroom condo Steve owned across the street from The Beachcomber. Ponto and Weasel, both bartenders at The Beachcomber, lived there. Both were stone alcoholics.

"I guess one more drunk wouldn't make a difference."

"Thanks. That'll work. I also need a tab."

"No problem," Steve said. I continued on my bender which turned out to be my last. When I got sick of The Beachcomber, I went across the alley to The Pennant and used my tab there.

Nanci knew I was on a roll. I imagined all my neighbors at the marina knew it, too. I really didn't give a shit what my neighbors thought or knew. They weren't going to be my neighbors much longer. The one person I didn't want to find out about my bender was Mike Thorsnes. Mike wanted me sober more than he wanted to win the lawsuit. One of his cronies spotted me in The Beachcomber and immediately went to the pay phone. I knew he was calling Mike.

A few days later, my suspicions were confirmed. I told Mike the whole story. I also told him that we received an offer on the boat and were moving to Lake Tahoe. He was delighted that we were moving. He thought the change would be good for both of us. I hoped he was right.

We sold the boat and moved to Lake Tahoe in June of 1997. It's a place of majestic beauty; it has a powerful feeling of spirituality. When I said that was my last bender in San Diego, it was. I've had beer and a little weed since then, but it's been few and far between. I was sober for over two years. I wish it was some sort of spiritual awakening, but the fact of the matter is that I just got tired of fighting it. Before I cut the booze and drugs loose, I spent most of my time lying or trying to hide my use. I was one devious son-of-a-bitch. Life wasn't a "bed of roses," but I was able to cope with problems instead of blanking them out with chemicals. It was like being fully awake after being semiconscious for years.

While at the Ranch, two of my brothers died: Bobby at the age of fifty-three, and Jimmy at sixty-five. Donald was sixty-nine when he passed away six months after I left Bethesda House. Their deaths saddened me. They made me think of my own mortality. I've stumbled through more than half my life and I hope to conduct myself with some dignity with the time I have left. Nanci has been through a lot of hell with me. I'd like to be the kind of person that she can lean on. So far in our marriage, I've done the leaning. She must be exhausted from holding me up.

For the most part, our time in Tahoe was good. I liked hitting the garage sales and once bought a book title *The Gladiators*. I liked this passage: "Every player has his own way of getting ready," (the Chargers offensive line coach Joe) Madro says. "Sweeney has so much natural ability that he doesn't need to do what a man of lesser ability may have to do. I used to coach Sweeney, and I know he hates to study. But I also know he'll be ready to play when I need him."

The NFL appeal date finally arrived. In June, Nanci and I drove down to Pasadena to the Ninth Court of Appeals. Thorsnes hired Sanford Svetc of from Landels, Ripley and Diamond to handle the appeal. Frank Rothman represented the NFL. I was disappointed that the usual hired gun from the NFLPA wasn't there. At our last court appearance, he had the shakes so bad that I knew he could relate to my drinking problem.

Rothman showed up with eight other attorneys. It was the old story of the little guy bucking big business. Each side had twenty minutes to present their case. When it was over, Svetcof, Nanci and I felt very good about how it went. The three panel judges would revue the information and make a decision in three to six months.

In November, my sobriety was put to the test when Svetcof called to informed us that we lost. Basically, the judges said that the NFL could do what they wanted to do. We were stunned at first. Everyone said we couldn't lose. The NFL didn't present any new evidence. Those people underestimated the power of the NFL. It is all-powerful and far-reaching.

Two days after we heard the news, I wrote a letter to the three judges. Their names were Hug, Fitzgerald, and Mazerky. I expressed my disappointment in their decision. I told them that they not only let me down, but hundreds of other former players who needed help.

I should have written, "I am in the process of writing a book and your chapter is going to be called *Three Chickenshit Judges.*

The At Long Last, Last Chapter

Before the appellate court decided our fate, Nanci and I would drive around the lake to look at homes for sale. After we lost, we drove around the lake looking for a room to rent. Losing the case bothered me for a while, but not for long. My immediate gut reaction was rage. I wanted to expose these people. I'd go to the press with details of the investigation my lawyers had uncovered about the practices of the NFLPA. I'd make all kinds of accusations. I had proof about what had happened to me. Over the years, whenever I've felt mistreated, my first reaction is always revenge. I can't help it, I'm Irish.

In the meantime, I had borrowed money from friends that I couldn't pay back. I also had to reimburse four months of stipulated treatment and $5,200 for each monthly payment the NFLPA made while my case was pending appeal. I didn't want to give the corrupt bastards a nickel, but I didn't have a choice. They're like the government. They controlled my pension and helped themselves until everything was paid off.

I was broke. I decided to write a book. I knew it would be a best seller and I had to make some money.

In 1999, I learned that Syracuse University selected me for their all-century football team. I may have been named to the team, but the school forgot to tell me about it. The headline of the feature story in the *Syracuse Post-Standard* sports page on November 5, 1999 was: "A Century of Stars." Bud Poliquin's column is adjacent to the "Century of Stars" story. His headline: "Sweeney's memories a bit grim."

Sitting out there in his Lake Tahoe home, he hadn't heard a word about Sadie's Place and the bloody mayhem seen on Halloween morning. Truth is, Walt Sweeney rarely keeps up with Syracuse football scores anymore, never mind the street fights involving his alma mater's athletes. So, when he was told about the knifings of David Byrd, Duke Pettijohn and Giovanni DeLoatch, Sweeney seemed to sigh into his telephone receiver.

"We've come a long way," he said, "haven't we?"

Forty years earlier, Sweeney had been an SU freshman who was drawn to the university from his Massachusetts high school because he liked Ben Schwartzwalder, the flinty Orange coach, and "because the drinking age in New York was 18." And upon arrival, the kid quickly impressed everybody with his performances on the field as a two-way lineman and in the saloons as a two-fisted pounder of anything alcoholic.

There was no Sadie's Place back then. But there was the Clover Club. And so much of what Sadie's Place was five days ago, the Clover Club had been 40 years earlier.

"It was right down at the bottom of the hill," Sweeney recalled Thursday. "It had been an old house, and in the basement there was a bar. You could get a beer for a quarter and a T-bone for $1.25, and that's where all the football players hung out. They'd cleared the place out a few years earlier before I got there. You know, it was theirs.

"That's where we'd always go. To the Clover Club. We kind of overran it. I remember there were rock fights out front. There was some racial stuff with people in the community. There was a stabbing in my freshman year. It was pretty wild."

Wild then ... wild now. Which means that, no, we haven't come such a long way at all.

He is a member of SU's all-century team that will be honored peior to the Orangmen's noon affair in the Carrier Dome against

Temple on Saturday. And Walt Sweeney, now 58 and a budding author with an artificial knee and an aching shoulder, is properly deferential.

"As I understand it, they picked 44 guys in the memory of Ernie Davis because 44 was Ernie's number," Walt said. "And any time I'm mentioned in the same breath as Ernie, I am very, very proud. He was a great guy and a great athlete."

So, of course, was Sweeney, who was an All-American at Syracuse before playing 13 professional seasons during which he never missed a single game for either the San Diego Chargers or Washington Redskins. He was a great guy and a great athlete...and a virtually hopeless drug addict. And now, Sweeney has written the first draft of his autobiography, "Off Guard," in which he includes mad tales of his times in Syracuse, the old AFL, the NFL and beyond.

"I'm not writing this as a celebrity, because I'm not a celebrity," Walt said. "I'm just a washed-up football player, an old man. I played a million years ago in a small market. But, hopefully people will read it and learn how things really were back in the '60s and '70s."

The book, which Sweeney has been reworking every morning for the past three weeks or so, is basically a litany of the man's near lifelong experience with booze and drugs—both before and after the Clover Club. Sometimes funny, but more often unsettling, "Off Guard" is 292 pages of mostly sad chronicling.

"I'm surprised I remembered as much as I did," said Sweeney, who spent too many of his days, weeks and months in hazes that cost him a marriage, another longstanding relationship, connection with his two children, fistfuls of dollars and countless job opportunities. "There's a lot of grim stuff in the book. I'm going to try to lighten it up."

Too, like every writer, he's going to try to make a buck on it. Having spent six years pursuing a lawsuit against the NFL Players

Association—a suit that would have provided him compensation in the form of a lump sum of more than $ 1 million and as much as $16,000 a month for life—he ended up without a dime. Oh, Walt, who believes the NFL is partially responsible for making him drug-dependent and therefore unemployable, initially won. But the NFLPA, so very powerful, claimed victories in the appeals process last year. And now, this former Orangeman is a would-be author.

He won't be at the Dome on Saturday. Because SU authorities were not able to track him down until just this past Tuesday, Walt Sweeny—who dislikes flying—could not commit to a trip east on such short notice.

"But," he said, "I'd love to be there. It would have been great to see the old guys."

Instead, Walt will remain in Lake Tahoe where he will continue laboring on his book, attempting to get the thing just right. The man wants to nail it, Clover Club and all. This all-century team is a great honor, sure. But it won't make the fingers dance across the keyboard. And, right now, that matters more than a humble wave to the crowd.

It was during this time, while writing extensively about my adventures and misadventures in San Diego that Nanci and I both became homesick for sunny Southern California. We decided to leave the cold and snow and return to perpetual summertime in San Diego.

I took a job driving elderly folks to doctor's appointments and the grocery store. I enjoyed many interesting characters from all walks of life. Among those who stand out in my memory was a little (4'10") lady doctor from Texas. She'd bark orders like a drill sergeant. She'd yell if I put her groceries in the wrong place. Her antics didn't bother me, but I didn't forget her, either.

I remember a 92-year-old Jewish man who sold mannequins in New York. He knew a lot of show business people in New York and LA. He was a colorful character who told great stories. I can't even recall his name, but he was a nice man.

There was another very nice lady who lived in North Park. She was from Holland. I'd take her shopping and to the eye doctor. She was a very sweet, old lady. She'd say, "There's nothing wrong with me, but I can't see and I have trouble walking." She didn't like living like that. I was impressed with her sense of dignity.

The price of gas got too high. The job didn't pay that much in the first place, but it kept me busy. I realized that the less activities I had, the more time I had to think about some of my unhealthy habits.

Where did I go wrong? As a kid, I was a hall monitor and an altar boy. I became a scholarship athlete who shined in college and the pros. Maybe playing games for half of my life was a contributing factor in my inability to grow up? The game of football became my life. I gave the game all I had to give.

I appreciate all the coaches and writers who say that I belong in the Pro Football Hall of Fame, but I take pride in the following quotes from great defensive linemen I faced.

"Mean Joe" Greene said, "I never have the troubles with other guys that I do with Sweeney. He will swing at you, bite you, hold you."

Joe, did I do all that to you?

I was surprised that Greene's Pittsburgh Steeler teammate Ernie Holmes went into detail about me. "Sweeney? He's the best guard I've ever seen. He plays the game the way it's supposed to be played. He's just a rough son of a gun. That's all I can say about him. He'll be all over the field with you."

When Ernie was asked if I was a dirty player, he repeated the question. "Is he dirty? Ask Joe Greene. Yeah, he's dirty. He don't take no swings at you, but you can't take your eye off him. You can't get by him. I use a push or pull on him and if you get by him, he'll kick or trip you. I use the club on him. I club him and he pulls me down with him while he's falling. If I run over him, he just falls back and pulls me down to the ground with him. If I pick him up and throw him off to the side, he lets me go by and trips you or holds your leg or anything. What does an offensive lineman do? He's got to use some protective techniques to keep a defensive lineman from running over him. I give him a lot of credit, but he is a dirty son of a gun."

Former Oakland Raiders All-Star defensive tackle Tom Keating said, "There is no better guard in pro football."

Defensive end Alan Page, leader of the Minnesota Vikings "Purple People Eaters," agreed with Tom Keating. Page was the first lineman to be honored as the Most Valuable Player of the NFL in 1971. Today, the Football Hall of Famer is the Honorable Alan C. Page, associate justice of the Minnesota Supreme Court.

As mentioned, Hall of Fame tackle Merlin Olsen, legendary member of the Los Angeles Rams "Fearsome Foursome" defensive line, quipped, "If I had to play against Sweeney every week, I'd rather sell used cars."

Every football player would like to be in the Hall of Fame, but I have no control over the selection process. If I were ever elected, it would be a great honor.

The NFL Network lists John Hadl and me among the all-time top ten Chargers. Assuming that Junior Seau and LaDainian Tomlinson are locks for enshrinement, John and I are the only two who are not in Canton.

So, where am I? Who am I? This manuscript was collecting dust and I was collecting dust. How does my story end? At one time, it was my goal to have my picture in every bar in San Diego. I didn't realize how many bars there are in San Diego.

I'm 71 years old now. In my playing days, I stood 6'4" and weighed 256 pounds. Today, I'm slightly taller than six feet and weigh less than 200 pounds. I've had four knee replacement surgeries and one hip replacement. Other than pain pills following surgery, I haven't used any drugs since returning to San Diego. I do smoke a little weed and drink an occasional beer (or two).

Today, my biggest vices are cigarettes, coffee and Spanish Omelets.

The last few years have been very hard on Nanci. The poor woman already had multiple sclerosis. She survived ovarian cancer when she was 30 years old. Two years ago, she was hospitalized for two months with endocarditis, a disease that infects the inner lining of the heart. In December 2011, she was diagnosed with bladder cancer. She survived surgery, but the cancer could not be removed. She's tough, she's courageous and she has a wonderful attitude.

She was instrumental in keeping me alive for all these years. Now it was my turn to do everything I could to make her as comfortable as possible. Nanci didn't like being in the hospital. When she realized there was nothing more that could be done, she came home. She missed her loyal German Shepherd dog, Duke, who slept beside her bed. Hospice came to ease her pain. We all cared for her until she died in her sleep in March 2012.

Shortly after her passing, I woke up one morning and realized that I had a chore to do. I thought Nanci was in the room with me. I had to do the chore right to please her.

But, she was no longer with me.

Then I realized Nanci will always be with me. If I do what is right, Nanci will be pleased.